The Path to Sustained Growth

Before the industrial revolution, prolonged economic growth was unachievable. All economies were organic, dependent on plant photosynthesis to provide food, raw materials, and energy. This was true both of heat energy, derived from burning wood, and mechanical energy, provided chiefly by human and animal muscle. The flow of energy from the sun captured by plant photosynthesis was the basis of all production and consumption. Britain began to escape the old restrictions by making increasing use of the vast stock of energy contained in coal measures, initially as a source of heat energy but eventually also of mechanical energy, thus making possible the industrial revolution. In this concise and accessible account of change between the reigns of Elizabeth I and Victoria, Wrigley describes how during this period Britain moved from the economic periphery of Europe to becoming briefly the world's leading economy, forging a path rapidly emulated by its competitors.

E. A. WRIGLEY is Emeritus Professor of Economic History at the University of Cambridge and co-founder of the Cambridge Group for the History of Population and Social Structure at the University of Cambridge.

The Path to Sustained Growth

England's Transition from an Organic Economy to an Industrial Revolution

E. A. Wrigley
University of Cambridge

CAMBRIDGE
UNIVERSITY PRESS

CAMBRIDGE
UNIVERSITY PRESS

University Printing House, Cambridge CB2 8BS, United Kingdom

Cambridge University Press is part of the University of Cambridge.

It furthers the University's mission by disseminating knowledge in the pursuit of education, learning and research at the highest international levels of excellence.

www.cambridge.org
Information on this title: www.cambridge.org/9781316504284

First published 2016

Printed in the United Kingdom by Clays, St Ives plc

A catalogue record for this publication is available from the British Library

Library of Congress Cataloguing in Publication data
Names: Wrigley, E. A. (Edward Anthony), 1931–
Title: The path to sustained growth : England's transition from an organic economy to an industrial revolution / E. A. Wrigley.
Description: New York : Cambridge University Press, 2016. | Includes bibliographical references and index.
Identifiers: LCCN 2015032902 | ISBN 9781107135710 (hardback)
Subjects: LCSH: Energy development – England. | England – Rural conditions. | Industrial revolution – England. | England – Economic conditions.
Classification: LCC HD9502.G72 W76 2016 | DDC 338.942 – dc23 LC record available at http://lccn.loc.gov/2015032902

ISBN 978-1-107-13571-0 Hardback
ISBN 978-1-316-50428-4 Paperback

For Mieke

Contents

Figures

Tables

Acknowledgements

The Cambridge Group for the History of Population and Social Structure recently held a conference to celebrate the fiftieth anniversary of the founding of the Group. It was a memorable occasion.

The Group has always consisted of a mixture of established staff, research assistants, graduate students, and a constant stream of visiting scholars from every continent. Its structure is not hierarchical and everyone present benefits from being able to call upon the expertise of others and finds pleasure in returning this favour. Coffee time is often the key period of the day when informal discussion stimulates thought and gives rise to new insights which would otherwise be missed. I have felt a particular gratitude to the Group in retirement since its nature has meant that it is readily possible to remain in touch with current research, and to receive the advice, help, and criticism so beneficial in developing initial ideas. This book is, indirectly, a tribute to the value of this contact.

I should also like to thank the two anonymous referees whom the Press appointed to comment on the text of the book. Some sections of the text have been altered as a result and are the better for it.

Introduction

The object of this book is to describe the transformation in the capacity to produce goods and services which took place in England over a period of three centuries between the reigns of Elizabeth I and Victoria, and which is conventionally termed the industrial revolution. At the beginning of the period England was not one of the leading European economies. It was a deeply rural country where agricultural production was largely focused on local self-sufficiency. In part this was a function of the low level of urbanisation at the time. England was one of the least urbanised of European countries: the only large town was London. The market for any agricultural surplus was limited other than close to the capital city. There was therefore little inducement to undertake improvement. Industry was little developed compared with the situation in the more advanced continental countries. Across a wide range of products there was little or no domestic production.[1] When an initiative was taken to create a domestic source of supply, it was often the case that foreign expertise was sought to enhance the chances of success. England was on the periphery of Europe economically as well as geographically. However, although other European economies were well in advance of England in the mid sixteenth century, all were subject to the limits to growth that were common to all organic economies.

The underlying constraint that prevented sustained growth in organic economies arose from the nature of its energy sources. All acts of material production, whether in the field, the forest, the workshop, or the household necessarily involved the expenditure of energy; and the same was true of all types of transport. But the quantum of energy that could be secured for these purposes was limited. It was based almost exclusively on the energy secured by the process of plant photosynthesis. The conversion of raw materials into finished products always involved the expenditure of either mechanical or heat energy, or both. The great bulk of the mechanical energy was provided by human or animal muscle power. This

[1] See pp. 86–8.

energy came from plant photosynthesis in the form of food or fodder. Wind and water power was of relatively slight importance.[2] Heat energy was secured from burning wood or charcoal. This too, therefore, was the product of plant photosynthesis. Most of the raw materials used by industry in organic economies were also vegetable, such as wood, wool, cotton, or leather. Even when the raw material was mineral, plant photosynthesis was essential to production, since converting ores into metals required a large expenditure of heat energy that came from burning wood or charcoal. When smelting iron or baking bricks no less than when operating a loom to produce woollen cloth or ploughing a field to prepare for next year's harvest, the energy involved was derived from plant photosynthesis. Directly or indirectly, therefore, almost all forms of material production depended on access to the energy available from this source.

The energy reaching the surface of the earth each year far exceeds the quantity of energy used by human societies even today, but plant photosynthesis captures only a very small fraction of such energy, and organic economies were constrained in what they could produce and transport by the degree of success they achieved in tapping this energy source. For reasons which are described in later chapters, the very nature of growth in organic economies at some stage necessarily involved rising costs per unit produced and falling output per head, a point familiar to the classical economists. They used a different framework of analysis to that used in this book, but came to the same conclusions about the constraints upon prolonged growth.

It is critical to the understanding of the difference between organic economies and those transformed by an industrial revolution that the energy available to organic economies was a *flow* from the sun whose scale scarcely varied from one year to the next. The quantity captured by a community might be increased if technical advance and invention made it possible to secure a larger fraction of this energy flow, but only within a ceiling set by the scale of plant photosynthesis. Small increases in the efficiency of energy capture for human use occurred from time to time and were cumulatively substantial. Occasionally, as in the era of the neolithic food revolution, a major advance in energy capture might lead to profound economic and social change, but the ceiling jointly set by the nature of plant photosynthesis and the productive technology of any given society prohibited prolonged economic growth.

The industrial revolution depended on securing access to vastly greater energy supplies. The energy required to produce, say, iron and steel on a large scale or to construct and operate a railway system implied that it

[2] See Table 3.2, p. 34.

was idle to expect that it could be secured from the annual *flow* of energy derived from plant photosynthesis. The possibility of bringing about an industrial revolution depended on gaining access to a different source of energy. Mining coal provided the solution to this problem. It enabled societies to escape from what Jevons termed 'the laborious poverty of early times'.[3] Coal consumption roughly doubled in each half-century between the reigns of Elizabeth and Victoria. Coal, however, is a *stock* not a *flow*. Each ton of coal dug from a mine marginally reduces the size of the stock, and the same is true of all fossil fuels. Since drawing upon a stock will ultimately lead to its exhaustion, the use of fossil fuels creates problems not faced when the energy source is a flow. In the long term, dependence on an energy stock is perilous, but there can be no doubt of the benefits that can follow from exploiting a stock of fossil fuel in the short term. It makes possible the attainment of a scale of production that is otherwise beyond reach.

This book shares an underlying theme with an earlier publication, *Energy and the English industrial revolution*, in stressing the importance of exploiting fossil fuel as a new energy source, but its scope is wider, covering many topics which did not figure in the earlier work, as may be inferred from the description of chapters which follows.

The first chapter defines the exceptional character of the industrial revolution by contrasting it with two earlier transformations of organic economies that are often compared to the industrial revolution; the conquest of fire and the neolithic food revolution. This helps to make apparent the sense in which the industrial revolution involved more radical change than anything that preceded it. Next, Chapter 2 describes the analysis of the character of organic economies made by the classical economists since this, too, is instructive as background to an appreciation of the nature of an industrial revolution.

There follows a group of chapters (Chapters 3–5) which describe the interplay between advances in the traditional forms of production and those arising from the increasing consumption of coal in production processes; in other words, the blending of growth which is possible within the constraints of an organic economy with the growth made possible by tapping a new energy source. A central topic is the exceptional nature of urban growth in England in the seventeenth and eighteenth centuries, which contrasts sharply with the virtual absence of urban growth in most of continental Europe. This was only possible because of the radical advances in agricultural productivity that was a *sine qua non* for the urban growth that took place. The extent to which London dominated urban

[3] Jevons, *The coal question*, p. 2.

growth in the seventeenth century contrasts vividly with the very different pattern of urban growth in the eighteenth century, reflecting the changing character of the national economy. The far more rapid rise of the English population compared with that on the continent between the mid seventeenth and mid nineteenth centuries was almost exclusively due to the scale of urban growth in England. Linked to the rapid urban growth, there were major changes in occupational structure and in the structure of consumer demand.

Chapter 6 is devoted to the country's population history. For reasons made clear by Malthus in his later writings, in organic economies the demographic characteristics of the country greatly influenced its economic circumstances and prospects. This was especially clear in relation to nuptiality. The conventions governing the timing and extent of marriage in each rising generation in England meant that the level of fertility was sensitive to prevailing economic circumstances, which kept the population a safe distance from the edge of a 'Malthusian' precipice. This in turn implied lower mortality than was common in most organic economies. In a 'low-pressure' system of this type living standards are likely to be higher than in 'high-pressure' systems in which both fertility and mortality are at higher levels. Because of the differing elasticities of demand for primary, secondary, and tertiary products, even modest differences in average incomes can produce significant differences in the structure of aggregate demand that is reflected in a country's occupational structure.

For many decades the release from earlier growth constraints by the increasing use of coal as an energy source was limited by the fact that although coal was widely used to supply heat energy, the sources of mechanical energy were unchanged. An industrial revolution could not be accomplished as long as mechanical energy continued to be provided principally by human and animal muscle. One key sector of the economy, land transport, remained primarily dependent on animal muscle as its energy source until a railway network was constructed in the middle decades of the nineteenth century. Chapter 7 describes the developments in transport taking place from the mid seventeenth century onwards, culminating in the building of the railway system. With the advent of the railway, the steam engine replaced human and animal muscle in powering land transport. More generally, by the mid nineteenth century the steady improvement in the efficiency of the steam engine meant that mechanical energy could be derived from coal as effectively as heat energy. The steam engine became the chief source of mechanical energy for industrial production in general. Once this was the case, the industrial revolution could be regarded as accomplished. Defining the industrial revolution in this way makes it possible also to date its completion, at least approximately.

Chapter 8 reveals the insights into the English economy made possible by the unusual character of the 1831 census, which provides the same level of detail for the smallest unit, the parish or township, as for the county or the country, and distinguishes between types of employment servicing only a local market and those dependent on a wider national or international market. This makes it possible, for example, to demonstrate that by the time of the census proto-industry had virtually disappeared.

Chapters 9 and 10 describe the rapid disappearance during the later nineteenth century of the advantage over continental economies that England had acquired over the three preceding centuries, and suggest the reason for this abrupt change. As long as coal was used only to supply heat energy, most of continental Europe continued to find that wood was cheaper than coal for this purpose, but when the steam engine made it possible to derive mechanical energy from fossil fuel, the situation was transformed. Between the mid nineteenth century and the outbreak of the First World War the growing economic advantage that Britain had enjoyed for two centuries rapidly disappeared. There are also reflections on the nature of the transformation of the economy that took place between the sixteenth and nineteenth centuries, and a brief discussion of the character and scale of change that followed the completion of the industrial revolution. As a coda to the volume as a whole, there is a brief discussion of what might be termed the downside of the industrial revolution, the imminent and growing danger of environmental disaster brought about by the large-scale use of fossil fuels.

The central concept used in providing structure to the description of the interaction between the changes that gave rise to the industrial revolution is the concept of *positive and negative feedback*. In organic economies negative feedback between different factors of production was common. For example, if the population increased it would involve at some point taking into cultivation marginal land, or farming existing land more intensively, or increasing the arable acreage at the expense of pasture, changes which tended to reduce labour productivity, inhibiting further growth and reducing living standards. In early modern England the rising importance of a fossil fuel as an energy source meant that many of the relationships which involved negative feedback in organic economies changed: positive feedback became more common. The growth process tended to foster further advance, whereas in organic economies the reverse was the case. One of the recurrent themes throughout the book is the significance of the replacement of negative feedback by positive feedback patterns in the interaction between different elements of the production system. It was unavoidably necessary to escape from the predominance of negative feedback within the production system if exponential economic growth was to be attained; or, in other words, if an industrial revolution was to take place.

As the subtitle of this volume suggests, it describes change in England and may therefore suggest that the accomplishment of an industrial revolution occurred in England exclusively. Only occasional reference is made to Wales, Ireland, or Scotland. In general, especially in the second half of the period covered, change took place in the British Isles as a whole rather than simply in England but I have focused on England because for some variables, notably but not solely those measuring demographic change, continuous data series are available for England over a longer period than for the other countries in the British Isles.[4] In the interests of simplicity and clarity I have told a story in purely English terms which was increasingly apposite for Britain, and indeed for the whole British Isles, notably from the mid eighteenth century onwards.

[4] It should be noted, incidentally, that in the population data set out in the tables in this volume England does not include Monmouth, even though it was treated as part of England in the early English censuses.

1 Organic economies

Before the industrial revolution all human societies laboured under a common constraint in attempting to increase their ability to produce even the basic necessities of life. Their degree of success in this regard varied enormously. It might seem ridiculous to regard those living in Renaissance Italy as similarly placed to the early tribes of hunter-gatherers. In many contexts such an assertion is indeed ridiculous; but in seeking to put into perspective the radical nature of the change implied by the occurrence of an industrial revolution, it is instructive to explore the sense in which the assertion is justified. All life on earth is dependent on the process of plant photosynthesis, by which a fraction of the energy reaching the surface of the earth from the sun is captured by plants. The energy thus captured creates the base of the pyramid comprising all life forms as, for example, in providing food for herbivores and therefore also indirectly for carnivores. Plant photosynthesis, however, captures only a tiny fraction of the energy contained in incident sunlight. One estimate suggests that 400,000 kilocalories of solar radiation reach each square metre of soil annually, of which 4,000 kilocalories, or 1 per cent of the energy involved, is translated into vegetable matter.[1] Other estimates suggest a lower figure. Pimentel indicates the wide range of efficiency with which different crops capture the energy from sunlight: maize captures 0.5 per cent, wheat only 0.2 per cent.[2] White and Plaskett calculate that the total of solar energy arriving on the surface of the United Kingdom from the sun each year translates into the equivalent of the energy contained in *c.* 26 billion tons of coal, an enormous figure, many times greater than current national energy consumption, implying that a total for England and Wales alone the figure would be perhaps *c.* 16 billion tons.[3] Assuming an average efficiency of energy capture of 0.35 per cent, this suggests

[1] Kander *et al.*, *Power to the people*, p. 39.

[2] Pimentel, 'Energy flow in the food system', p. 2.

[3] White and Plaskett, *Biomass as fuel*, p. 2. Their estimates are made in terms of billions of tons of oil, that I have converted into coal equivalents assuming the quantity of energy in 1 ton of oil as equivalent to that in 1.5 tons of coal.

that the equivalent of the energy in 56 million tons of coal might have been secured from the products of plant photosynthesis in early modern England and Wales.[4]

There are wide bands of uncertainty round any estimates of this kind. It is clear, however, that in reality the energy limit imposed by plant photosynthesis on the English economy was very much lower than any suggested in the last paragraph. Only a part of the land surface of England and Wales consists of farmland or forest. Large tracts are too high, too steep, or too lacking in soil depth to be cultivated or to afford good grazing. Agricultural yields per acre in England in the reign of Elizabeth I were only a fraction of the yields used in making the estimates for crops in the last paragraph, and a substantial fraction of the arable acreage was in fallow each year.

Moreover, there was a wide difference between the energy obtained from food consumption and the energy that this made available to perform work. The plants consumed by people and their draught animals provided the great bulk of the mechanical energy available for production processes, since human and animal muscle provided the energy in question, but a large proportion of the food and fodder consumed served to meet the basic metabolic requirements of the men, women, horses, and oxen concerned. Since only the surplus after meeting these needs was available to perform work, mechanical energy derived from human and animal muscle was only a proportion of the energy represented by the intake of food. For example, at least 1,500 kilocalories are needed each day to keep a man alive even if no work is performed. Therefore, if his daily food intake provides 2,500 kilocalories, only 1,000 kilocalories, or 40 per cent of his total energy consumption, will be available for work. If, on the other hand, his intake is 3,500 kilocalories, this will double the amount of energy he can put to productive purposes since it increases the surplus after meeting basic metabolic needs from 1,000 to 2,000 kilocalories. Both figures are maxima since in the course of an average day much of the energy theoretically available to perform work will be devoted to other activities. Both for men and for draught animals any decline in food intake will have a disproportionate effect in limiting the amount of mechanical work that can be performed. In early modern Europe wind and water power provided only a tiny fraction of the mechanical energy secured from human and animal muscle.[5] In all forms of production,

[4] White and Plaskett also present estimates of the efficiency of energy capture which are higher than those of Pimentel, in the range 0.4 to 1.0 per cent, *ibid.*, p. 2.

[5] For example, in 1820, consolidating information covering eight European countries, Warde found that water and wind provided 1.7 per cent of energy consumption, whereas the combined total for food and fodder, the other two sources of mechanical energy,

whether in agriculture, manufacture, or transport, the ceiling set by the available muscle power severely limited the output that could be attained.

Heat energy came from burning wood; 2 tons of thoroughly dried wood yields roughly the same amount of heat as 1 ton of coal. An acre of woodland has been estimated to have yielded approximately 1 ton of dry wood each year on a sustained yield basis.[6] On this estimate of woodland productivity, therefore, it would be necessary to reserve 2 million acres of land for forest to produce the same quantity of heat energy each year as could be secured from burning 1 million tons of coal. A particular example may serve to illustrate the contrast between the comparative energy poverty of an organic economy and the situation that arose in the wake of the industrial revolution. In early modern England to produce a ton of bar iron using charcoal as the source of the heat energy expended in smelting the ore and in its subsequent processing required the consumption of *c.* 30 tons of dry wood.[7] If woodland had covered 30,000 square miles of the land surface of Britain, therefore, it would have sufficed to produce only about 650,000 tons of bar iron each year. As long as plant photosynthesis was the energy base of all human economies it was clearly physically impossible to construct, for example, large fleets of steel cargo vessels, still less to provide a car for every family.

Plant photosynthesis was at the base of all productive activity in organic economies. What could be undertaken depended on the degree of success that a given community experienced in securing as large a fraction as possible of the energy unlocked by plant growth. The degree of success achieved varied massively between hunter-gatherer tribes and societies with settled agriculture. In relatively advanced organic economies there was sometimes a clear recognition that energy availability set a ceiling to what could be achieved. This was admirably analysed in the writings of the classical economists that are discussed in Chapter 2, but it had been recognised in earlier centuries. The problem was well captured in a picturesque fashion in the writings of Sir Thomas More, when he

was 31.7 per cent of total energy consumption. Heat energy from firewood and coal accounted for the balance, with firewood still the bigger of the two. Since England and Wales was one of the eight countries, the dominance of firewood over coal would be far more pronounced in the other seven at this date. Warde, 'The first industrial revolution', Table 5.1, p. 133.

6 Van der Woude *et al.*, *Urbanization in history*, p. 8. It is suggested that well-managed forests in early modern Europe produced 2 tons of firewood per hectare, or 0.8 tons per acre. This estimate may be slightly pessimistic. I have used a figure of 1 ton per acre in these calculations, but it is simple to establish the implications of making an alternative assumption.

7 Wrigley, *Energy and the English industrial revolution*, p. 16.

reflected on the pressures associated with the expansion of wool production in Tudor times. He wrote 'your sheep that were wont to be so meek and tame and so small eaters, now, as I hear say, be become so great devourers and so wild, that they eat up and swallow down the very men themselves'.[8] If the woollen industry was flourishing and the demand for wool therefore rising, more land would be devoted to sheep pasture, but this must mean less land available to grow corn for human consumption, or less land under forest. Expanding the production of woollen cloth must at some point create difficulties for the supply of food, or of fuel for domestic heating, or for the production of charcoal iron. If the land was the source of virtually all the material products of value to man, expansion in one area of the economy was all too likely to be secured only by shrinkage elsewhere.

The ceiling to energy availability set by plant photosynthesis was intrinsic to the nature of all organic economies, but its existence was of little relevance to the lives of men and women in societies whose ability to gain access to such energy was severely limited by the primitive nature of their technologies. The ceiling set by plant photosynthesis was orders of magnitude greater than the energy to which they had access and was therefore largely irrelevant to their attempts to succeed in raising their 'standard of living'. In contrast, in advanced organic economies a much higher fraction of the energy made available by plant photosynthesis was captured, which brought this ceiling closer and made further advance more difficult. As a background to describing the relatively advanced organic economies of early modern Europe in the centuries that ended with the industrial revolution, it may be helpful briefly to review the two earlier radical transformations of productive capacity that are sometimes mentioned as comparable in importance to the industrial revolution. To do so serves to clarify the nature of the difference between the industrial revolution and the earlier transformations within the setting of an organic economy. The two earlier events in question were the mastery of fire and the neolithic food revolution.

Earlier transformations of energy supply

The mastery of fire

Charles Darwin was very conscious of the significance of the mastery of fire, remarking that, 'This discovery of fire was probably the greatest ever made by man, excepting language'.[9] Before the mastery of fire, the energy

[8] More, *Utopia*, p. 26. [9] Darwin, *The descent of man*, p. 49.

available to mankind to secure food and for all other purposes, like that available to other animal species, consisted exclusively of the mechanical energy exerted through the use of muscles. All movement, whether in walking, climbing, running, and swimming, or in lifting, pulling, and throwing, was of this nature. In this respect life for men and women paralleled that of other animals. The mastery of fire for the first time set human populations apart from all other creatures. Wood fires produced heat energy, and mankind found an increasing range of uses for this new energy source. Over time heat energy became an essential element in a wide variety of production processes: the cooking of food; the brewing of beer; the production of bricks, pottery, and glass; the smelting of ores and the production of metals. Fire was also of great value in ways which were only indirectly linked to production, as for example in scaring away predatory animals or in creating a circle of warmth round a fire in cold weather. Extension of human settlement into areas where the winters were cold was greatly assisted by the mastery of fire.

The mastery of fire began in the distant past. Goudsblom suggests that it may have begun as much as 400,000 years ago and that it was the achievement of *homo erectus*, well before the appearance of *homo sapiens*. In addition to providing warmth in winter and assisting in the preparation of an increased range of foodstuffs, it may have been used from an early date in the burning of woodland to provide more grassland for grazing animals, an important food source for hunter-gatherers. The use of fire for this purpose was still widely practised by Indian tribes in some parts of North America at the time of European settlement there. It produced more grazing for the buffaloes and other herbivores that they hunted.[10]

The neolithic agricultural revolution

Control of the energy produced by fire was also crucial in the second transformation of the productive capacity of society, the neolithic agricultural revolution, which began about 10,000 years ago. The neolithic agricultural revolution made it possible for populations to rise by an order of magnitude. Rather than competing with other animals to secure as large a share as possible of the edible products afforded by the plants and animals in the natural environment, new environments were created in which communities could be confident of securing for their use a large fraction of the whole product of the land. Vast tracts of land that had previously supported a wide range of plants and animals were transformed by the advent of settled agriculture. In these areas, the result was to obtain

[10] Goudsblom, *Fire and civilization*, p. 31.

for exclusive human use a far larger proportion of the products of photosynthesis than had earlier been possible. Only those plants of direct use to man were grown. Only those animals which were valued as a source of food, or whose muscle power could be harnessed for human use, or which produced raw materials such as wool or hides, were supported. Other plants were weeds to be uprooted where possible. Other animals were at risk to be treated as pests to be destroyed. The natural vegetation was replaced by cereals and other edible food plants, or by grassland to provide fodder for domesticated animals.

The prior mastery of fire was of critical importance in making possible the neolithic agricultural revolution. It is probable, for example, that it was a necessary precondition for the large-scale cultivation of cereals which were the most important food crop planted in the new agrarian lands. Cereals have a high nutritional value and are easier to store for long periods than most vegetable products but they are not readily digestible in a raw state. The ability to cook or bake cereals overcame this difficulty. Baking a loaf of bread depended on making use of the heat energy gained from the controlled burning of wood. Again, in many parts of the world the neolithic food revolution was based on slash and burn agriculture, underlining the interconnection of the mastery of fire and the development of agriculture. The ability to provide heat energy from burning wood was also a necessary condition for the provision of many of the tools, domestic equipment, building materials, and other facilities that were widely employed in the permanent settlements which had been made possible by the neolithic agricultural revolution.

This revolution brought about profound changes in social and economic life generally. Any given area was able to support a far larger population. Since in many cases the agricultural population produced more than enough food to meet the needs of the peasants who tilled the land, a surplus was available to enable a proportion of the population to specialise in secondary and tertiary activities. Settled agriculture meant settled populations living not only in villages but also in towns. Trade links and transport facilities were developed, enabling exchange to take place and thus to extend the division of labour. The towns housed craftsmen, retail traders, and merchants. Social and political hierarchies developed. An elite, a priesthood, and a military hierarchy were able to lay claim to part of the rural surplus. Legal, religious, and administrative structures were established and were described, codified, and given coherence by the development of writing.

By replacing the natural vegetation cover with a limited range of plants that were exclusively for human use, the resources platform was much enlarged. Much of the annual harvest was food for human consumption, but a substantial part was fodder consumed by pigs, sheep, goats, cattle, and other livestock. Much of the fodder fed to animals was also intended indirectly for human consumption, since their slaughter provided supplies of meat. Raising domestic livestock made it unnecessary to send out hunting parties to secure meat for the cooking pot. Domesticated livestock, moreover, provided many products other than meat. The animal hides were the raw material used in a wide range of leather products, notably shoes and clothing for the human population and harnesses and saddles for draught animals and riding stock. The wool shorn from sheep flocks, when converted into woven cloth, kept human populations warm and clad through much of northern Europe. In Britain in 1770 Crafts' estimates suggest that the woollen and leather manufactures were the two largest industries by value added, accounting for more than half of the overall total of value added in British industry.[11] In both cases, the raw material was largely domestically supplied.[12] The agricultural revolution that took place in neolithic times provided a base for substantial industries which had only a very limited scope in earlier times.

The supply of food and raw materials was thus greatly increased by the neolithic agricultural revolution. There was, moreover, also an entirely new departure of great significance. Part of the fodder fed to animals was given with a new purpose in mind. They were not bred to provide meat, hides, or wool but to increase the mechanical energy available for a variety of productive ends. The muscle energy exerted by draught animals played an important and novel role in these economies. Horses, oxen, and donkeys were used to haul carts, pull ploughs, carry panniers, support human riders, provide the power to drive machines, and for a host of other activities in primary, secondary, and tertiary production.

This aspect of the new era deserves special emphasis since in many ways it can be regarded as equivalent to increasing the average bodily strength of the human workforce. A particular example may bring home the implications of the new situation. A horse can produce about ten times as many foot-pounds of effort in an hour as a man; an ox perhaps two-thirds as much as a horse. Enjoying the assistance of a horse or an ox in carrying out a task can therefore increase the output of a man very considerably. A study of Mexican agriculture in the middle of the twentieth century illustrates the point. Maize was cultivated in Mexico both by hand and with the use of oxen. If a hectare of maize was cultivated entirely by hand it required 1,140 man-hours of labour. If the same work

11 Crafts, *British economic growth*, Table 2.3, p. 22.

12 Clarkson, 'The manufacture of leather', p. 466; Holderness, 'Prices, productivity, and output', p. 174.

was carried out with the assistance of oxen it required 380 man-hours, plus 200 hours of work by oxen. In this case, therefore, 1 ox-hour saved the equivalent of 3.8 man-hours of work.[13]

The potential benefits to levels of output per head associated with the employment of animal muscle in place of human muscle are clear. It is the equivalent of endowing each worker who has the muscle power of an ox or horse to assist him with the strength of several men rather than being dependent solely on his own muscle power. The advantage gained by employing draught animals was perhaps greatest in relation to overland transport. The output in terms of ton-miles performed during a working day by a man with a sack on his back or pushing a wheelbarrow is almost derisory compared with what is possible by a man with a horse and cart on a firm road surface. In many agricultural systems draught animals were essential. This was normally true of the cultivation of cereals such as wheat. If the yield per acre of a cereal is modest, it may be beyond the physical capacity of one man to cultivate a large enough area by his own efforts to support himself and his family. The land had to be ploughed by oxen or horses. Because yield per acre of rice was much higher than that of wheat, draught animals figured less prominently in east and south-east Asia than in Europe.

But the potential difficulties associated with the widespread employment of draught animals are no less evident. If the produce of 5 acres of land is needed to feed a working horse, the area available to feed people is reduced commensurately. As Cottrell remarked: 'Where land is plentiful, population sparse and draught animals available, there may be an economy in substituting draught animals for manpower; but with increased population and competition for land for the production of food and feed, the situation may be reversed, the survival of man being more important than the feeding of work animals.'[14] It was an unfortunate feature of organic economies after the neolithic agricultural revolution that a period of growth and prosperity when the population was rising tended to restrict the area that could be devoted to growing fodder for draught animals unless productivity per acre was rising sufficiently to offset the population rise. The relatively rapid rise in European populations in the twelfth and thirteenth centuries produced increasing difficulties for this reason. This was one of the many ways in which the very process of growth in organic economies involved changes that tended to bring growth to a halt or to reverse it. Nonetheless, the appearance of draught animals was the first example of a means of escape from dependence

[13] Pimentel, 'Energy flow in the food system', pp. 5–6.
[14] Cottrell, *Energy and society*, p. viii.

almost exclusively on human muscle power as a source of mechanical energy for productive purposes. Where the ratio of cultivable land to population was high, so that draught animals as well as a human population could be supported, it created the possibility of achieving a higher standard of living than was possible where only human muscle could be employed.

The mastery of fire and the neolithic agricultural revolution gave human societies access to an increasingly large fraction of the energy produced by plant photosynthesis. The total volume of the necessities of life (food, fuel, housing, and clothing) which could be produced each year increased in parallel with the rise in available heat and mechanical energy. The successive gains in the aggregate power to produce made possible the sophisticated civilisations that developed across the Eurasian continent. Greek, Roman, Egyptian, Turkish, Mesopotamian, Indian, and Chinese civilisations made striking achievements in a wide range of human activities, both those which raised the power to produce, and those which supported a much more complex development of administrative, artistic, religious, and political systems. It remained the case, however, that the bulk of the population in all these societies, despite their enhanced productive capacity as settled agrarian economies, remained poor. Periodically, their living standards in the wake of a bad harvest declined to the level of bare subsistence or fell still further, triggering great suffering and many deaths.

The tension between the potential rapidity of population growth rates and the pace at which production could be increased, to which Malthus drew attention, inhibited decisive progress. Even though mortality was always high by the standards of the developed world today, population growth rates in organic economies where economic circumstances were favourable sometimes exceeded 0.5 per cent per annum, and might even approach 1.0 per cent per annum. A population growth rate of 0.5 per cent per annum would result in a doubling of the population in *c.* 140 years, and a quadrupling in *c.* 280 years. Rates of economic growth, which were ultimately determined by the productivity of the land, were far more modest. The tendency for population growth rates to outstrip gains in productive capacity often meant misery for the bulk of the population. In a land of recent settlement as, for example, in areas of European settlement in North America in the eighteenth and nineteenth centuries, it was readily possible to increase agricultural and forest production faster than the growth of population. Where this was the case, high rates of population growth were compatible with rising real incomes for the mass of the population. In contrast, in a land long settled the intrinsic nature of all organic economies ruled out escape from the inevitable tension created, as Malthus expressed the problem, by the difference between arithmetic and geometric growth rates, the first representing a convenient way of highlighting the highest rate by which output could be increased, the second the inherent tendency of all animal populations to grow rapidly and at a constant rate until checked by a shortage of food and the other basic necessities of life.

The situation was not necessarily static in organic economies. On the land better methods of cultivation, the introduction of new crops, the breeding of improved farm animals, and the drainage of marshlands; these and other initiatives might lead to a larger output, and in some cases to rising output per head, at least for a time. Similarly, in industry improved techniques might secure greater output volumes from any given level of raw material inputs, but human and animal muscle provided the great bulk of the mechanical energy used by organic economies, and its scale was therefore bounded by the quantity of food and fodder which could be produced by their agricultures. Harnessing wind or water power might alleviate the problem to a degree without causing additional pressure on the output of the land, but only for a restricted range of productive activities and to a comparatively limited extent. The cumulative rise in productive capacity over a period of centuries brought about by agricultural improvement could be considerable, but measured in terms of an annual rate of increase it fell well short of the growth potential of populations in most organic societies.

In a period of economic growth advanced organic economies might experience greater difficulties than less advanced economies in raising their aggregate output still further. The quantity of energy made available by the annual round of plant photosynthesis was finite. For this reason, the more successful an organic economy was in capturing the heat and mechanical energy that was made available through the growth of plants, the more difficult it was to achieve a further advance. This is an assertion that should be hedged about with qualifications. As has been noted, the quantity of solar energy reaching the surface of the earth each year is enormous and does not in itself represent a constraint. It was the degree of success with which the vast flow could be captured for human use that determined the height of the barrier to exponential economic growth. The height of the barrier was influenced by many factors. Since different plant species differ substantially in their ability to capture solar energy, the level of the ceiling to energy availability set by photosynthesis is less absolute than might be suggested by a simple formulation of the problem. For example, the introduction of maize and the potato into European agriculture raised energy capture per acre substantially compared with the level achieved when the same area of land was used to grow wheat or barley. Nevertheless, as a broad generalisation it seems justifiable to regard the problem as more pressing in advanced organic economies than in their predecessors.

The major advances in output per head in agriculture taking place in early modern England brought substantial benefit, facilitating the very rapid expansion of the urban sector. These agricultural advances occurred in a sector of the economy that remained essentially organic in character, but England was also benefiting simultaneously from a novel development of very great long-term significance. Plant photosynthesis was no longer the sole source of all food, raw materials, and fuel. The substitution of coal for wood as a source of heat energy was steadily reducing the area of woodland needed to meet the country's heat energy requirements. Consider, for example, domestic heating in towns. Bairoch estimated that each town dweller typically needed between 1.0 and 1.6 tons of firewood each year, which Van der Woude *et al.* estimated would represent the annual product of 0.5 to 0.8 hectares of woodland, or roughly 1.25 to 2 acres.[15] For simplicity, I assume that 1.6 acres would cover the firewood needs of the average town dweller. A town with 10,000 inhabitants, therefore, would need access to the annual growth of wood taking place in woodland covering 16,000 acres. For an urban population totalling, say, half a million people and therefore needing 650,000 tons of firewood a year, it would be necessary to devote the wood growth of roughly 800,000 acres to meeting their domestic heating needs. The same quantity of heat energy could be secured from burning approximately 325,000 tons of coal, since burning 1 ton of coal produced as much heat as 2 tons of dry firewood. By 1700 the population of London had passed the half million mark and its fuel needs were predominantly met from burning coal. The switch from wood to coal therefore enabled approximately 800,000 acres of woodland to be used instead to produce food, or wool and hides, rather than fuel. The massive growth in the sea-borne coal trade between Newcastle and London is a symbol of the new age. As John Cleveland had remarked: 'England's a perfect world! has Indies too! correct your maps! Newcastle is Peru.'[16]

Conclusion

The discussion of the main characteristics of organic economies in this chapter centred on energy supply, and in particular on the restrictions imposed by the fact that almost all the energy available in organic

[15] Van der Woude *et al.*, 'Introduction', pp. 8–9.
[16] Quoted by Jones, *Agriculture and the industrial revolution*, p. 8.

economies was the product of plant photosynthesis derived from the annual *flow* of energy arriving on the earth's surface from the sun. An industrial revolution was not possible as long as this situation continued since the quantity of energy needed to underwrite the scale of production achieved in the industrial revolution greatly exceeded what was possible in an organic economy. One essential prerequisite for production on this scale was discovery of a different source of energy. This proved possible because fossil fuels could provide access to a massive *stock* of energy. Fossil fuels embodied the product of plant photosynthesis accumulated over geological ages. Indefinite dependence on fossil fuels is impossible because the size of the *stock* available is reduced each time a ton of coal is dug, or an equivalent quantity of oil is pumped, but the use of fossil fuel can provide an interlude during which exponential growth is possible, something which could not happen when an economy could only count on the energy *flow* derived from the annual round of plant photosynthesis.

Expressing the limits to growth in organic economies in terms of energy supply and consumption is convenient because it enables both the restrictions under which all organic economies laboured and the character of the escape from these restrictions to be described in a common framework; but there is much to be learned from considering the different framework of analysis used by the classical economists. They explained most persuasively the nature of the economies with which they were familiar and stressed the impossibility of prolonged growth in such economies. Since they were writing in the period that was once regarded as the heyday of the industrial revolution their insistence on the impossibility of engendering exponential growth gives a special interest to their analyses. Their writings are the subject of the next chapter.

2 The classical economists

For those living in the centuries after an event that changed the nature of their society fundamentally, achieving an understanding of how the world appeared to their ancestors living at the time of its occurrence is apt to be challenging. That the industrial revolution changed societies fundamentally is evident to people today, but not to contemporaries. The very fact that the term 'industrial revolution' only came into common usage towards the end of the nineteenth century is indirect evidence of this. To those living in the decades during which the industrial revolution was long supposed to have reached its climax, the possibility of prolonged, rapid growth appeared an idle fancy. It may be difficult today to appreciate the weight of arguments that had once carried conviction. But the very fact that the significance of some aspects of the changes taking place during the industrial revolution were so difficult for contemporaries to appreciate can itself be helpful in investigating its character.

Partly for this reason, the reflections of the classical economists, Adam Smith, Thomas Malthus, and David Ricardo, are instructive when seeking to understand the nature of organic economies. They were eloquent in stressing the benefits of market economies in which the state ensured the operation of a legal system that enabled entrepreneurs when assessing risk to have confidence in the enforcement of contracts. They identified the scope for the increase in productivity that could flow from specialisation of function if the size of the accessible market was enlarged, and in turn the connection between this and improvements in transport. They were conscious that developments of this sort had brought about substantial economic advance in England during the two preceding centuries. They demonstrated the economic benefits associated with what has subsequently come to be described conventionally as a capitalist economy. They are even sometimes portrayed as demonstrating the possibility of what came to be termed exponential economic growth. Yet they were explicit in rejecting such a possibility. They saw no reason indeed to suppose that the lot of the bulk of the population would be any better at the end of an expansionary cycle than it had been at its beginning.

In short, they saw clearly that, unhappily, the very nature of growth in what has recently come to be termed an organic economy must eventually entail a loss of momentum and probable decline. Negative feedback must always eventually prevail. They were unconscious of the fact that developments already well in train in their lifetimes were rendering their analysis obsolete.

The analysis of the classical economists

Adam Smith followed the lead taken by Bernard Mandeville earlier in the eighteenth century. In *The fable of the bees*, Mandeville had expounded the apparent paradox that it was not the qualities in mankind that were normally taken as praiseworthy but those conventionally denounced as vicious which do most to promote general prosperity and wellbeing. He wrote, 'by setting forth what of necessity must be the consequence of general honesty and virtue and national temperance, innocence and content, I demonstrate that if mankind could be cured of the failings they are naturally guilty of they would cease to be capable of being rais'd into such vast, potent and polite societies, as they have been under the several great common-wealths and monarchies that have flourish' since the creation.'[1] As might be supposed from the subtitle of his book, *Private vices, public benefits*, Mandeville's views were found deeply shocking by his contemporaries. John Wesley's reaction was typical of many. He had 'imagined there had never appeared in the world such a book as the works of Machiavel. But de Mandeville goes far beyond them in wickedness.' It attracted attention widely. 'In France the book was ordered to be hanged by the common hangman, and Mandeville was burned in effigy.'[2]

Mandeville's analysis of the aspects of human character which promoted rising prosperity in *The fable of the bees* caused horror in 1714, when his views were first set out more fully, but became a commonplace of thinking and writing in England towards the end of the century. He was born and grew up in the Netherlands. Possibly his thinking reflected life in a society that was more fully commercialised than England in the later seventeenth century.

Mandeville had a more deliberately provocative style than Adam Smith, but Smith echoed his thinking. In a well-known passage in the second chapter of *The wealth of nations*, he noted that 'In almost every other race of animals, each animal, when it is grown up to maturity, is entirely independent – But man has almost constant occasion for the help of his

[1] Mandeville, *The fable of the bees*, p. 54.
[2] McKendrick, 'Commercialization and the economy', pp. 16–17.

brethren, and it is in vain for him to expect it from their benevolence only. He will be more likely to prevail if he can interest their self-love in his favour, and show them that it is for their own advantage to do for him what he requires of them.'[3] Expanding on this generalisation Smith then penned a passage strongly reminiscent of Mandeville's thinking:

It is not from the benevolence of the butcher, the brewer, or the baker, that we expect our dinner, but from their regard to their interest. We address ourselves, not to their humanity but to their self-love, and never talk to them of our own necessities but of their advantages. Nobody but a beggar chuses to depend chiefly upon the benevolence of his fellow-citizens.[4]

Although the operations of a market economy, recognising the reality of human motivation, might give rise to notable gains in efficiency with general benefit, the classical economists explicitly rejected the possibility of sustained economic growth of the kind that occurred in the wake of the industrial revolution. Adam Smith summarised his view in a paragraph that ended with the following sentence:

In a country which had acquired that full complement of riches which the nature of its soil and climate, and its situation with respect to other countries, allowed it to acquire; which could, therefore, advance no further, and which was not going backwards, both the wages of labour and the profits of stock would probably be very low.[5]

Musson once remarked that: 'Adam Smith provided the gospel for the industrial revolution, in denouncing outdated, ineffective and hampering mercantilist controls and in lauding economic freedom, free trade or *laissez-faire*, as the essential basis for increasing the wealth of nations.'[6] Musson's description of the changes that Smith advocated is accurate but the implication that they were sufficient to engender an industrial revolution is at odds with Smith's own conclusions.

The span of years between the publication of *The wealth of nations* in 1776 and Ricardo's *On the principles of political economy* in 1817 represents a large fraction of the period once regarded as the classic period of the industrial revolution. Malthus' *Essay on population* was published in 1798 at the midpoint between the other two classics, but the three men were all reflecting on the nature of the organic economies. They were unaware of the nature and significance of the transformation already in train. They were providing an authoritative description of the limitations to growth

3 Smith, *The wealth of nations*, I, p. 18. 4 *Ibid.*, I, p. 18.
5 *Ibid.*, I, p. 106. 6 Musson, *The growth of British industry*, p. 73.

inherent in organic economies on the eve of the emergence of a radically different economic system.[7]

In essence their pessimism about future prospects mirrored the view of the character of organic economies that I have discussed in terms of energy supply, though they approached the question using a different framework. The classical economists saw all activity giving rise to material production as involving three component elements: capital, labour, and land. The quantity of capital and labour available to allow production to take place might in principle be increased as necessary and without apparent limit, but the same was not true of land. The area of land was limited and could not be increased. Advances in technology might permit significant improvements in aggregate output. The output from any given area of land might be increased by the introduction of a new crop, as when the potato arrived from the Americas; or by innovations which reduced the proportion of arable land kept in fallow each year; or the area of land under cultivation might be increased by drainage of marshland, enclosure of heath, or reclamation from the sea, but the general problem was permanent and insoluble. If growth occurred it must at some point increase the pressure on the land since the land was the source of all food and the great bulk of the raw materials of industry. If either poorer land was taken into cultivation or existing land used more intensively, this must tend to involve declining returns both to capital and labour, and eventually growth would grind to a halt or be reversed. Though expressed differently, this was in essence a recognition of the problems associated with the character of the annual round of plant photosynthesis.

Because the productivity of the land was the prime constraint on increasing output generally, Adam Smith regarded investment in agriculture as intrinsically more productive than all other forms of investment:

> The capital employed in agriculture, therefore, not only puts into motion a greater quantity of productive labour than any equal capital employed in manufacture, but in proportion too to the quantity of productive labour which it employs, it adds a much greater value to the annual produce of the land and labour of the country, to the real wealth and revenue of its inhabitants. Of all the ways in which a capital can be employed, it is by far the most advantageous to the society.[8]

[7] McCloskey drew attention to the unprecedented nature of the changes in train and their curious invisibility to contemporaries in an essay on the industrial revolution: 'In the eighty years or so after 1780 the population of Britain nearly tripled, the towns of Liverpool and Manchester became gigantic cities, the average income of the population more than doubled, the share of farming fell from just under half to just under one fifth of the nation's output, and the making textiles and iron moved into the steam-driven factories. *So strange were these events that before they happened they were not anticipated, and while they were happening they were not comprehended* [my italics].' McCloskey, 'The industrial revolution', p. 103.

[8] Smith, *The wealth of nations*, I, p. 385.

The belief that the productivity of agriculture determines the scale of output generally is reflected in many passages of *The wealth of nations*. Consider, for example, the following:

The inhabitants of the towns and those of the country are mutually the servants of one another. The town is a continual fair or market, to which the inhabitants of the country resort, in order to exchange their rude for manufactured produce. It is this commerce which supplies the inhabitants of the town both with the materials of their work, and the means of their subsistence. The quantity of the finished work which they sell to the inhabitants of the country, necessarily regulates the quantity of the materials and provisions which they buy. Neither their employment nor subsistence, therefore, can augment, but in proportion to the augmentation of the demand from the country for finished work; and this demand can augment only in proportion to the extension of improvement and cultivation. Had human institutions, therefore, never disturbed the natural course of things, the progressive wealth and increase of the towns would in every political society, be consequential, and in proportion to the improvement and cultivation of the territory or country.[9]

The elapse of time between the publication of *The wealth of nations* and Ricardo's *Principles* did not cause Ricardo to qualify the pessimism which Adam Smith had expressed. Rather the opposite, since Ricardo made it clear that his gloomy conclusion was due not to institutional shortcomings, the character of economic systems, or the failure of human judgement, but to the operation of the laws of nature. He summarised his analysis in a manner that left no grounds for optimism about the secular trends of real wages or profit levels. His reasoning excluded any possibility of the type of sustained growth that came to be termed an industrial revolution:

Whilst the land yields abundantly, wages may temporarily rise, and the producers may consume more than their accustomed proportion; but the stimulus which will thus be given to population, will speedily reduce the labourers to their usual consumption. But when poor lands are taken into cultivation, or when more capital and labour are expended on the old land, with a less return of produce, the effect must be permanent. A greater proportion of that part of the produce which remains to be divided, after paying rent, between the owners of stock and the labourers will be apportioned to the latter. Each man may, and probably will, have a less absolute quantity; but as more labourers are employed in proportion to the whole produce retained by the farmer, the value of a greater proportion of the whole produce will be absorbed by wages, and consequently the value of a smaller proportion will be devoted to profits. *This will necessarily be rendered permanent by the laws of nature, which have limited the productive powers of the land* [my italics].[10]

[9] *Ibid.*, I, pp. 403–4. [10] Ricardo, *Principles*, pp. 125–6.

In organic economies it was widely recognised that this problem was unavoidable. Immediately preceding his betrayal by Judas, Jesus told his disciples that he was about to be betrayed and crucified. Shortly afterwards in the house of Simon the Leper a woman in sympathy poured a precious ointment over his head. This caused indignation among the disciples who argued that it should have been sold to raise money to be distributed to the poor. But Jesus defended her action, saying that she did it with his approaching burial in mind: 'For ye have the poor always with you; but me ye have not always.'[11] To modern ears his statement concerning the poor may seem somewhat unfeeling, but to those listening to a reading of the passage in a parish church in Tudor England it would pass unnoticed since it was no more than a statement of fact. Similarly, to someone sitting in a congregation today the sentence in the Lord's Prayer, 'Give us this day our daily bread', may occasion mild surprise. It is seldom a grave concern in societies that have been transformed in the wake of the industrial revolution, but would have had pressing and immediate relevance from time to time for congregations in Tudor times. Poverty and the difficulty of securing an adequate supply of basic food were ever-present features of organic economies.

Malthus, the third member of the triumvirate of classical economists, published his *Essay on population* in 1798, shortly before the taking of the first census in 1801. The information contained in the early censuses, and his increasing knowledge of the demographic circumstances of populations in other European countries and in countries elsewhere in the world, caused him to modify substantially the analysis that he set out in the *Essay on population*, but it was his initial formulation which made him both famous and infamous. The *Essay* was published when Malthus was only thirty-two years old. He had been provoked by what he regarded as the groundless optimism of men such as Wallace, Condorcet and Godwin about the possibility of transforming the human condition.[12] His central argument was not new. Adam Smith had previously expressed it bluntly:

> Every species of animals naturally multiplies in proportion to their means of subsistence, and no species can ever multiply beyond it. But in civilized society it is only among the inferior ranks of people that the scantiness of subsistence can set limits to the further multiplication of the human species; and it can do so in no other way than by destroying a great part of the children which their fruitful marriages produce.[13]

[11] St Matthew, 26:11. [12] Malthus, *Essay on population* [1798], Chapters 8–15.
[13] Smith, *The wealth of nations*, I, p. 89.

Malthus, however, formulated the issue in a way that was simple, eye-catching, and difficult to ignore. He had read mathematics at Cambridge and was familiar with the difference between arithmetic and geometric progressions. He suggested that, at best, output might rise arithmetically, but that the population, if unchecked, would rise geometrically. The nature of the two progressions is such that on these assumptions living standards must always be under pressure from the fact that production could not keep pace with population. In times of prosperity the population would rise quickly, outpacing production. Living standards would therefore fall and, as the bulk of the population became poorer, mortality would rise, eventually to the point where it matched the level of fertility. The population would therefore cease growing and the labouring poor would hover on the verge of destitution.

Ironically, in later life Malthus took a much more nuanced attitude to the balance between production and population than he had taken in his *Essay on population*. His thinking changed after the first census was taken in 1801. Rickman, who directed the taking of the first four censuses, was much interested not only in the current totals of population but also in population movements in preceding centuries, and he required Anglican ministers to make returns of the totals of baptisms, burials, and marriages recorded in their parish registers for certain years which he specified. He then made estimates of national population trends based on these data. It became clear to Malthus that his initial assumptions about demographic behaviour were wide of the mark. There was no simple and invariant relationship between levels and trends of production and population. His increasing knowledge of the demographic characteristics of other European populations and of populations in other parts of the world further reinforced his recognition that his initial stance had been too simplistic.

In particular, Malthus came to appreciate that nuptiality played a very important role in determining population trends, influencing both fertility levels and, indirectly, also mortality levels. Population growth might cease well short of the point at which most families were living close to the point of bare subsistence. Where the marriage system found in much of western Europe prevailed and the decision to marry was heavily influenced by prevailing economic conditions and by long-term economic trends, the living standards of a population might remain above, even well above, bare subsistence even in difficult times. He also became conscious of the fact that the economic–demographic process was subject to long-term 'oscillations' during which living standards might move in either direction for substantial periods of time.

Malthus' model of the interplay between production and population in its later formulation was less harsh and uncompromising than that either of Adam Smith or of Ricardo. But his initial formulation remained highly influential because of its simplicity and dire implications. Its influence extended well beyond economics and the other social sciences. Reading the *Essay on population* provided Darwin with an engine to drive the process of natural selection. In the context of the attempt to portray the nature of organic societies and to identify characteristics that prepared the way for an industrial revolution to occur, however, it was Malthus' later writings that are more relevant.

Malthus' insight into the significance of the west European marriage system is important in considering the range of characteristics of an organic economy which could facilitate the occurrence of an industrial revolution. It contrasted with the stance taken by Adam Smith. If Smith's view of population behaviour were correct, the vast majority of people in every society would be living in poverty, close to bare subsistence. Their incomes would be almost exclusively devoted to the four essentials; food, fuel, housing, and clothing.

The character and attributes of the west European marriage system are discussed at greater length in Chapter 6. Its potential importance is clear. What was distinctive about the system when compared with other marriage systems was that decisions to marry were strongly affected by economic circumstances. This in turn was the result of the convention that on marriage a couple should create a new household. Instead of joining an existing household, a couple on marriage was expected to establish a new one. This involved accumulating the resources necessary to acquire and equip a household. For many couples it was necessary to save from income over a period of time to make the marriage possible. If incomes were depressed or irregular it took longer to do so than in more prosperous times. As a result the average age of marriage might rise or fall in sympathy. In western Europe societies, moreover, a significant fraction of each rising generation never married, and this proportion was also influenced by economic circumstances. In other societies the timing of marriage was governed by the prevailing conventional norms that meant that the vast majority of women married young. The norms in extra-European societies were not, of course, everywhere the same but it was frequently the case that celibacy was almost unknown and the average age of marriage for women was far lower than in western Europe, often close to the attainment of sexual maturity. The fact that in western Europe between a tenth and a fifth of each generation never married, combined with a relatively late average age at marriage for women, implied that fertility levels were normally lower than in other societies. This generalisation is too sweeping. Fertility levels were influenced by many factors other than age at marriage and celibacy levels. Relatively modest levels of general fertility sometimes prevailed through the effect of social and personal conventions and practices very different from the west European system. And the west European marriage system itself took varying forms. Nevertheless, Malthus' recognition that the 'preventive checks of moral restraint' implied the possibility of stationing a society at some distance from the Malthusian precipice is relevant to any consideration of the circumstances in which escape from the constraints of an organic economy might occur.

With the benefit of hindsight it is not difficult to see that the classical economists' dismissal of the possibility of escaping from the confines of an organic economy was mistaken. Focusing on the fact that the supply of land, unlike the supply of labour or capital, was incapable of expansion, as the central issue which enforced a gloomy conclusion proved a less insoluble problem than they supposed. Since expressing the same problem in terms of gaining access to a different source of energy clarifies the nature of the change which proved capable of overcoming the constraint which they viewed as insuperable, it is intriguing to note how Adam Smith accounted for the tendency of industries to locate on coalfields and assessed the significance of access to cheap coal:

> In a country where the winters are so cold as in Great Britain, fuel is, during that season, in the strictest sense of the word, a necessary of life, not only for the purpose of dressing victuals, but for the comfortable subsistence of many different sorts of workmen who work within doors; and coals are the cheapest of all fuel. The price of fuel has so important an influence on that of labour, that all over Great Britain manufactures have confined themselves principally to the coal countries; other parts of the country, on account of the high price of this necessary article, not being able to work so cheap.[14]

It is also instructive to recognise the difficulty that near-contemporaries experienced in disputing the validity of the arguments that the classical economists advanced. Even at a date at which it is now generally agreed that the industrial revolution had become established, those best placed to judge whether exponential growth was possible were often reluctant to abandon the conclusion to which the classical economists had come. John Stuart Mill published the first edition of his *Principles of political economy* in 1848 and several subsequent editions in the next quarter-century. He was very widely read and much respected. He discussed the significance of the land as a constraint upon indefinite expansion in the following terms:

[14] Smith, *The wealth of nations*, II, p. 404.

The materials of manufacture being all drawn from the land, and many of them from agriculture, which supplies in particular the entire material of clothing: the general law of production from the land, the law of diminishing return, must in the last resort be applicable to manufacturing as well as to agricultural history. As population increases, and the power of the land to yield increased produce is strained harder and harder, any additional supply of material, as well as of food, must be obtained by a more than proportionally increased expenditure of effort.[15]

Mill was hesitant, however, in ruling out entirely the possibility of ameliorating the situation. He recognised that in manufacturing there was scope for increasing productivity by the use of machinery and the division of labour. Even though it was likely that labour productivity in agriculture would tend to decline:

– the productive power of labour in all other branches of industry might be so rapidly augmenting, that the required amount of labour could be spared for manufactures, and nevertheless a greater produce be obtained and the aggregate wants of the community be on the whole better supplied, than before.[16]

Mill remained unsure about the long-term prospects for society. He followed Malthus in regarding the extent of the restraint on fertility as a key variable in this regard, but did not recognise that the industrial revolution was producing a radically new situation in which the traditional restrictions on prolonged growth had ceased to apply. His writing is a salutary reminder that what looms large in hindsight may not be easy to appreciate at the time. But an appreciation that a new age had dawned, an age in which poverty for the masses was not inevitable, and that not only the necessities of life but comforts and even luxuries might be widely enjoyed, came to be increasingly widely recognised. The reason for the changed situation is well encapsulated in Jevons' book, *The coal question*. The first edition was published in 1865. His subject was the 'Age of Coal'. He remarked:

Coal in truth stands not beside, but entirely above all other commodities. It is the material source of the energy of this country – the universal aid – the factor in everything we do. With coal almost any feat is possible or easy; without it we are thrown back on the laborious poverty of early times.[17]

But Jevons also had a clear appreciation of the hazards and uncertainties of the new age, of the danger of depending upon a *stock* of energy rather than a *flow*. He was deeply concerned about the depletion of coal reserves generally and the export of coal in particular:

15 Mill, *Principles of political economy*, I, p. 182.
16 *Ibid.*, p. 182. 17 Jevons, *The coal question*, p. 2.

> To part in commerce with the surplus yearly interest of the soil may be unquestioned gain; but to disperse so lavishly the cream of our mineral wealth is to be spendthrifts of our capital – to part with that which can never be reproduced.[18]

In short, the export of corn was less hazardous than the export of coal because the former was the product of an energy *flow*, whereas the latter was an exhaustible *stock*.

The fact that the supply of land could not be increased proved not to be the insuperable obstacle to prolonged growth that the classical economists had posited, and this was not solely because they were not aware of the significance of making use of fossil fuel. The scope for advance within the context of an organic economy proved substantial in England in the seventeenth and eighteenth centuries. Organic economies were not as rigidly constrained as contemporaries sometimes believed. This fact suggests a re-evaluation of some of the changes taking place in early modern England. Success in freeing the country from sole dependence on plant photosynthesis as an energy source was the fundamental reason for the change, but major advances were also achieved within the context of an organic economy. Without the momentum that this afforded it is debatable whether an industrial revolution would have occurred, an issue explored further in Chapter 4.

Conclusion

Medieval philosophers distinguished between what they termed *fungibles* and *consumptibles*. A field was a fungible because its use in any one year did not prevent using it for the same purpose in the next. A loaf of bread was a consumptible because after it had been consumed its use was ended. This distinction clarifies an important difference between organic economies and an economy based on fossil fuels, such as that which emerged first in Britain. The supply of energy in organic economies was fungible in nature. The use of the product of plant photosynthesis in any one year did not normally affect its availability in the following year. In contrast, fossil fuels are consumptibles. Each ton of coal burned slightly reduces the stock left to be burned in the future. In the long run dependence upon a *stock* of energy invites disaster since it must eventually be exhausted, but for a while it removes the constraint that is imposed by dependence on a limited annual *flow* of energy. For the provision of mechanical energy, Britain continued to depend on fungible sources long after it had become dependent on coal, a consumptible, for heat energy.

[18] *Ibid.*, p. 455.

The position began to change early in the eighteenth century, when steam power increasingly replaced animal muscle in the evacuation of surplus water from coal mines, but further progress was relatively slow. A century later, however, when engines using steam as an energy source had become far more efficient, fossil fuel, a consumptible, had become the dominant energy source across the whole range of productive activities, whether involving the use of heat energy or mechanical energy. Thereby, the industrial revolution was accomplished.

Chapter 3 describes the changing pattern of energy consumption between the sixteenth and nineteenth centuries as a preliminary to the consideration of the changes brought about by dramatic urban growth, major advances in agricultural productivity, and linked changes in occupational structure and in the scale of consumer demand, which are the subject matter of Chapters 4 and 5.

3 Energy consumption

Adding access to a vast *stock* of energy in the shape of coal to the *flow* of energy derived from plant photosynthesis was central to many of the changes that transformed the English economy from the mid sixteenth century onwards. The history of the changing balance between new and traditional energy sources in this period therefore deserves attention. It provides a background to many aspects of the economic and social changes that are the subject of the subsequent chapters of this book. There was a major increase in energy consumption per head of population due almost entirely to the increasing use of coal, but it is important to note that until the end of the eighteenth century coal was almost exclusively a source of *heat* energy. The principal traditional sources of *mechanical* energy, animal and human muscle, remained dominant until the early decades of the nineteenth century. It was only when the development of the steam engine made coal a convenient source of both types of energy, and it had proved possible to harness the steam engine to a very wide range of productive tasks, that the industrial revolution could be regarded as accomplished. If mechanical energy had continued to be provided almost exclusively by human and animal muscle, the constraints of an organic economy would have continued to limit growth. Because draught animals were the most important single source of mechanical energy in early modern England, increasing use of mechanical energy would only have been possible by devoting a larger and larger acreage to animal fodder, thus experiencing once again the constraint on growth that afflicted all organic economies. As Sieferle remarked, 'The history of energy is the secret history of industrialisation'.[1]

The growth of coal production

Table 3.1 provides coal production estimates and population totals for England over a period of three centuries. Coal production rose massively.

[1] Sieferle, *The subterranean forest*, p. 137.

Table 3.1 *Coal production per annum and population growth in England*

	1560s	1700	1750	1800	1850–5
	Coal production (000 tons)				
	177	2,430	4,295	11,195	48,300
	Population (000)				
	3,036	5,211	5,922	8,671	16,732
	Coal production per 1,000 population (tons)				
	58	466	725	1,291	2,875
	Annual growth rates (per cent)				
		1560s/1700	**1700/50**	**1750/1800**	**1800/1850–4**
Production		1.89	1.15	1.93	2.97
Population		0.39	0.26	0.77	1.32
Production per head of population		1.50	0.89	1.16	1.61

Sources: Hatcher, *The history of the British coal industry*, I, Table 4.1, p. 68; Flinn, *The history of the British coal industry*, II, Table 1.2, p. 26; Church, *The history of the British coal industry*, III, Table 1.1, p. 3.

In the mid nineteenth century, it was 270 times larger than it had been in the 1560s, and 20 times larger than in 1700. Over the three centuries in question, however, the population more than quintupled, rising from 3.04 million in 1561 to 16.73 million in 1851.[2] Rather than considering only absolute totals of coal production, it is therefore also helpful to consider consumption per head of population in assessing change over time, and the growth rates for each of them. The annual growth rate for coal production varied between 1.2 and 1.9 per cent per annum throughout the period from the 1560s to 1800, with only limited variation. In the final half-century 1800 to 1850/4, however, the annual rate of growth accelerated markedly to 3 per cent, in part a reflection of the fact that coal was an increasingly important source of mechanical as well as heat energy. The comparable growth rates per head of population were between 0.9 to 1.5 per cent between the 1560s and 1800 and 1.6 per cent per annum in the final half-century. Since the rate of

[2] Wrigley *et al.*, *English population history*, Table A9.1, pp. 614–15.

population growth rose markedly during the later eighteenth century and the population total almost doubled in the first half of the nineteenth, the acceleration in the rate of growth of coal production per head in the final half-century was substantially less marked than that for the coal production total.

Recent work by Warde makes it possible to specify approximately the quantity of all major forms of energy consumed in England and Wales from Elizabethan times onwards. The total rose massively between the mid sixteenth and mid nineteenth centuries. In 1560–9 the annual average figure was 65 petajoules, a quantity roughly equivalent to the energy contained in 2.2 million tons of coal. Three centuries later, in 1850–9, energy consumption had risen to 1,833 petajoules, a total more than 28 times as large as the earlier figure. The very large increase in energy consumption that took place was mainly due to the rapid expansion in coal production over the three centuries in question. Coal provided an annual average of 7 petajoules in 1560–9; in 1850–9 the equivalent figure was 1,689 petajoules. Other energy sources increased only from 58 to 144 petajoules.[3] Table 3.2 reflects the changes that occurred in greater detail, expressed in megajoules per head of population rather than as gross totals.

It should be noted, of course, that the quantity of energy consumed greatly exceeds the quantity of useful work performed. In men and animals, much of the energy consumed in the form of food is taken up in bodily maintenance, and when coal is burned only a fraction of the heat energy released performs useful work, but the variables involved vary so greatly over time and in different contexts that it makes sense that consumption data should be used when making a general survey.

Over the first two centuries from the 1560s to the 1750s consumption per head of population in each energy category was largely stable, apart from the rapid growth in the coal figure, which rose ten-fold, and a halving in firewood consumption, as coal began to replace firewood as a source of heat energy. The expansion of merchant shipping largely accounts for the increase in the wind power figure. During the final century the consumption per head of firewood as an energy source declined sharply and the mechanical energy per head of population supplied by draught animals halved. In this period the only category other than coal in which consumption per head rose was again wind power as the number and size of sailing vessels continued to expand, though expansion was slowing towards the end of the period as steam began to replace sail for propulsion. As already noted, the rate of growth in coal

[3] Warde, *Energy consumption*, Appendix I, 1, pp. 115–22.

Table 3.2 *Annual energy consumption per head in England and Wales (megajoules)*

	Human	Draught animals	Firewood	Wind	Water	Coal	Total
1560–9	4,373	6,210	6,324	59	162	2,039	19,167
1600–9	4,161	4,647	4.729	85	152	3,153	16,927
1650–9	4,521	4,802	3,849	153	156	6,772	20,253
1700–9	4,789	5,744	3,939	238	173	14,719	29,602
1750–9	4,519	5,113	3,429	427	198	21,403	35,089
1800–9	4,233	3,471	1,877	1,282	111	41,373	52,347
1850–9	3,564	2,633	118	1,280	89	88,779	96,463
	Totals above expressed as percentages of the overall total						
1560–9	22.8	32.4	33.0	0.3	0.8	10.6	100.0
1600–9	24.6	27.5	27.9	0.5	0.9	18.6	100.0
1650–9	22.3	23.7	19.0	0.8	0.8	33.4	100.0
1700–9	16.2	19.4	13.3	0.8	0.6	49.7	100.0
1750–9	12.9	14.6	9.8	1.2	0.6	61.0	100.0
1800–9	8.1	6.6	3.6	2.4	0.2	79.0	100.0
1850–9	3.7	2.7	0.1	1.3	0.1	92.0	100.0

Note: Estimated population totals for England and Wales were obtained by multiplying the totals for England alone by 1.07. Rounding the percentages means that the sum of the individual percentages does not always equal 100.0.
Sources: Warde, *Energy consumption in England and Wales*, Appendix 1, Table 1, pp. 115–22; Wrigley *et al.*, *English population history*, Table A9.1, pp. 614–15.

consumption per head changed little over the three centuries, approximately doubling every half-century, and eventually dominating the pattern of energy consumption as a whole.

The upper half of Table 3.2 provides a striking contrast between on the one hand the comparative stability of energy consumption per head, which relates to the energy *flows* derived from plant photosynthesis, and on the other hand the huge increases in energy consumption per head, which took place where the source was an energy *stock*. Coal supplied only 11 per cent of total energy consumption in the 1560s, rising to 33 per cent in the 1650s, 61 per cent in the 1750s, and no less than 92 per cent in the 1850s.

The lower half of Table 3.2 brings home forcefully the scale of the transformation involved in moving from an organic economy to an industrial revolution. In the mid sixteenth century mechanical energy represented 56.4 per cent of the total (human and animal muscle plus wind and water) while heat energy accounted for 43.6 per cent (firewood and coal). Human and animal muscle provided 98 per cent of the mechanical energy total; wind and water power were relatively unimportant, contributing only 2 per cent. In this period firewood accounted for three-quarters of the heat energy total with coal supplying the balance.

By 1750–9 there had already been substantial change in the relative importance of the different energy sources. The share of human and animal muscle power had halved from 55.2 to 27.5 per cent. The share of wind power had quadrupled, but it remained only a minor element among the sources of mechanical energy. The combined total for all four sources of mechanical energy (human and animal muscle, wind, and water) was 29.2 per cent, a large reduction compared with the situation two centuries earlier, when the comparable figure was 56.3 per cent. In contrast, heat energy, with 70.8 per cent, greatly increased its share of energy supply, far outweighing mechanical energy in the overall energy picture. In the mid sixteenth century firewood had accounted for three-quarters of the consumption of heat energy, but two centuries later consumption per head of firewood had halved and its share of heat energy consumption had fallen from three-quarters to less than one-sixth.

By the middle of the nineteenth century coal dwarfed all other energy sources, supplying more than nine-tenths of the total. However, because overall energy consumption per head had risen so notably over the preceding three centuries, the decline in the totals in each column in the top half of Table 3.2, which shows the quantity of energy consumed per head of population, was comparatively modest, apart from firewood and to a lesser extent animal muscle.

Down to the middle of the eighteenth century the division of all the energy sources into two groups, heat and mechanical energy, causes no problems, but thereafter it becomes increasingly meaningless. Until the mid eighteenth century coal was almost exclusively a source of heat energy. Thereafter the invention and progressive improvement of the steam engine meant that coal eventually became the dominant source of mechanical as well as heat energy. Setting flame to coal had provided heat energy in abundance but initially had no similar effect in increasing the scale of mechanical energy available for industrial production and transport. The discovery of a method of turning heat into controlled movement by harnessing steam for this purpose meant that the stock of energy present in the coal measures could be harnessed to meet energy needs across the board.

The degree to which the constraints of an organic economy had produced marked similarities between patterns of energy consumption in early modern Europe is illustrated in Table 3.3. Malanima, like Warde, is one of a group of scholars who are reconstructing the history of energy consumption in a number of European countries using the same

Table 3.3 *Energy consumption in England 1561–70 and in Italy 1861–70*

	Human	Draught animals	Firewood	Wind	Water	Fossil fuel	Total
	Annual consumption per head (megajoules)						
Italy 1861–70	3,831	3,058	8,894	46	127	1,206	17,162
England and Wales 1561–70	4,373	6,210	6,324	59	162	2,039	19,167
	Percentage share						
Italy 1861–70	22.3	17.8	51.8	0.27	0.74	7.0	100.0
England and Wales 1561–70	22.8	32.4	33.0	0.31	0.85	10.6	100.0

Sources: Malanima, *Energy consumption in Italy*, Appendix 1, Tables 2 and 3, pp. 96–101; Warde, *Energy consumption in England and Wales*, Appendix 1, Table 1, pp. 115–22.

definitions of the various types of energy and standard methods of measurement. The similarity in the scale of consumption of energy per head in England in the mid sixteenth century and Italy three hundred years later is striking. As late as 1861–70 coal was a very minor source of energy in Italy and energy consumption per head was closely similar to that in England three centuries earlier. Draught animals were of less importance in Italy than in England, reflecting no doubt, among other factors, the difference in the relative importance of arable and pastoral agriculture between the two countries. The opposite was the case with firewood, which was of greater importance in Italy. Coal was already beginning to be a significant source of heat energy in England even in the Elizabethan age.

The pattern and level of energy consumption found in Tudor England and Victorian Italy was characteristic of almost all the countries in early modern Europe for which estimates have been made before the nineteenth century. Because of lower winter temperatures, the consumption of firewood was higher in Scandinavian countries than around the Mediterranean or in those parts of western Europe benefiting from the northward flow of the Gulf stream, but almost everywhere the bulk of the mechanical energy available to the economy came from human and animal muscle, and firewood was the prime source of heat energy. Much of Europe remained 'organic' in its economic structure until the mid nineteenth century, or even later, though a few countries, notably Belgium, France, and Germany were steadily increasing their consumption of coal throughout the whole of the nineteenth century.

Apart from England, the only country in the early modern period whose energy consumption differed radically from the organic norm was Holland, and for the same reason. Both countries had access to a large *stock* of energy created by plant photosynthesis in the past rather than being dependent on the *flow* of energy derived from the annual round of plant photosynthesis. As a result, they were both drifting apart from the normal European level and pattern of energy consumption. The prime source of additional energy in Holland was peat; in England coal. The scale of the energy derived from peat in Holland has been the subject of dispute. De Zeeuw suggested a figure that equates to about 13,000 megajoules per annum per head of population on average in the seventeenth century. Unger considered that this figure was much too high and provided a revised, and probably more accurate, estimate for total consumption of 1.2×10^{12} kcal., which results in a much smaller average per head of 2,700 megajoules.[4]

The Netherlands in its 'golden age', however, was not solely dependent on peat to gain access to a *stock* of accumulated photosynthesis. As was the case with London, the low cost of water transport meant that coal from Newcastle and other coalfields that lay close to the sea was accessible even though the distance involved was measured in hundreds of miles.[5] Unger estimated that in the seventeenth century coal provided about two-fifths as much energy as peat in Holland, suggesting a combined total for peat and coal of *c.* 3,800 megajoules, and that by 1800 coal was supplying the Dutch economy with as much energy as peat had done in the seventeenth century. By this date, peat was supplying only half as much energy as coal.[6]

Peat represents an accumulation of the product of plant photosynthesis over thousands of years; coal a similar accumulation over millions of years. Sieferle estimated that in the seventeenth century 0.3–0.5 per cent of the stock then existent in the Netherlands was used annually, suggesting that over the century as a whole approaching half of it was consumed.[7] The increasing attraction of coal as an alternative to peat was reflected, for example, in the attempts made by Amsterdam to limit its use by sugar refineries in the city. Between 1614 and 1674 a variety of restrictions on its use during certain periods of the year were imposed by the city authorities, but in 1674 'the burgemeesters caved in altogether before the refiners' threats of closing down their operations, and gave permission for the burning of coal on a year-round basis'.[8] In the eighteenth and still more in the nineteenth century, when coal production was

[4] De Zeeuw, 'Peat and the Dutch golden age', Table III, p. 16; Unger, 'Energy sources', p. 227. The Dutch population total was taken as 1.875 million: De Vries and van der Woude, *The first modern economy*, Table 3.1, p. 50.

[5] The Netherlands was not the only country with a North Sea coastline to benefit from access to Tyneside coal. Denmark is a more dramatic instance of this, see pp. 186–8.

[6] Unger, 'Energy sources', p. 246.

[7] Sieferle, *The subterranean forest*, p. 38.

[8] De Vries and van der Woude, *The first modern economy*, p. 329.

measured in millions and then tens of millions of tons, the big coal-producing countries dominated the energy supply scene, but the Dutch example is a reminder that any means of escaping dependence exclusively on the energy flow which was characteristic of all organic economies brought with it novel opportunities.

In England in the seventeenth century the average annual consumption of energy derived from coal was about 7,400 megajoules,[9] almost twice the quantity secured from a combination of peat and coal in the Netherlands, though both figures are at best rough approximations. What is not in doubt, however, is that heat energy consumption in both countries was significantly higher than comparable levels in neighbouring countries. In both countries the availability of relatively cheap and abundant heat energy favoured the growth of industries such as brewing, brick and tile making, salt boiling, sugar refining, and dyeing, which were heat energy intensive.

It is of interest to note incidentally that, just as with coal, the use of peat as an energy source was feasible only where the cost of transport could be kept to a minimum, and this constraint is especially severe in the case of peat because of its greater bulk in relation to its energy potential. Van der Woude *et al.* made a calculation that brings home forcefully how strong this constraint was in an organic economy:

> Water transport was essential to the economical digging and transporting of this bulky commodity. Had road transport been used to bring the peat to its urban markets, 110,000 horses would have been required, and to feed these horses 230,000 hectares – one third of the nation's arable land – would have been withdrawn from the production of crops destined for human consumption.[10]

Other aspects of the huge rise in coal output

Manpower productivity and its implications

In most of the major industries in which output increased dramatically during the industrial revolution, employment rose less rapidly, often much less rapidly, than output. Output per worker increased substantially. The coal industry was a notable exception. Pit drainage was transformed by the employment of steam pumps, but work at the coal face changed very little over the centuries down to the First World War. Paradoxically, although the use of coal as an energy source transformed industrial production and productivity, the coal industry was perhaps the

9 Warde, *Energy consumption*, Appendix I, 2, pp. 123–5 and Appendix I, 3, pp. 131–3.
10 Van der Woude *et al.*, *Urbanization in history*, p. 11.

only major industry in which output per worker was broadly stationary from the seventeenth century to the end of the nineteenth. Indeed manpower productivity probably declined during the nineteenth century, and may not have been much different in *c.* 1900 from *c.* 1700. In England as a whole the average annual quantity mined per worker was 310 tons in *c.* 1830 and 247 tons in *c.* 1910.[11] Estimates of output per head at earlier dates are few and involve significant margins of error. Flinn estimated output per man-year on the north-east coalfield at 290 tons 'in the early decades of the nineteenth century' (for *c.* 1830 and *c.* 1910 the figures for this coalfield were 332 tons and 241 tons, respectively).[12] For earlier dates very few reliable estimates are available, but it is interesting that Hatcher used data for the Cumberland collieries of Howgill and Greenbank in the late 1690s and early 1700s which suggest that output per man-year in Howgill was *c.* 185 tons and in Greenbank 272 tons, figures which are in rough accord with Nef's estimate that annual output per man 'must have approached 200 tons' in the north-east field in the seventeenth century.[13] Estimates relating to the north-east coalfield are particularly valuable since throughout the whole period from Tudor times to the First World War it was substantially the largest producer of the several English coalfields.

The absence of any clear rise in output per coalminer meant that the pit workforce increased roughly in line with the increase in coal output, and considerably faster than employment growth in manufacturing industries generally. This meant that coalmining claimed a steadily increasing proportion of the male labour force. Church noted that the coalmining workforce constituted 5 per cent of the combined employment in mining, manufacturing, and building in 1830 and that this figure had risen to almost 12 per cent in 1913. The marked rise in this percentage implies that while manufacturing employment doubled and building employment tripled during the same period, the mining workforce increased ten-fold.[14]

The growth of the coal industry, combined with the fact that manpower productivity was static, resulted in large population increases linked to coalmining growth. An early example of this occurred in the seventeenth century when London became dependent on 'seacoal' for domestic

11 Church, *The history of the British coal industry*, III, Table 1.2, p. 3, and Table 3.1, p. 189.

12 Flinn, *The history of the British coal industry*, II, p. 365.

13 Hatcher, *The history of the British coal industry*, I, p. 346; Nef, *The rise of the British coal industry*, II, p. 138.

14 Church, *The history of the British coal industry*, III, p. 188. The period to which the ten-fold increases is attributed is 1841–1913, but the accompanying table (Table 3.3) and the earlier text suggests that the period was 1830–1913.

Table 3.4 *The seven fastest-growing counties 1801–1911 (ratios to the base 100 in the first year of each period)*

1801–21		1821–51		1851–81		1881–1911		1801–1911	
Lancashire	152.6	Durham	198.9	Durham	230.3	Essex	240.7	Durham	923.9
Sussex	143.0	Lancashire	191.6	Surrey	230.2	Surrey	196.6	Surrey	818.0
Middlesex	140.6	Staffordshire	176.8	Lancashire	165.6	Nottinghamshire	163.6	Lancashire	669.1
Staffordshire	139.9	Warwickshire	167.8	Middlesex	164.5	Northumberland	160.7	Essex	604.6
Yorkshire, W.R.	138.8	Middlesex	167.7	Yorkshire, W.R.	161.4	Durham	159.9	Staffordshire	535.2
Cheshire	136.2	Yorkshire, W.R.	163.6	Essex	158.0	Hampshire	157.4	Middlesex	525.5
Cambridgeshire	135.1	Cheshire	159.7	Staffordshire	157.5	Cheshire	148.8	Yorkshire, W.R.	511.0

Notes: The county totals were drawn from a recent exercise designed to produce population totals for unchanging units for the whole period 1801–1911. Because the boundaries of units used by successive censuses changed, this meant that some of the small units at parish level were amalgamated to form larger units. If the boundary of a parish was changed, this created a larger unit whose boundary did not change. Occasionally, the enlarged unit crossed the boundary between two administrative counties, causing a fractional difference between the county total recorded in the census and the total resulting from producing an unchanging unit.

Sources: The county totals for 1801 to 1851: Wrigley, *The early English censuses*, Table M1.1, pp. 254–5. Thereafter census totals drawn from the censuses 1861–1911, slightly modified in some cases as indicated in the notes.

heating and for providing heat energy for an increasing range of industries. London's coal came by sea from Tyneside. Between 1600 and 1700 her imports increased from *c.* 150,000 tons to 400,000–450,000 tons.[15] On the assumption that each miner was producing 200 tons annually this implies that mining employment in the north-east rose by about 1,400 over the century. If mining families contained on average five members, and allowing for the rise in employment linked to the growth of coalmining, for example in the supply of food, in construction, and in inland and water transport, the growth in coalmining probably increased population totals by 15–20,000. It is therefore of interest that during the seventeenth century the percentage growth of population was greater in Northumberland and Durham than in any of the other English counties, apart from Middlesex (essentially London).[16] Without the London coal trade it is probable that other counties would have taken their places.

The absolute level of coal output in the seventeenth century meant that coalmining employment was relatively small. In the nineteenth century output levels and employment were many times greater. In 1830–4 annual output on the English coalfields averaged 23 million tons, rising to 175 million tons in 1910–13.[17] The comparable employment totals were 76,000 and 709,000. With employment so substantial and highly concentrated geographically, it was to be expected that the growth rates of some county populations would be strongly affected by coalmining. Table 3.4 lists the seven fastest-growing counties over the whole period 1801–1911 and for four subdivisions of the period.

It is striking that the fastest-growing county over the whole period 1801–1911 was Durham, heading both the suburban county of Surrey, whose rapid growth reflected the expansion of the metropolis, and Lancashire, the county *par excellence* of the industrial revolution. Durham's population in 1911 was more than nine times larger than it had been in 1801. The subperiods also reveal much of interest. As might be expected, given the presence of the rapidly expanding cotton industry and its general prominence during the industrial revolution, Lancashire headed the list in the first subperiod but thereafter steadily lost momentum, slipping down the table until in the last subperiod it was no longer in the top seven, finishing fifteenth. In the final subperiod, 1881–1911, Northumberland joined Durham in the list of fastest-growing counties, and the fact that Nottinghamshire finished higher than either of them was largely a reflection of the rapid expansion of coal mining in the county.

15 Hatcher, *The history of the British coal* industry, I, p. 41.
16 Wrigley, 'Rickman revisited', Table 4, p. 723.
17 Church, *The history of the British coal industry*, III, Table 1.1, p. 3.

The annual rate of growth in coalmining employment in the East Midlands field was higher than in any other coalmining region in England in the 1860s, 1870s, 1880s, and 1890s.[18] There are other features of this table that would call for comment in a different context, notably the vigour of metropolitan expansion. The three 'London' counties, Middlesex, Surrey, and Essex figure prominently, especially in the second half of the nineteenth century.

It is an interesting irony of the period during which the English economy was transformed by the energy derived from coal that manpower productivity in the coalmining industry barely changed, whereas in agriculture, the universal energy source in organic economies, manpower productivity increased markedly. Yet, while both contributed to bringing about an industrial revolution, it was the former which made the decisive difference.

Coal transport

Perhaps the most important change brought about by the increasing production of coal, other than its transformation of the scale of energy supply, was its impact on the transport system. Coal is heavy and bulky. As an illustration of the challenge that its transport presented, consider the scale which coal production had reached by the later eighteenth century compared with the comparable figure for grain, the principal product of arable agriculture. In 1750 England mined 4.3 million tons of coal; in 1800 this figure had risen to 11.2 million tons (Table 3.1). In 1800 the total weight of grain produced in England and Wales may be estimated at 4.4 million tons.[19]

The great bulk of both coal and grain were consumed at a distance from their points of production and therefore in both cases their cost at the point of consumption included significant transport costs.[20] Although the total weights of each product to be transported were broadly similar

[18] Church, *The history of the British coal industry*, III, Table 3.2, p. 190. In some of these decades there was faster growth in the Scottish and Welsh coal regions.

[19] Based on the estimates in Wrigley, 'The transition to an advanced organic economy', Table 1, p. 440 and Table 2, p. 443. In 1800 there were 7.63 million acres in grain, divided between four grains – wheat, rye, barley, and oats – whose shares were 41.0, 1.3, 24.4, and 33.3 per cent, respectively. The acreages in each grain were therefore 3.13, 0.10, 1.86, and 2.54 million, respectively. Bushels of wheat, barley, and oats were taken to weigh 56, 48, and 38 lb, respectively: Overton, *Agricultural revolution*, p. xiv. I have assumed a figure of 50 lb for rye.

[20] In the case of grain there was one major exception to the rule that consumption took place at a distance from production. In 1800 *c.* 70 per cent of the production of oats was consumed on the farm: Overton and Campbell, 'Statistics of production and productivity', Table 7.11, p. 201.

in the middle decades of the eighteenth century, the problems they posed differed fundamentally, arising from the fact that the production of corn, like that of all agricultural products, was *areal*, whereas the production of coal was *punctiform*. To produce the country's grain crop meant devoting millions of acres to the crop. To produce comparable tonnages of coal might mean gaining access to underground beds of the mineral spread over a considerable area, but once brought to the surface the pitheads were a scattering of points covering only a few acres rather than millions of acres. As a result, the transport network needed to take grain to market was *dendritic*, that is, resembling the structure of a tree. The route from the farm to a neighbouring village represented a twig which linked first to a thin branch and then through thicker branches to boughs, before finally reaching the main trunk. In contrast the transport network needed to bring coal to the settlement or industrial plant where it was consumed was *linear* in character. Large volumes moved from the minehead to a limited number of final destinations, thus simultaneously creating the need to improve transport facilities between the points in question and encouraging the necessary investment.

To describe the difference between the transport needs of corn and coal in this fashion fails to do justice to the complexities of the historical past. Much of the coal that was carried in large volumes along a canal to an industrial city, for example, made the last few hundred yards of its journey by horse and cart to the cotton mill or domestic consumer, and assumed a more dendritic character in so doing. Yet the basic fact about coal transport and its market price was simple. The cost of coal was highly sensitive to the cost per ton-mile of transporting it. Characteristically, it doubled within about ten miles from the pithead when carried on horseback or by horse and cart, but alternative forms of transport could transform the size of the accessible market area. Movement costs over navigable water were far lower than over land. Costs per ton-mile were lowest of all when using sea transport by collier vessel. London had long benefited from this. Its ability to meet its heat energy needs with coal dug in Northumberland or Durham from Tudor times onwards depended on the coastal location of both the capital and coalfield.

The fact that coal production was punctiform, that coal was bulky and heavy, and that its transport to market was often linear rather than dendritic in character, created a powerful incentive to invest in transport improvements. In particular, it transformed the economics of canal construction. A large proportion of canal construction was explicitly undertaken to reduce the cost of coal in centres that promised to become large-scale consumers if the price could be lowered. Canal construction took place predominantly in rising industrial regions, encouraged by the fact that whereas in the seventeenth century coal was mainly a fuel for domestic heating, in the following century it became the fuel of choice for an increasing range of industrial processes in which heat energy was needed on a large scale. Canals passing through predominantly rural areas brought many benefits to farms close to the canal route by reducing the cost of lime, marl, coal, and other bulky or heavy materials, but they seldom proved profitable investments if largely dependent on rural custom, since traffic volumes were modest compared to canals linking coalfields to industrial and commercial centres.

Ironically, although the nature of coal production and its rapidly increasing scale encouraged major improvements in transport facilities, until the early decades of the nineteenth century the transport improvements were all made subject to the limitations inherent in organic economies. The mechanical energy source used in moving raw materials and finished goods by road and canal remained animal muscle, and therefore the scope for increasing the scale, speed, and reliability of transport facilities remained limited. It was only with the construction of a national railway system in the middle decades of the nineteenth century, using coal rather than muscle as its source of mechanical energy, that transport could achieve advances to parallel those already long achieved in the branches of industry in which cheap and abundant heat energy was the key to rapid expansion.

The fundamental importance of gaining access to a new and far more abundant source of energy in the form of coal is unmistakable in considering the gathering momentum of growth in the quarter-millennium between the reigns of Elizabeth I and Victoria, which set England apart from her continental neighbours. But there were other changes in train whose significance in causing the English economy to diverge so notably is equally unmistakable. Perhaps the most striking of these changes was the notable gain in agricultural productivity interlinked with the remarkable surge in urban growth taking place during the seventeenth and eighteenth centuries, which is the subject of Chapter 4.

4 Urban growth and agricultural productivity

In organic economies it was always the case that the size of the urban sector was strongly influenced by the productivity of agriculture. City dwellers needed food and drink no less than those living in the countryside and since they produced little food themselves, they depended upon the existence of a rural surplus. If, for example, the agricultural sector produced 25 per cent more food than would cover the needs of the rural population, the food needs of an urban population that constituted a fifth of the total population could be satisfied. Agricultural productivity set limits to the urban growth that could take place, but agricultural productivity was itself strongly influenced by urban demand. In the absence of a substantial urban sector, in rural areas there was little incentive to produce an output greater than that needed to meet local needs. In other words, agricultural productivity and urban growth might be characterised by either negative or positive feedback. If the urban sector was trivially small and stagnant there would be minimal incentive for increased agricultural output since any surplus over local rural needs would be unable to find a market. If, however, the urban sector was significant and growing it created an incentive to increase agricultural output, thus ensuring that demand and supply remained in balance as urban growth progressed. Positive feedback between urban growth and improved agricultural productivity was always possible in organic economies. If it occurred, however, although the level of urbanisation might increase for a time, matched by an increasing rural surplus, the positive feedback could not continue indefinitely, because of the implications of the fixed supply of land which the classical economists described so effectively.

The scale of urban growth in England and the continent

Perhaps the most striking and important of all the contrasts between England and her continental neighbours in their economic development in the early modern period was in the speed, scale, and nature of the urban growth taking place. It was striking in England but muted to the point of non-existence in most of continental Europe. This in turn, necessarily meant that throughout this period English agriculture was making notable progress, given that the island remained broadly self-sufficient in food production. The balance between home demand and home supply was not always exact. In the early eighteenth century there was a substantial export of grain, and towards the end of the century the balance tipped in the other direction, but in neither period was the imbalance substantial.[1]

Table 4.1 provides some basic data relating to the urban growth taking place between 1600 and 1800 in England and continental Europe. The urban totals refer to large towns with 10,000 or more inhabitants because de Vries, from whose work the totals for continental countries were taken, found difficulty in securing consistent data for smaller towns in Europe in the early part of the period.[2] The table is intended to illustrate the extent to which urban growth in England came to dominate trends in Europe as a whole in the course of the seventeenth and eighteenth centuries. Columns (2)–(4) in the top two sections are self-explanatory. The totals in column (5) show how urban totals would have risen if the urban percentage had remained at its level in 1600, thus causing urban growth to parallel the rise in the total population. For example, in Europe as a whole including England 8.0 per cent of the population was urban in 1600. In 1700 if the urban percentage had remained the same the urban total would have been 6.0 million but it had in fact risen to 7.13 million, and therefore the 'net' gain in population, shown in column (6) was 1.13 million. This is an informative statistic since a town whose share of the total population did not change would nonetheless grow in absolute size if the urban percentage remained unchanged. Indeed, a town's

[1] Deane and Cole provide estimates of corn exports and total corn production which suggest that over the period from 1700 to 1760 corn exports represented 3.1 per cent of total corn production in England and Wales: Deane and Cole, *British economic growth*, Table 17, p. 65. Overton made estimates of agricultural output and net imports which suggest that in 1791 net imports were 2 per cent of total output and in 1801 5 per cent: Overton, *Agricultural revolution*, Table 3.5, p. 75. Jones' calculations suggest that 90 per cent of the food consumed by the British population in 1800 was produced domestically. In contrast, in 1700 domestic needs were fully covered by local production, leaving a surplus equivalent to 1 per cent for export: Jones, 'Agriculture, 1700–80', Table 4.1, p. 68.

[2] Conscious of drawbacks of relying on estimates of urban trends based only on large towns, de Vries also estimated at half-century intervals the overall populations of towns with 5,000 to 10,000 inhabitants as well as the urban populations in larger size ranges above 10,000 inhabitants for which he had direct information. His estimates suggest that in 1600 including the population of towns in the 5,000 to 10,000 size range would increase the overall total of all towns with 5,000 or more inhabitants by 41 per cent compared to that for towns with 10,000 plus inhabitants. The comparable figure in 1800 was 29 per cent: De Vries, *European urbanization*, Table 4.13, p. 72.

Table 4.1 *Urban populations in England and the continent of Europe 1600–1800*

(1)	(2) Total population (million)	(3) Urban population (million)	(4) Urban percentage	(5) Urban total at 1600 proportion (million)	(6) 'Net' gain on 1600 (million) (col.(3) – col.(5))	(7) 'Net' gain on last date (million)
Europe						
1600	70.6	5.65	8.0	5.65		
1700	75.0	7.13	9.5	6.00	1.13	1.13
1750	86.6	8.57	9.9	6.93	1.64	0.51
1800	111.8	11.85	10.6	8.94	2.91	1.27
England						
1600	4.16	0.249	6.0	0.249		
1700	5.21	0.680	13.1	0.313	0.367	0.367
1750	5.92	1.012	17.1	0.355	0.657	0.290
1800	8.67	2.079	24.0	0.520	1.559	0.902
English percentage of total European 'net' urban gain						
1700/1600	32 ((0.367/1.13) × 100)					
1750/1700	57 ((0.290/0.51) × 100)					
1800/1750	71 ((0.902/1.27) × 100)					

Note: The countries comprising 'Europe' are: the British Isles, France, Germany, Italy, the Low Countries, Portugal, Scandinavia, Spain, and Switzerland. The urban totals relate to towns with 10,000 or more inhabitants.
Sources: For English population totals: Wrigley *et al.*, *English population history*, Table A9.1, pp. 614–15. Other population totals: Wrigley, 'Urban growth and agricultural change', Table 7.7, p. 179.

population might grow, even though its percentage share of the national population total was falling if the country was growing faster than the town. The same holds true at times not merely for individual towns but for an entire urban category. For example, in the eighteenth century county towns and regional centres that had long figured prominently in the English urban scene lost momentum compared with both the national population and the urban sector as a whole. The combined populations of Norwich, York, Salisbury, Chester, Worcester, Exeter, Cambridge, Coventry, Shrewsbury, and Gloucester stood at *c.* 103,000 in 1700 rising to *c.* 153,000 in 1800, a rise of 49 per cent.[3] The national population rose by 66 per cent and the urban sector as a whole increased by 206 per cent.

[3] Wrigley, 'Urban growth and agricultural change', Table 7.1, pp. 160–1.

The totals in column (7) of Table 4.1 show the net gain between the date in question and the previous date. For example, in the section for Europe, the total of 0.51 million in 1750 represents the net gain between 1700 and 1750 (1.64–1.13 million). This in turn makes it possible to calculate the proportion of the net gain in urban population in Europe as a whole (including England) that took place in England alone. This is shown in the bottom section of the table. The English share of overall European urban growth was 32 per cent in the seventeenth century, rising to 57 in the first half of the eighteenth century, and to a truly remarkable 71 per cent in the second half of the eighteenth century, even though the English population was less than 8 per cent of the European total in this period. The trio of percentages shown in this section of the table captures very effectively the depth of the contrast in urban growth trends on either side of the English Channel.[4]

Table 4.1 leaves no room for doubt that the scale of urban growth in England was exceptional, but this was also true of some of its other characteristics. Over the early modern period the rank order of the largest cities changed only slightly in most European countries. In the Netherlands, of the 20 largest towns in 1550, 19 were still among the top 20 in 1800. In Spain the comparable proportion was 15 out of 20, comparing 1600 and 1800. In England, in contrast, the urban rank order was transformed. London, of course, was always by far the largest city but in 1800 of the next six towns only Bristol was also in the top seven in 1600.[5] None of the other five towns (Manchester, 89,000; Liverpool, 83,000; Birmingham, 74,000; Leeds, 53,000; and Sheffield, 46,000), appear in the list of towns with 5,000 or more inhabitants in 1600.[6]

Other features of English urban growth deserve comment. London had headed the surge in the urban population total in the seventeenth century. In that century 60 per cent of all urban growth in towns with 5,000 or more inhabitants took place in London alone (Table 4.2). In the eighteenth century, however, the capital no longer dominated the urban growth scene. It continued to grow substantially. Its population rose by 67 per cent between 1700 and 1800, but this simply kept pace with the overall national growth rate (66 per cent). In this century it grew little faster than the county towns and regional centres whose collective growth has already been noted.[7] Indeed, in the eighteenth century the combined

[4] There are helpful surveys of the wider aspects of urban growth in England in Clark and Slack, *English towns in transition* and in Chalklin, *The rise of the English town*. There is also an excellent discussion of the same topic in Poussou, 'Les villes anglaises'.

[5] De Vries, *European urbanization*, Appendix 1, pp. 269–304.

[6] Wrigley, 'Urban growth and agricultural change', Table 7.1, pp. 160–1.

[7] See p. 47.

Table 4.2 *Urban and national population totals 1600–1800 (000)*

	1600	1700	1800
London	200	575	960
Other towns with 5,000 plus inhabitants	135	275	1,420
Total urban	335	850	2,380
England	**4,162**	**5,211**	**8,671**

Sources: Wrigley, 'Urban growth and agricultural change', Table 7.2, p. 162; Wrigley *et al., English population history*, Table A9.1, pp. 614–15.

population of the capital and the county towns probably experienced a marginal fall in their percentage share of the population of England. The very rapid growth in the urban sector as a whole in the eighteenth century occurred because of the exceptional expansion taking place in the industrial and commercial centres in the north and midlands. The combined populations of Manchester, Liverpool, Birmingham, Leeds, and Sheffield rose more than ten-fold during the century from *c.* 33,000 in 1700 to *c.* 345,000 in 1800. Urban growth in the seventeenth century might perhaps be regarded as an extreme example of urbanisation in an organic economy, followed in the eighteenth century by the type of urban growth produced by a nascent industrial revolution. As will become apparent, however, this view may fail to do justice to the complexity of the changes taking place.

Another aspect of the urban growth taking place in England in the early modern period deserves emphasis. Table 4.3 records the growth of urban and non-urban populations in England and continental Europe during the seventeenth and eighteenth centuries. Both urban growth and total growth were substantially faster in the island than on the continent, but it is notable that non-urban growth was remarkably similar, indeed in the eighteenth century virtually identical (46 per cent in England; 47 per cent on the continent). Over the whole two-century period the non-urban population in England rose by 69 per cent; on the continent by 53 per cent, a relatively minor difference. The comparable percentages for urban growth were 732 and 81 per cent, a massive difference. The difference in urban growth rates was what caused overall growth rates to differ as they did (108 per cent compared to 55 per cent). The key point brought to light by Table 4.3 is that the faster overall population growth in England was almost entirely due to the very rapid growth of the urban sector.

Table 4.3 *Urban and non-urban growth in England and continental Europe 1600–1800*

	Population totals (million)		
	Urban	**Non-urban**	**Total**
England			
1600	0.25	3.91	4.16
1700	0.68	4.53	5.21
1800	2.08	6.59	8.67
Continental Europe (excludes British Isles)			
1600	5.40	61.04	66.44
1700	6.45	63.34	69.79
1800	9.77	93.36	103.13
		Percentage change	
England			
1600/1700	172.0	15.9	25.2
1700/1800	205.9	45.5	66.4
1600/1800	734.9	68.5	108.4
Continental Europe (excludes British Isles)			
1600/1700	19.4	3.8	5.0
1700/1800	51.5	47.4	47.7
1600/1800	80.9	52.9	55.2

Source: For total population totals and urban population totals, see Table 4.1.

Given the nature of organic economies, an increase in the urban sector as striking as that which occurred in early modern England must imply comparably notable advances in agricultural productivity since the country remained broadly self-sufficient in foodstuffs. Moreover, several English industries relied largely upon domestic agriculture for their supply of raw materials, including major industries such as those dependent on wool and leather.[8] As with urban growth, advances in agricultural productivity set England apart from the continent in a striking fashion, and the two developments were closely connected.

Urban growth and the provision of food and fuel

Adam Smith once remarked: 'Had human institutions, therefore, never disturbed the natural course of things, the progressive wealth and increase

[8] See p. 13.

of the towns would, in every political society, be consequential, and in proportion to the improvement and cultivation of the territory or country.'[9] The course of events in early modern England suggests that 'the natural course of things' progressed without disturbance.

The two most important demands made by towns upon any rural surplus arising from 'the improvement and cultivation of the territory' were those arising from their consumption of food and fuel. In organic economies, each requirement could be satisfied only by devoting substantial areas of land to producing the grain and firewood which were the most significant elements in meeting food and fuel needs generally. Each is considered in turn.

Meeting urban food requirements

As an introduction to the scale of the changes involved in meeting urban food requirements generally it is helpful to take advantage of the existence of estimates of the scale of London's grain requirements *c.* 1600 before the major advances in agricultural productivity that occurred over the next two centuries.

The size of London's population meant that the area needed to satisfy its food requirements was large even in 1600. Gras estimated London's annual consumption of grain as 0.5 million quarters (4 million bushels) at the beginning of the seventeenth century when the population of the city was *c.* 200,000, an estimate accepted by both Chartres and by Glennie and Whyte.[10] This suggests that each Londoner was consuming 20 bushels annually on average.[11] Chartres considered that food and drink, bread and beer, contributed roughly equally to the total of grain consumed.[12] The gross yield per acre of a combination of grains at the time is not known with any certainty. I assume a figure of 12 bushels per acre for a mixture of wheat and barley, the two main food and drink

9 Smith, *The wealth of nations*, I, p. 404.

10 Chartres, 'Food consumption and internal trade', Table 21, p. 178; Glennie and Whyte, 'Towns in an agrarian economy', p. 173. Chartres suggested a slight modification of Gras' estimate, but not of a size to alter the picture significantly, and showed that roughly equal quantities of corn were consumed in providing bread and drink for the population of the metropolis.

11 It is worth noting that van der Woude *et al.* in their admirable discussion of the problems of meeting urban food and fuel needs in the past assume a bread grain requirement 'for all purposes' of 1 kilogram per person each day. This equates to an annual bread grain consumption of 800 lb, or approximately 14 bushels, depending on the mix of grains consumed. This is broadly similar to the estimate made for London given that one estimate relates solely to bread grain whereas the other also includes the grain used for drink. Van der Woude *et al.*, 'Introduction', p. 8.

12 Chartres, 'Food consumption and internal trade', Table 21, p. 178.

cereals.[13] When calculating the acreage of arable land needed to supply the food and drink needs of the population, however, the gross yields are misleading. Account must be taken of two factors that reduce it considerably. Net yield may be taken as 9 bushels after allowing for the reservation of 3 bushels as seed for the next harvest. Furthermore, about 30 per cent of the arable acreage was fallowed each year.[14] This means that the quantity of grain available for consumption from each arable acre should be taken as only 6.3 bushels ($9 \times 0.7 = 6.3$).[15]

To provide 20 bushels for each Londoner therefore meant securing the grain output from about 3.2 acres of arable land, implying that London's 'footprint' in meeting the grain needs of its 200,000 inhabitants in 1600 extended to 640,000 acres, or 1,000 square miles. On the same assumptions in 1800 with a population of 960,000 London's grain 'footprint' would have covered 3,100,000 acres or 4,800 square miles; and the national urban requirement in 1800, when the national urban population total was 2,380,000, would have been 11,900 square miles, an impressively large total, given that the total arable acreage in England and Wales is estimated to have been 11.5 million acres, or 18,000 square miles.[16] Moreover, the urban 'footprint' resulting from the urban demand for food is considerably understated by this calculation since meeting the urban demand for meat, cheese, butter, fruit, and vegetables would have enlarged its size substantially; and providing fodder to feed the horses used to transport rural produce to the towns would have extended the 'footprint' still further.[17]

[13] Overton provides a table of cereal yields *c.* 1600 for several southern counties that suggests a lower figure, but notes that the poor harvests of the 1590s depress his estimates: Overton, *Agricultural revolution*, Table 3.7, p. 77. It is of interest to note that Bairoch estimated that in Europe as a whole (excluding Russia and the United Kingdom) wheat yields in 1800 were about 8 quintals per hectare, equivalent to 12 bushels per acre: Bairoch, 'The impact of crop yields', p. 137. Bairoch's estimate accords well with the assumption I am making but there were, of course, wide local variations within countries. Pollard, for example, also using data for the early nineteenth century, noted that in Germany in 1800–20 the yield:seed ratio in East Friesland was 12:1 but in the rest of Germany 5:1; and that in France in the late eighteenth century, though again the average was again 5:1, it reached 11.0 in French Flanders but was only 3:1 or 4:1 in Roussillon and Limoges: Pollard, *Peaceful conquest*, p. 48.

[14] This percentage embodies the assumption that the fallowing percentage had declined somewhat from a figure in the range of 36–40 per cent in the medieval period: Wrigley, 'Transition to an advanced organic economy', pp. 441–2.

[15] For simplicity, other factors that affected this quantity, such as the consumption of grain by rodents in granaries, is not taken into account in this order of magnitude calculation.

[16] Overton, *Agricultural revolution*, Table 3.6, p. 76.

[17] It is convenient and broadly accurate to treat rural areas as food producers and urban areas as food consumers but food production within the boundaries of a city was not always trivial. London breweries and distilleries produced large volumes of food waste downstream from the production of beer and gin: Mathias, 'Agriculture and

It seems plain that if the circumstances of urban food provision, determined by cereal yields per acre, which prevailed throughout Europe in, say, 1500 had continued to hold good thereafter, urban growth in England would have come to a halt well short of the level it had actually reached in 1800. What, then, had changed?

The immediate cause of the reduction in the urban 'footprint' was a remarkable advance in net agricultural output per acre. For example, gross grain yields roughly doubled between the end of the sixteenth century and the beginning of the nineteenth century, rising from 12 to 24 bushels per acre.[18] Allowing again 3 bushels for seed, the net yield was 21 bushels at the end of the period. The proportion of arable land that was fallowed each year had declined substantially to *c.* 16 per cent.[19] As a result, the net output secured from an acre of arable land used for grain production rose to 17.6 bushels per acre ($21 \times 0.84 = 17.6$) from 6.3 bushels two centuries earlier. London's claim on arable land in 1800, therefore, may be taken as 1,100,000 acres, or 1,700 square miles compared with a figure of 4,800 square miles if the yield per acre and fallowing percentage had remained at their levels two centuries earlier. The comparable figure for the English towns as a whole is 2,700,000 acres, or 4,200 square miles compared with 11,900 square miles if yields had not changed. In 1800 the national urban population total in towns with 5,000 or more inhabitants had risen seven-fold from 1600 but an area only two-and-a-half times as large as in 1600 could supply their grain requirements.

The most significant feature of the transformation of English agriculture in the seventeenth and eighteenth centuries, however, was not the increase in yields that occurred but the fact that it was achieved with an agricultural workforce whose size was largely unchanging. The rise in the productivity of the agricultural labour force was truly exceptional. For the reasons so forcefully expounded by the classical economists, in a land long settled it was logical to assume that any substantial increase in agricultural output could only be secured at the cost of a decline in the marginal productivity of the farm labour force. Both working existing farmland more intensively and taking into cultivation land of inferior

the brewing and distilling industries'. One eighteenth-century author estimated that 50,000 pigs were fattened annually from distillery waste alone: *ibid.*, p. 84. Many cattle were also fattened similarly. The original raw material came, of course, from the countryside but the later stages of 'production' were urban.

18 The figure of 24 bushels may be a little conservative but it is a simple matter to calculate the implications of any alternative assumption. Overton's estimates of wheat and barley yields in 1801 are 22 and 29 bushels per acre, respectively: Overton, *Agricultural revolution*, Table 3.7, section (d), p. 77.

19 Wrigley, 'The transition to an advanced organic economy', Table 1, p. 440.

quality tended to involve this penalty: output could be increased only by increasing the labour force more than proportionately. Early modern England avoided the normal fate. The agricultural labour force was little larger in 1800 than it had been in 1600, even though the population had more than doubled.

The 1831 census was the first to provide reliable information about the size of the male agricultural labour force. It recorded totals for males aged 20 years old and above. It recorded only men in active employment, excluding those who were retired, sick, or crippled whereas subsequent censuses, apart from the 1841 census, included elderly men who were long past working age and so substantially inflated employment totals.[20] The male agricultural labour force total in 1831 numbered 973,114, constituting 32.6 per cent of active males aged 20 or more.[21] An earlier study in which estimates were made of the adult male labour force in agriculture in England in the first half of the nineteenth century concluded that the total of men aged 20 and above rose from 910,000 in 1811 to 1,010,000 in 1851.[22] The size of the agricultural labour force in 1600 can only be estimated with substantial margins of error, but it is reasonable to suppose that *c.* 70 per cent of the workforce was employed on the land at that date.[23] The English population total in 1600 was 4.16 million, and approximately 53 per cent of the population were in the age group 20–64. This age range was chosen on the assumption that the active labour force aged 20 and above in 1831 closely approximated the 20–64 age range. Assuming that 48 per cent of the population in this age group was male, the number of men of prime working age in agricultural employment may be estimated as *c.* 750,000.[24] Recent work has provided an estimate of the proportion of the labour force engaged in agriculture at the midpoint between the 1600 and 1831 totals. Using occupational data drawn from Anglican baptism registers, the estimate relates to *c.* 1710. Agriculture in *c.* 1710 is estimated to have employed 49.8 per cent of the labour force.[25] The population total at that date was 5.382 million, and the proportion of the population in the age group 20–64 was approximately 52 per cent. If men are again assumed to constitute 48 per cent of this age group, this suggests a total in agriculture

[20] See pp. 155–6. [21] *1831 Census*, Enumeration Abstract, II, pp. 832–3.
[22] Wrigley, 'Men on the land', Table 4.12, p. 124 and accompanying text.
[23] Leigh Shaw-Taylor will shortly publish evidence that supports this estimate.
[24] The proportion male in this age group is unknown at this date, but was almost certainly less than half. The percentage at the time of the 1841 census when the age information, though far from perfect, appears broadly reliable, was 48 per cent. *1841 Census*, Age Abstract, part I, pp. 366–73.
[25] Shaw-Taylor and Wrigley, 'Occupational structure and population change', Table 2.2, p. 59.

of about 670,000 men. It should be noted, however, that because in the parish registers an agricultural labourer was usually recorded simply as a 'labourer' the estimated total is sensitive to the allocation of 'labourers' between those working on the land and those in other employment sectors. Estimating agricultural employment total for men aged 20–64, of course, understates the overall total of men working on the land, but captures effectively changes in the relative size of the male agricultural workforce.

In summary, the available evidence leaves little doubt that the number of men working in agriculture rose only moderately between 1600 and 1831, perhaps by 30 per cent, with the increase taking place during the latter half of the period. Incidentally, the total of 1.35 million for agricultural employment in 1851 shown in Table 5.2 is misleading. In the 1851 census agriculture was given a much broader definition than in 1831 or 1841 and after correction the total in all three censuses is very similar.[26] Since the English population more than tripled between 1600 and 1831, from 4.16 to 13.25 million, but the agricultural workforce probably increased only by about a third, combined with the fact that even in 1831 it is probable that only about a tenth of the total of temperate foodstuffs was imported, there is little doubt that output per farmworker more than doubled in this period.[27]

The sharp rise in cereal yield per acre which occurred in England in the early modern period set it apart from most of continental Europe, where there was little change in yield during the seventeenth and eighteenth centuries. There were a few exceptions to this generalisation. In parts of Flanders, for example, agricultural practices had been advanced from an early date and yield per acre was as high as in England. Indeed, it was the import of these improved practices that accounted for much of the rise in yields achieved in England. Dejongh and Thoen describe the wide range of innovations, such as the introduction of turnips and clovers and the reduction in fallow, which underwrote the high yields achieved. However, they then noted: 'the progress of Flemish agriculture was not primarily the result of technical revolution but rested rather upon the high input of

[26] A full description of the changes made in 1851 is outside the scope of this discussion, but the following points may be noted. Landed proprietors, farm servants (indoors), bailiffs, and woodmen were included, as were all sons, grandsons, brothers, and nephews resident on the farm. Further, not only those currently active in a given occupation but also all those who had once been active in it were included. There was no separate category for the aged and retired. As a result 10 per cent of agricultural labourers were over 65, 6 per cent were over 70, and there were even well over 2,000 agricultural labourers over 85. When adjustment is made for these differences it is clear that agricultural employment changed very little between 1831 and 1851.

[27] See pp. 57–60 for a discussion of the degree of dependence on temperate food imports.

labour per unit of land. In most areas, the intensification of arable production went along with a splitting up of peasant holdings and *declining labour productivity* [my italics].'[28] A decline in labour productivity may have occurred at times in medieval England as the population increased between the twelfth and early fourteenth centuries, though the evidence is not clear-cut. Since providing food for people will always take priority over providing fodder for draught animals, and an area of land cannot be used simultaneously to meet both demands, a rising population always has the potential to create problems in an organic economy.[29]

An increase in the productivity of the land achieved only by a disproportionate increase in the size of the agricultural labour force, rather than making possible an increase in urbanisation, will have the opposite effect. After meeting the needs of those working on the land, the food surplus available for urban consumption will decline rather than rise. The fact that whereas the urban percentage was rising strongly in England during the eighteenth century, in Belgium it declined from 23.9 to 18.9 per cent, may exemplify the difference between the effects of rising and falling productivity in the agricultural labour force.[30] It may be worthy of note that Bairoch summarised a wide-ranging discussion of this topic by remarking that, 'in the context of traditional societies – in the absence of agricultural imports, the maximum possible proportion of the population that could live in towns (with a criterion of 5,000 inhabitants for a town) was of the order of between 13 and 15 per cent'.[31]

Urban growth and agricultural productivity are necessarily interrelated in organic economies, but the relationship may be one of either positive or of negative feedback. Normally, in organic economies the relationship was negative. By providing a market for any rural surplus, an increase in the urban population might for a time stimulate additional output, but at some point as output increased it could only be secured by an increase in the agricultural labour force that outstripped the increase in output. Meeting the food needs of the rural population would then take an increasing proportion of total output, making it impossible also to satisfy the needs of the urban population and inducing a decline in its size. The ratio of agricultural output to the food needs of the local rural population was bound to fall if the marginal productivity of the

28 Dejongh and Thoen, 'Arable productivity in Flanders', p. 57.

29 The complexity of the interaction between the factors which are involved in attempting to measure labour productivity in medieval England are well exemplified in Campbell, 'Land, labour, livestock'.

30 De Vries, *European urbanization*, Table 3.7, p. 39. The percentages refer to towns with 10,000 or more inhabitants.

31 Bairoch, 'The impact of crop yields', p. 146.

agricultural labour force declined, thus setting a limit to the scale of urban growth. Only if output per head rose as fast as or faster than aggregate output could urban growth continue. In early modern England this desirable but unusual pattern continued for the three centuries during which an organic economy was transformed and which culminated with an industrial revolution. Accounting for the exceptional nature of the prolonged period during which England escaped from the normal consequence of rapid urban growth, when positive feedback continued in a fashion unknown elsewhere in Europe, is challenging. The fact that it occurred, however, was of great significance in making possible the advent of an industrial revolution.

The period during which England's food needs were met very largely by local agriculture continued into the early nineteenth century as agricultural production continued to rise, though by the later decades of the century imports played an increasing role in providing food for the population. Population growth in the first half of the nineteenth century was exceptionally rapid: England's population almost doubled between 1801 and 1851, rising by 93 per cent from 8.7 to 16.7 million, or by 1.32 per cent per annum.[32] An increase on this scale in earlier periods of English history would have been impossible. If in the past the rate of growth had risen, even briefly, to the level which prevailed in the late eighteenth and early nineteenth centuries, it would have resulted in deep misery, great suffering, and increased mortality, but no such ill consequences occurred in the early nineteenth century. It is of interest to examine for how long the increase in food consumption implied by the population rise continued to be met principally from local agriculture rather than by food imports. In the second half of the century food imports clearly played an increasing role in supplying the increased demand. Was this change, as is sometimes supposed, already well in train in the first half of the century?

Since the population increased by roughly 90 per cent between 1801 and 1851, it is reasonable to assume that the consumption of foodstuffs increased approximately in parallel. Unfortunately, continuous national agricultural output statistics were collected by the state only from 1867 onwards. Initially, the returns were somewhat defective and even after 1875, by which time coverage had improved, Mitchell warned that 'Whilst it may be that overall figures need to be treated with less caution after 1875', he considered that the deficiencies had not been entirely eliminated.[33] Nevertheless, attempts have been made to estimate the scale of agricultural production earlier in the nineteenth century. For

[32] Table 3.1, p. 32. [33] Mitchell, *British historical statistics*, p. 182.

example, Overton used three different indirect methods to estimate the scale of English agricultural output over varying periods of time. Two of them make it possible to estimate the extent of the rise in output between 1801 and 1851. One produces a rise of 71 per cent; the other a rise of 49 per cent.[34] The first of the two also provided estimates of net imports at both dates: 5 per cent in 1801, 16 per cent in 1851. The second made no estimate of the scale of net food imports but, assuming that in 1800 the country was self-sufficient, the implied level of net imports in 1851 would be *c.* 28 per cent. An authoritative figure for net food imports is probably beyond reach, but consideration of the extent to which cereal production rose in the early decades of the century raises points of interest, and other scattered data helps to narrow uncertainties.

Davis touched on the general issue of British food self-sufficiency in his volume on British exports and imports covering the period from the 1780s to the 1850s. Imported foodstuffs accounted for more than 40 per cent of total imports by value in the early decades of the period he covered, declining thereafter to *c.* 35 per cent in the later decades, but the great bulk of the imported foodstuffs consisted of produce from warmer climes (wines and spirits; tea, coffee, cocoa; and sugar). What he termed 'temperate' foodstuffs (grain, meat, butter, cheese) until the 1840s accounted for only a tenth of the overall total of imported foodstuffs.[35] He commented that 'Down to the 1840s imported foodstuffs were on the whole the products of warmer lands than Britain – Britain was still essentially self-sufficient in the "temperate foodstuffs".'[36] He pointed to the late 1830s as the period when dependence on imports to meet the demand for temperate foodstuffs began to rise. What follows is an attempt to make use of quantitative rather than value data to determine how far his conclusion is supported.

Broadberry *et al.* have recently provided estimates of English production of the major grains from the thirteenth to the nineteenth centuries. Their estimates are net of grain reserved as seed and consumed by horses and oxen. They suggest that the output of wheat, barley, and oats rose by 86, 34, and 16 per cent, respectively between the 1800s and the 1850s.[37] As noted, the English population rose by 93 per cent between the censuses of 1801 and 1851. During the preceding century wheat increasingly replaced other cereals as the bread grain. At the beginning

[34] Overton, *Agricultural revolution*, Table 3.5, p. 75.
[35] Davis, *The industrial revolution and British overseas trade*, Table 23, p. 36 and Table 24, p. 37.
[36] *Ibid.*, p. 37. [37] Broadberry *et al.*, *British economic growth*, Table 3.07, p. 98.

of the nineteenth century about 65 per cent of the population of Britain was wheat-eating and the percentage in England and Wales was substantially higher, probably about 75 per cent; by 1850, these percentages had increased to 80 per cent, and *c.* 90 per cent.[38] Therefore, the estimate of the increase in wheat production made by Broadberry *et al.*, which initially suggests that dependence on wheat imports only rose marginally over the first half of the nineteenth century, is consistent with a greater gap between production and consumption than might be inferred at first sight. However, any estimate of the output of individual agricultural commodities is subject to very wide margins of error for this period. Some estimates suggest a far greater growth in the output of the main cereals. The estimates collated by Arthur John and published in *The agrarian history of England and Wales*, for example, suggest a very large rise in cereal output. Between 1810–19 and 1840–9 the average annual output of wheat, barley, and oats (measured without deduction of seed or taking account of consumption by horses and oxen), using these estimates, rose by 158, 97, and 10 per cent, respectively.[39] The scale of the increase in cereal production appears to defy precise measurement, but that it was very substantial seems clear. It is probably consistent with the observation that Davis made.

A related point should be noted. Broadberry *et al.* regard the agricultural labour force as having risen by 37 per cent between 1801 and 1851 and conclude that 'labour productivity growth in agriculture slowed to rates last seen before 1700'.[40] The figure of 37 per cent is substantially overstated, probably because the 1851 census total is misleadingly high if used for comparison with the available data for agricultural employment earlier in the century. A more accurate figure for the increase of men engaged in agriculture over this period would be *c.* 10 per cent.[41]

It is probable that the relative importance of imports of other products of arable agriculture in England in the early nineteenth century was smaller than was the case with cereals. Products such as beans and peas, potatoes, and hops were largely home produced, as were perishable vegetables and fruits. It is much harder to assess the situation for pastoral products, though it is clear that imports from Ireland figured prominently. In 1825, Ireland ceased to be treated as a foreign country and therefore imports from Ireland were no longer included in returns of imports. The last period for which Davis was able to provide details of the sums

[38] Petersen, *Bread and the British economy*, Table 7.11, pp. 205–6 and associated discussion.
[39] John, 'Statistical appendix', Table III.4, C, pp. 1054–5.
[40] Broadberry *et al.*, *British economic growth*, Table 9.09, p. 365 and p. 368.
[41] Wrigley, 'Men on the land', esp. pp. 304–18 and Table 11.12, p. 332.

expended on each import category was 1824–6.[42] The annual average total of all temperate food imports was £8.01 million. Corn imports were much the largest individual item (£4.16 million, of which £2.91 million was from Ireland). Meat, butter, and cheese made up the remainder. In total Ireland supplied temperate food imports valued at £5.60 million. This demonstrates the importance of Ireland as a source of temperate foodstuffs but suggests that pastoral products were less important than arable products. This, however, is to ignore the cattle trade. Large numbers of cattle and other animals were imported from Ireland. The average number of Irish cattle imported in 1824–5, for example, was 63,000, and the total appears to have tripled by the mid 1840s.[43] In the same years the average number of cattle brought for sale at Smithfield market was 161,000.[44] Assuming that Smithfield was the chief source of beef for London and that the capital housed *c.* 1.5 million people, and further that meat consumption per head was similar throughout England and Wales, this would imply the slaughter of about 1.5 million cattle each year, of which perhaps 5 per cent were Irish.

Needless to say, there must be substantial margins of error around any calculation of the degree to which the country was dependent on imports from abroad in meeting its need for temperate foodstuffs down to the 1840s. Many of the relevant data are missing, but in the light of the evidence that is available, it seems unlikely that more than a tenth was supplied from abroad.[45] What, however, is not in doubt is that there was again a marked rise in labour productivity in agriculture. The number of men employed on the land rose far less than the output increase. The early decades of the nineteenth century were a period in which the gains both in aggregate output and in labour productivity in England continued to be substantial.

Meeting urban fuel requirements

The need for fuel was just as fundamental to urban life as that for food. Urban fuel needs had been met by burning fuel wood, which in turn meant devoting large areas to coppiced woodland.[46] Using Bairoch's estimate, the average town dweller consumed 1.3 tons of firewood each

42 In order to provide a figure for Ireland in 1826, he took an average of the totals for the two preceding years.

43 John, 'Statistical appendix', Table II.5, pp. 1021–2.

44 *Ibid.*, Table III.9, p. 1064.

45 For an alternative view of the importance of Irish imports and the scale of the rise in food production in Britain, see Thomas, *The industrial revolution and the Atlantic economy*, Chapter 4, 'Britain's food supply, 1760–1846: the Irish contribution'.

46 The large-scale use of peat, of course, enabled the Netherlands to escape this restriction.

year, which in turn represented the product of 1.6 acres of woodland on a sustained yield basis.[47] Since the comparable figure to cover a town dweller's grain requirement was 3.2 acres, an area of 4.8 acres was needed to provide for his or her combined grain and fuel requirements. If, therefore, English towns throughout the seventeenth and eighteenth centuries had supplied their fuel needs solely by burning wood, and grain yields had remained at the level prevailing *c.* 1600, the area needed to provide for the whole urban sector would have risen to 17,900 square miles by 1800 (11,900 for grain; 6,000 for fuel). For London alone the comparable figure is 7,200 square miles (4,800 for grain; 2,400 for fuel). 17,900 square miles represents 31 per cent of the land surface of England and Wales and a substantially higher proportion of the area that could be used as farmland or to produce fuel wood. Moreover it falls well short of the total urban 'footprint' which would have been needed in the circumstances hypothesised, since it does not take into account land used to provide other foods, nor the wood needed for building rather than fuel, nor the area needed to provide raw materials for a wide range of urban industries, such as wool and hides. Plainly urban growth would have ground to a halt long before reaching the level that it had actually reached by the end of the eighteenth century.

The reduction in the size of the urban 'footprint' made possible by the rise in grain yields per acre has already been described. There was an equally remarkable reduction in the size of the urban 'footprint' associated with the changing balance between wood and coal as sources of urban fuel supplies. In the case of London the change was already virtually complete at the beginning of the seventeenth century. Hatcher estimated the capital's coal consumption as *c.* 15,000 tons in the middle of the sixteenth century, *c.* 150,000 tons at the start of the seventeenth century, and *c.* 425,000 tons at the end of the seventeenth century.[48] The population of London in 1550, 1600, and 1700 was *c.* 80,000, *c.* 200,000, and *c.* 575,000, respectively. The annual consumption per head was therefore approximately 0.2 tons in 1550 and 0.75 tons at the two later dates. By 1700, coal supplied almost all London's fuel needs, and the fact that consumption per head of population was the same in 1600 suggests that this was already the case at the earlier date. Half a century earlier in 1550 the relative size of its coal consumption per head suggests that about a quarter of its fuel needs came by ship from the Tyne rather than from woodland in the surrounding counties. In 1600, on the assumption that firewood had already been relegated to a marginal role in meeting London's heating needs, coal was supplying heat that would

[47] See p. 17. [48] Hatcher, *The history of the British coal industry*, I, p. 41.

otherwise have been supplied from 320,000 acres (500 square miles) of woodland. By 1800, in the absence of coal, the area would have risen to 1,550,000 acres (2,400 square miles).

In 1600 other English towns still made extensive use of firewood as fuel, but in 1800 Flinn considered that the average urban consumption of coal per head was probably between 2.25 and 2.5 tons.[49] Coal had largely replaced firewood as a source of heat energy in an urban setting. Flinn's estimate was based on data from Kendal and Edinburgh and included both domestic and urban industrial use. It suggests that by this date the great bulk of urban domestic heating was provided from coal. Drawing a bow at a venture, I assume that 80 per cent of urban domestic heating needs in towns other than London was provided from firewood in 1600 but that the corresponding figure in 1800 was 10 per cent. In that case, assuming that the area of woodland needed to provide domestic heating for a town dweller was 1.6 acres, the use of coal in towns other than London was reducing the woodland area which would otherwise have been devoted to firewood production by 70 square miles in 1600 and 3,240 square miles in 1800.

Table 4.4 summarises the comparisons which have just been described between the areas of arable and woodland which would have been required to supply urban needs in the conditions for meeting cereal and fuel requirements which characterised the organic economies of continental Europe in the early modern period, and those which were operative in England in 1600 and 1800. Columns (1) and (2) headed 'Pure organic' show the areas needed to meet urban needs for cereals and fuel assuming that the net cereal yield was 6.3 bushels per acre and that all heating was by firewood. Columns (3) and (4) headed 'Actual situation' shows the areas devoted to grain and fuel production in 1600 and 1800. Columns (5) and (6) show the savings brought about by greatly increased agricultural productivity and the substitution of coal for firewood at the two dates. All the totals are at best rough approximations, but setting them out in this fashion has the advantage that it is simple to follow through the implications of making different assumptions.

The area of land involved in meeting urban grain and fuel needs rose in round numbers from 2,000 square miles in 1600 to 4,500 square miles in 1800, a rise of 125 per cent during a period when the urban population rose from 335,000 to 2,380,000, or by more than 600 per cent. Column (6) shows that the savings that transformed the situation were split fairly evenly between those arising from the near-tripling in net cereal yields and those resulting from the substitution of coal for

[49] Flinn, *The history of the British coal industry*, II, p. 232.

Table 4.4 *Meeting urban food and fuel requirements in 1600 and 1800 (square miles)*

	Pure organic		Actual situation		Saving	
	1600 (1)	*1800* (2)	*1600* (3)	*1800* (4)	*1600* (5)	*1800* (6)
London						
Grain	1,000	4,800	1,000	1,700	0	3,100
Fuel	500	2,400	0	0	500	2,400
Total	1,500	7,200	1,000	1,700	500	5,500
Other towns (>5,000)						
Grain	675	7,100	675	2,500	0	4,600
Fuel	340	3,600	270	360	70	3,240
Total	1,015	10,700	945	2,860	70	7,840
Urban England						
Grain	1,675	11,900	1,675	4,200	0	7,700
Fuel	840	6,000	270	360	570	5,640
Total	2,515	17,900	1,945	4,560	570	13,340

Note: Some of the totals in the table are rounded for simplicity of presentation.

wood as the main method of domestic heating, though the agricultural contribution was somewhat the larger of the two.[50] The size of the urban 'footprint' in 1800 was only a quarter as large as it would have been if the normal methods of satisfying urban demand in most European countries in the early modern period had remained unchanged (4,560 compared to 17,900 square miles). It is not possible, of course, to say at what point urban growth would have ceased if methods of urban provisioning had remained as they had been at the beginning of the Tudor period, but deceleration might well have begun at some point in the seventeenth century. Urban growth would have ceased far short of the urban total reached by the end of the eighteenth century.

Reviewing the scale of urban growth in continental Europe in the seventeenth and eighteenth centuries enables developments in England to be put into context. The urban population of towns with 5,000 or more inhabitants in continental Europe stood at 8.0 million in 1600

[50] It is of interest to note that van der Woude *et al.*, in commenting on the surge of growth in early modern England and especially in London, remarked: 'Both features of England's rapid urbanization – its rapid growth and its concentration in one great city – appear to be related to the character of its energy supply': Van der Woude *et al.*, 'Introduction', p. 12.

and 15.4 million in 1800.[51] Much of the increase was associated with the general rise in numbers. The proportion of the population living in towns rose much less steeply from 11.3 to 13.8 per cent of the total population.[52] On the assumptions used in calculating the 'pure organic' areas in Table 4.4 (that is assuming that cereal net yields were 6.3 bushels per acre and that domestic heating was by firewood), the area devoted to supporting the urban population on the continent rose from 40,000 square miles to 77,000 square miles between 1600 and 1800, or by 93 per cent.[53] The rise in England ('actual situation' columns in Table 4.4) was larger at 134 per cent, but the difference in the percentages is relatively modest when compared with the massive differences in the urban population increases in the two areas (the continent 89 per cent, England 730 per cent[54]).

Conclusion

There are many fascinating topics related to the positive feedback between urban growth and agricultural improvement in England. Local self-sufficiency in food and fuel was always a prime concern of rural populations in organic economies; any failure to achieve and sustain it meant suffering and loss to the community. Incentives to produce an increasing surplus for sale elsewhere were slight or absent when the urban percentage was small and urban growth minimal. Often distance from the nearest town removed any incentive to seek an urban market. The needs of small towns could be met from the countryside immediately surrounding them, leaving large tracts of the countryside without this stimulus. Poor roads and high transport costs reinforced the geographical constraint. Accessible markets were rarely of a size to repay the introduction of methods that radically increased the productivity of either the land or the husbandman. Specialisation in the production of arable or pastoral

[51] These totals are larger than those in Table 2.1 because the urban populations in that table relate to towns with 10,000 or more inhabitants. They were increased as suggested in n. 2, p. 46.

[52] Urban population totals for continental Europe from Table 4.1, p. 47. They were corrected as noted in n. 51.

[53] The assumption that urban fuel needs were always met by burning wood is too simplistic. In many Dutch towns peat was the main fuel, and it was common for continental towns close to the North Sea coast to import coal, notably in Denmark and Holland, where coal was often the main fuel source by the eighteenth century.

[54] Note that the European population totals in Table 4.1 include England, and that therefore the English totals were deducted from the European totals in calculating the percentage increase in the continental total.

products had little point in the absence of accessible urban markets of substantial size. Conversely, if for whatever reason the urban sector was substantial, and more especially if it was expanding and gave promise to expand further, the farming sector had a powerful incentive to find ways of increasing output, ideally at a reduced cost per unit. In organic economies, this rarely happened.

Early modern England was exceptional in that a positive feedback between urban growth and agricultural advance was maintained over several centuries rather than losing momentum as pressure on the land increased. It is perhaps symbolically significant in assessing the extent of the changes in the English farming community that between 1600 and 1800 the terms 'yeoman' and 'husbandman' were replaced by 'farmer' and 'labourer' as the descriptors most commonly used when referring to men working on the land. The mere fact of this change in terminology underlines the basic character of the transformation of agriculture and rural life that occurred. It symbolises the increasing power of rising market demand to change practice. The existence of a large and expanding urban market for agricultural products was a necessary condition for the changes in agriculture which took place, but in organic economies it was normally the case that the penalty paid for securing a substantial increase in agricultural output was a decline in the average output per man in the agricultural labour force. It may prove challenging to produce a comprehensive and convincing account of the circumstances which led England to strike out on a novel path in the seventeenth century, not only raising total agricultural output greatly but raising output per head in agriculture in parallel. The fact that it occurred, however, was an important element in the gradual supplanting of the normal features of an organic economy by structures and practices that foreshadowed and facilitated an industrial revolution.

Similarly, escaping from sole dependence on wood for heat energy was a portent of the new age. It illustrates the way in which access to a new energy source played a gradually increasing role in enabling an expanding economy to avoid the penalty that had always previously attended economic growth in organic economies. Since coal was a product of plant photosynthesis in the past rather than the present, an increase in heat energy consumption derived from coal did not involve a reduction in the area of land that could be used for other purposes. It was a claim on an energy *stock* rather than an energy *flow*, an early example of a change that ultimately transformed the whole productive landscape of the country. Reviewing the early modern period, Coleman suggested that 'One of the central, unanswered questions of European history in this period is why and how England became sufficiently differentiated from the rest of pre-industrialized Europe by 1750 so that its economy could take off into the first industrial revolution'.[55] An important element in providing a satisfactory answer to this question lies perhaps in the novel form of the feedback between urban growth and rising labour productivity in agriculture that set England apart from continental Europe during the seventeenth and eighteenth centuries.

55 Coleman, *The economy of England*, p. 2.

5 Changing occupational structure and consumer demand

The changing balance between primary, secondary, and tertiary employment in early modern England provides a valuable insight into the nature of the changes that were gradually transforming an organic economy into the first example of a completed industrial revolution. In organic economies it was normal for 70–80 per cent of the workforce to be employed on the land, reflecting the fact that labour productivity in agriculture was low. The secondary and tertiary sectors were always dwarfed by the primary sector. Ten peasants might produce enough food for their own families and perhaps two or three other families who were then able to engage in textile manufacture, handicrafts, building, retailing, transport, etc., but the surplus in question was limited and might prove fragile in hard times. For the same reason, the proportion of the population living in towns and cities was always modest. Labour productivity in agriculture was too low to support a large urban sector. Equally, the absence of a large urban demand for food meant that there was little incentive for a peasant farmer to increase his output since there was no guarantee that it would find a market.

Recently new estimates of the changing occupational structure of England in the early modern period have been made. They differ substantially from earlier estimates; they suggest that the rise in the proportion of the workforce in the secondary and tertiary sectors occurred earlier, and was larger than was once supposed. The revised estimates and their implications for the nature and timing of the changes that ultimately brought about an industrial revolution are the subject of this chapter. It should be noted that the estimates normally relate to the male labour force only.

The expansion of the secondary and tertiary sectors

Given the relative income elasticities of demand for the products of the primary, secondary, and tertiary sectors in organic economies, a very high proportion of the labour force engaged in agricultural production normally indicated a modest standard of living and sometimes deep poverty. The bulk of the population, if they engaged in market transactions, spent much of any income at their disposal to obtain food. Equally, if a substantial proportion of the labour force was no longer working on the land, it implied an increase in the proportion of overall employment in the secondary sector and a rise in the importance of the products of manufacture and handicrafts in the structure of overall demand. Similarly, increasing incomes in a developing market economy boosted employment in trade, transport, and the professions, causing tertiary employment to increase. Employment in the tertiary sector was normally smaller than in the secondary sector but as incomes rose and an economy became more complex and sophisticated, it was normally the tertiary sector that experienced the faster growth.

Obtaining information about the occupational structure of England in the early modern period presents many problems. For example, the first census that provides reliable data on the number of men working on the land was the census of 1831. The earlier censuses used the family rather than the individual in describing the country's occupational structure and collected information only for three broad categories (agriculture; trade, manufacture, and handicraft; other). Before national censuses were taken occupational data can be found in several sources but the information they contain was collected for a variety of purposes, for example to provide a basis for tax collection, or to identify men capable of serving in the militia, and the information about occupation was incidental to the prime object of the exercise.

Attention has turned recently to the parish registers as a source of occupational data. Under the provisions of Rose's Act, when a baptism was registered the occupation of the father had to be stated. This Act came into force in 1813; before 1813 there was no obligation to include the occupation of the father when registering a baptism but some parishes did so for longer or shorter periods. There were more than 10,000 parish registers in England when Rose's Act came into force and in a recent research exercise the occupational data which they contain were abstracted for a period of eight years, 1813–20. The percentage distribution of occupations for this period is shown in Table 5.1 in the column headed '*c.* 1817'. Prior to 1813, although there was no obligation to record the father's occupation in the baptism register, there were periods when a substantial proportion of parishes did so. Several hundred parishes recorded the occupation of the father in the late seventeenth and early eighteenth centuries, often for a decade or more. This has made it possible also to construct estimates of the occupational structure *c.* 1710.

Table 5.1 *Male occupational structure of England and Wales* c.*1700–1851 (percentages)*

Sector	**c. 1710** %	**c. 1817** %	**1851** %
Primary	**50.8**	**39.4**	**32.4**
Agriculture	49.8	35.7	26.9
Mining	0.6	3.2	4.9
Rest of primary	0.4	0.5	0.6
Secondary	**37.2**	**42.1**	**44.7**
Clothing	4.5	3.4	3.4
Footwear	3.2	3.8	3.9
Textiles	7.5	7.8	6.8
Iron and steel manufacture and products	3.4	3.0	3.8
Machines and tools, making and operation	0.9	1.1	1.6
Building and construction	6.1	7.4	7.5
Rest of secondary sector	11.6	15.6	17.6
Tertiary	**12.0**	**18.4**	**22.8**
Dealers and sellers	2.5	3.4	4.7
Services and professions	5.1	8.7	10.4
Transport and communications	4.4	6.4	7.7
Total	**100.0**	**100.0**	**100.0**

Source: Shaw-Taylor and Wrigley, 'Occupational structure and population change', Table 2.2, p. 59.

Earlier estimates had suggested that the secondary sector was relatively small at the beginning of the eighteenth century and that it had more than doubled in size at the time of the 1841 census when the percentages in each sector can be measured with precision. For example, Crafts' estimate for the secondary sector in 1688 was 18.5 per cent.[1] This figure has sometimes been taken as equivalent to a measure of the size of the secondary sector. Because of the nature of the exercise Crafts was undertaking, however, this should be regarded a minimal figure. He was basing his estimates on those made by Lindert and Williamson, who in turn drew heavily upon the social tables of Gregory King, Joseph Massie, and Patrick Colquhoun, and he was seeking to establish the maximum proportion engaged in agriculture which could be inferred from the estimates in Lindert and Williamson's table. To ensure this, he allocated all labourers and cottagers to agriculture. Dividing those included in these two categories on different assumptions would produce a higher figure

[1] Shaw-Taylor and Wrigley, 'Occupational structure and population change', Table 2.1, p. 56.

for the secondary sector, but not a figure as high as that suggested using parish baptism registers, which indicate that 37.2 per cent of the labour force *c.* 1710 was in this category, a figure which then rose relatively slowly during the eighteenth century to reach 42.1 per cent *c.* 1817 and 44.7 per cent when the 1851 census was taken. The comparable percentages for the tertiary sector were 12.0, 18.4, and 22.8 per cent. The new estimates therefore suggest that the period of most rapid percentage gain for the secondary sector occurred in the seventeenth century. At present an authoritative figure for the late sixteenth century is lacking, but it is unlikely that the percentage in agriculture alone was less than 70 per cent, which suggests that the highest possible figure for the secondary sector was little more than *c.* 20 per cent. It may well have been significantly less.

There are few major changes in the relative size of the individual occupations in each sector in Table 5.1. Perhaps the most striking was the very rapid growth of mining within the primary sector, balanced by a marked reduction in the agricultural percentage that fell more sharply than the decline in the primary sector as a whole. In the secondary sector the 'Rest of secondary sector' share of the sectoral total increased from 31 per cent to 39 per cent between *c.* 1710 and 1851, suggesting a vigorous expansion in a wide range of industries.

It is also helpful in following occupational change over the seventeenth and eighteenth centuries to convert the percentages into estimated totals of men employed in each sector or occupational group. National population totals are available throughout the two centuries and also the distribution of the population by age group. The male population totals of those aged 15–64 were calculated by assuming that 48 per cent of the population was male and using the age distributions derived from inverse projection. Since population growth was far faster in the eighteenth than in the seventeenth century, comparison of the two methods of presentation can be illuminating. Table 5.2 presents the results of this exercise. Note that the agricultural totals are larger than the comparable totals in Chapter 4 since they relate to those aged 15–64 rather than 20–64.

It should immediately be stressed that the data for 1600 represent at best a rough sketch. The percentage split between primary, secondary, and tertiary employment is based on the assumption that 70 per cent of the workforce was engaged in agriculture and basing the estimates for the primary, secondary, and tertiary sectors on what seems plausible rather than on empirical material. In due course, it will be possible to produce more firmly based estimates. It is unlikely that these would produce radically different figures, but this remains uncertain. There are,

Table 5.2 *Estimated male occupational totals in the primary, secondary, and tertiary sectors 1600–1851*

	1600	c. 1710	c. 1817	1851
	Percentage of labour force			
Primary	71.0	50.8	39.4	32.4
Secondary	21.0	37.2	42.1	44.7
Tertiary	8.0	12.0	18.4	22.8
	Male population aged 15–64 (000)			
	1,242	1,576	2,910	4,812
	Male labour force (000)			
Primary	**882**	**801**	**1,147**	**1,559**
Agriculture	869	785	1,039	1,294
Mining		9	93	236
Rest of primary		6	15	29
Secondary	**261**	**586**	**1,225**	**2,151**
Clothing		71	99	164
Footwear		50	111	188
Textiles		118	227	327
Iron and steel manufacture and products		54	87	183
Machines and tools, making and operation		14	32	77
Building and construction		96	215	361
Rest of secondary sector		183	454	847
Tertiary	**99**	**189**	**575**	**1,097**
Dealers and sellers		39	99	226
Services and professions		80	253	500
Transport and communications		69	186	371
Total	**1,242**	**1,576**	**2,910**	**4,812**

Sources: Shaw-Taylor and Wrigley, 'Occupational structure and population change', Table 2.2, p. 59; Wrigley *et al.*, *English population history*, Table A9.1, pp. 614–15.

moreover, reasons to be cautious about some estimates for later dates. For example, the rise of 25 per cent in the total for agricultural employment between *c.* 1817 and 1851 is certainly a massive overstatement of the scale of the increase. Using a uniform definition of what should be included shows that there was very little change in agricultural employment in the first half of the nineteenth century.[2] The agricultural totals in *c.* 1710 and *c.* 1817 are affected by a different problem, which is also present in some census data. Many men are described simply as 'labourer'. Of these, a high proportion were agricultural labourers, and the totals for

[2] For a discussion of the problems in reducing occupational information from censuses in early decades of the nineteenth century to a common basis: Wrigley, 'Men on the land' and 'The occupational structure of England'.

agricultural labourers are sensitive to the assumptions made in dividing the labourers between agriculture and other occupations.

Converting percentages into estimated totals brings home some features of change that are cloaked when using percentages alone. For example, the secondary sector percentage rose from 21.0 to 37.2 in the seventeenth century but rose more modestly in the following century, from 37.2 to 42.1. In the seventeenth century, the absolute totals rose from 261,000 to 586,000, an increase of 325,000. In the eighteenth century, the increase was almost twice as large, at 639,000, since in *c.* 1817 the secondary sector total had risen to 1,225,000 (for simplicity I have referred to the seventeenth and eighteenth centuries although in both cases the periods were a little more than a century in length).

Between 1601 and 1711 the English population rose by 29 per cent; between 1711 and 1816 by 97 per cent.[3] In the seventeenth century the population was rising slowly; in the eighteenth its rate of growth became almost hectic by comparison. As a result, expressing change in terms of employment totals rather than percentages suggests a more stable pattern of change. The number of men employed in the secondary sector roughly doubled in both the seventeenth and eighteenth centuries.

The percentages of two of the secondary sector occupations, clothing and iron and steel manufacture, declined during the eighteenth century even though the secondary sector's share of the national occupational total as a whole was expanding, but because the population was rising rapidly the absolute totals increased substantially, from 71,000 to 99,000 in the case of clothing, and from 54,000 to 87,000 in the case of iron and steel manufacture. Equally, what appears as a modest increase when expressed in percentage share can appear much more dramatic as an absolute total. For example, employment in building and construction rose from 6.1 to 7.4 per cent of the national total in the eighteenth century, but the number of men in the industry more than doubled from 96,000 to 215,000. The tertiary sector was growing more rapidly than the secondary sector in the eighteenth century and some of the absolute rises were therefore even more dramatic than was the case in the secondary sector. The total of men in the services and professions tripled from 80,000 to 253,000. Its percentage share, of course, also rose but the increase was substantially less dramatic, from 5.1 to 8.7 per cent, an increase of only 70 per cent.

The radical revision in the estimated percentages of the workforce in the secondary and tertiary sectors set out in Table 5.2 may occasion surprise. It suggests a much greater growth in the secondary and tertiary

[3] Wrigley *et al.*, *English population history*, Table A9.1, pp. 614–15.

sectors in the seventeenth century than was once widely assumed. The combined percentage of these two sectors rose from an estimated 29 per cent in 1600 to 49.2 per cent in *c.* 1710, a striking rise. There is, however, other evidence that suggests that the rise is readily credible, indeed that a substantial rise in the combined percentage for the secondary and tertiary sectors must have taken place. Urban growth over this period was brisk, driven by the huge rise in the population of London. The percentage of the national population living in towns with 5,000 or more inhabitants rose from 8.0 to 16.3 per cent. In towns of this size it is safe to assume that the percentage of the workforce engaged in agriculture was negligible, and that therefore the increase of 8.3 per cent in the urban share of the national population consisted of people virtually all of whom depended on employment in secondary or tertiary activity for their livelihood. Urban growth measured in this way therefore accounts for more than 40 per cent of the increase in the combined secondary and tertiary percentage. For three reasons, however, this calculation understates the importance of urban growth in explaining the changing balance between the primary, secondary, and tertiary sectors.

The first reason is that defining an urban settlement as one with 5,000 or more inhabitants is too restrictive; there were many smaller towns. Normally, only a small fraction of the workforce in these towns were farm labourers: most men worked in the secondary or tertiary sectors. If, for example, towns with 2,500 or more inhabitants are included in the national urban total, the urban percentage in 1700 rises from 16.3 to 18.7 per cent, and the increase in that percentage over the preceding century rises to a figure of between 9 and 10 per cent.[4] At this level the increase in the urban percentage in itself accounts for almost half the increase in the percentage of the male workforce engaged in secondary and tertiary employment that occurred during the seventeenth century.

The second reason why urban growth and the changing balance between the three major employment sectors are so closely linked lies in the wider changes which were set in train by urban growth. Much employment is in a sense urban-generated though not entailing residence in a town. Urban growth, for example, invariably entails increased transport activity. This is true in the direct sense that meeting a town's food and fuel requirements involves the performance of many ton-miles in the course of a year. As an example of the scale of this activity it has been estimated that to meet its firewood requirements, 'A town of 10,000 inhabitants would need to witness the annual arrival of between 10,000

[4] Corfield, *The impact of English towns*, Table 1, p. 8. Her calculation was for England and Wales; the percentage for England alone would be marginally higher.

and 16,000 horse-drawn carts' carrying the firewood in question.[5] But it is also true in that indirectly the growth of towns induced other changes that had this effect. If the growing market for agricultural produce in towns led to local specialisation, it would imply a growth in the exchange of produce between the agricultural areas that had moved in this direction. In short, urban growth undermined local self-sufficiency and in so doing increased secondary and tertiary employment. Or, again, increased contact with towns meant that an increasing fraction of the rural population had direct experience of urban life and 'luxuries'. It excited interest in novel forms of expenditure in rural areas, symbolised in the appearance of the village shop. The increasing penetration of the market economy even into the remote countryside, and the mind set this induced, was closely linked to the urban growth that was taking place.

Thirdly, the estimates of urban growth relate to the years 1600 and 1700 whereas the estimates of secondary and tertiary percentages relate to 1601 and *c.* 1710. If there were estimates of the urban percentages for 1710, and the estimates of the contribution of urban growth to explaining the changes in occupational structure were revised to reflect this, the importance of urban growth in accounting for occupational change would be further enhanced. In large measure, therefore, the steady and substantial rise in employment in the secondary and tertiary sectors may be seen as an aspect of the surging growth of the urban sector in seventeenth-century England.

Consumer demand

As Adam Smith remarked: 'Consumption is the sole end and purpose of all production.'[6] The very marked growth in the secondary and tertiary sectors during the seventeenth century must imply a comparable rise in the demand for their products and a change in the structure of aggregate demand to match.[7] This in turn suggests that real income per head was increasing. Given the relative elasticities of demand for basic necessities on the one hand and for consumer durables, other industrial products, and tertiary services on the other, the rise in average real incomes needed to produce a rise in the demand for the products of the secondary and

[5] Van der Woude *et al. Urbanization in history*, p. 8.

[6] Smith, *The wealth of nations*, II, p. 179. He added, 'and the interest of the producer ought to be attended to, only so far as it may be necessary for promoting that of the consumer'. He went on to note that in the mercantile system the opposite was the case.

[7] This assertion is perhaps too categorical. It ignores the possible importance of overseas demand in providing a market for English industrial production. But the great bulk of the output of the secondary sector was consumed domestically, and indeed even if exports had been more substantial, unless they were increasing in relative importance, the domestic market would have increased in step with overall production.

tertiary sectors to match the increase in its output is considerably smaller than might initially be supposed.

As a simple illustration of the point at issue, suppose that a family enjoys an income of 100 units and spends 75 units on basic necessities, predominantly food, leaving 25 units available to spend on other consumer goods and services. Its income then rises by 20 per cent to 120 units. Its spending on basic necessities rises but only moderately to 85 units, or by 13 percent. The units of income available for spending on what contemporaries sometimes termed 'comforts' and 'luxuries' rises from 25 to 35, or by 40 per cent. It is not likely that this example captures the seventeenth-century reality but it may be correct in suggesting that comparatively small changes in average incomes could produce greater structural change than might at first sight seem probable.

Attempts to identify the causes of the rise in aggregate demand and changes in its structure, which would serve to parallel the increase in the output of the secondary and tertiary sectors implied by their increasing prominence in the workforce, have sometimes focused on the behaviour of real wage trends. Many other research topics, of course, provoked interest in real wage trends, notably the fortunes of the working class caught up in the pressures and perils associated with the industrial revolution. In the context of the explanation of the sources of the surge in demand that must have paralleled the rise in the production of goods and services, however, focusing on real wage trends as the key factor is foredoomed to failure because other factors were of equal or greater importance. Using a real wage series based on wage levels in a small number of occupations as a guide to the trend of average incomes is unsatisfactory because implicitly it assumes that the relative size of individual occupations and occupational groups does not change over time. In a period when the economy is in a process of transformation this assumption is mistaken. Since some occupations will increase in size relative to others that will shrink, there can be significant changes in overall average incomes, even if the wages paid to those in each occupational group do not change.

An experimental calculation using the estimates of the average family incomes of a wide range of social groups and occupations in the 'long' eighteenth century illustrates this point. Thanks to Peter Mathias' work in enabling the information in the social tables of Gregory King, Joseph Massie, and Patrick Colquhoun to be reduced to a common format, the size of the change in average incomes that can arise from a changing occupational structure can be illustrated.[8] Although the data relate to the eighteenth century, the calculation has a general relevance. The derivation

[8] Mathias, 'The social structure in the eighteenth century'.

of the average incomes of each social group is described elsewhere.[9] Table 5.3 shows the scale of the change in overall average incomes which would occur if the proportion of the workforce engaged in agriculture declined from 55 to 40 per cent over the eighteenth century, with a consequent rise in the proportion in other occupations, but with no change in the *relative* size of each non-agricultural occupational group, and with no change in the average income of each group.

The top section of Table 5.3 shows the average incomes of the individual economic groups and consolidates the individual groups into two larger groups, all those engaged in agriculture and all those in other categories. The second section shows the overall average income which results from assuming a 55/45 split in agriculture/non-agriculture and from making the split 40/60. At the foot of this section the ratio between the two results is set out. Thus, using King's data, a fall in the agricultural percentage from 55 to 40 increases average income per head by 16.6 per cent, while the comparable increases based on Massie and Colquhoun are 15.7 and 22.8 per cent, respectively. The new estimates of the decline in the percentage of the workforce in agriculture (Table 5.1) differ from those used in this experimental calculation but its implications are virtually unchanged using the more recent estimates.[10] Given the relative income elasticity of demand for primary, secondary, and tertiary products, the fall in the proportion of the workforce in agriculture could, for this reason alone, result in a substantial rise in the demand for the products of industry and for a range of services. In short, an increase in the proportion of the workforce in the secondary and tertiary sectors with a consequent fall in the proportion in agriculture will result in a significant rise in average real incomes.

Changes of the sort assumed in constructing Table 5.3 and rising urbanisation were closely related. In the case of England, therefore, when considering the factors influencing average real incomes, the rapid increase in the proportion of the population living in towns should be noted, particularly as in this respect change in England contrasted sharply with the pattern on the continent. This contrast was one of the main themes of Chapter 4, which provides detailed statistics of the contrast. Here it is sufficient to note that the proportion of the English population living in towns with 5,000 or more inhabitants rose from 8 to 27 per cent between 1600 and 1800, and that the contrast with the continent was so marked that in the second half of the eighteenth century 70 per cent

[9] Wrigley, *Energy and the English industrial revolution*, Table 5.5, p. 129 and associated text.

[10] Wrigley, *ibid.*, Tables 5.5 and 5.6, pp. 129–31.

Table 5.3 *The effect on aggregate income of a decline in the proportion of families in agriculture*

	King		Massie		Colquhoun	
	Average income (£)	Weighting	***Average income*** (£)	Weighting	***Average income*** (£)	Weighting
Farmers	51.3	1	46.4	1	73.5	1
Farm labourers	10.5	3	16.8	3	10.0	3
Average agricultural income	**20.7**		**24.2**		**25.9**	
	Families **(000)**	***Total income*** **(£000)**	***Families*** **(000)**	***Total income*** **(£000)**	***Families*** **(000)**	***Total income*** **(£000)**
Nobility and gentry	16.6	6,286	18.0	8,720	27.2	32,800
Professions, office holders	90.0	5,770	83.0	4,822	172.5	31,300
Artisans, handicraft	60.0	2,400	80.0	4,200	541.0	51,080
Merchants, shopkeepers, seamen	100.0	5,200	277.5	15,400	242.9	48,725
Vagrants	30.0	60			123.5	2,385
Total	296.6	19,716	458.5	33,142	1107.1	166,290
Average income (non-agricultural)	**66.5**		**72.3**		**150.2**	
	Part shares	***Total income*** **(£000)**	***Part shares***	***Total income*** **(£000)**	***Part shares***	***Total income*** **(£000)**
Agriculture	55	1,140.8	55	1,330.5	55	1,424.2
Other than agriculture	45	2,991.3	45	3,252.8	40	6,759.1
Total (A)	**100**	**4,132.1**	**100**	**4,583.2**	**100**	**8,183.3**
Agriculture	40	829.7	40	967.6	40	1,035.8
Other than agriculture	60	3,988.4	60	4,337.0	60	9,012.2
Total (B)	**100**	**4,818.1**	**100**	**5,304.6**	**100**	**10,048.0**
Ratio Total B/Total A		**116.6**		**115.7**		**122.8**

Note: There is additional information about the incomes of the constituent categories in the farming and non-farming households in Wrigley, *Energy and the English industrial revolution*, Table 5.5, p. 129. Vagrants were included in the calculations for King and Colquhoun (Massie provides no comparable data). To do so is debatable since they are individuals rather than families and, furthermore, it is not clear that they should be regarded as 'belonging' outside agriculture. The last jobs of many vagrants may well have been agricultural. But their inclusion must reduce the contrast between the average income of the agricultural and non-agricultural sectors, helping to ensure that the ratios shown on the bottom line of the table can be regarded as minimal estimates of the impact of the posited change in occupational structure.
Source: Wrigley, *Energy and the English industrial revolution*, Table 5.6, pp. 130–1.

of the urban growth in Europe as a whole (including England) took place in England alone even though the English population represented only about 8 per cent of the European total.[11] The increase in the urban percentage was the dominant element in the rise in the percentage of the workforce in secondary and tertiary employment. Moving from the countryside to the town frequently meant a change of occupation and often a rise in the wage received. Table 5.3 embodied the restrictive assumption that as the percentage in agriculture declined the relative size of the component elements in the non-agricultural sector did not change. If there was change, it might well imply that the rise in income suggested in Table 5.3 understates the scale of change that occurred.

It should also be noted that, given the importance of urbanisation in changing the occupational structure, it is probably too restrictive to assume that there was no change in the average income of each occupation. Urban wages in a given occupation were normally higher than rural wages.[12] Where it was the case that the wage difference exceeded the difference in living costs, the real as well as the nominal wage of workers in a given occupation would rise in the wake of urban growth. An increase in the proportion of men in that occupation living in towns would raise the average level of real wages in that occupation in the country as a whole.

A further reason for considering that a focus on changes in the real wages of particular occupations as a guide to changes in the purchasing power of the wider community may be mistaken is to be found in the notion of an 'industrious revolution' advanced by Jan de Vries. He suggested that in parts of north-west Europe, and notably in England, an 'industrious revolution' took place in the early modern period. The key to restoring a balance between the scale of consumption demand and productive activity, he argued, lay in the recognition that the unit on which to focus should be the household rather than the individual or, in his words, 'The industrious revolution concept argues for a shift of attention from the *daily wage of individuals* to the *annual earnings of households*'.[13] He summarised his thesis in the following terms:

> my historical claim is that north-western Europe and British North America experienced an 'industrious revolution' during a long eighteenth century, roughly 1650–1850, in which a growing number of households acted to reallocate their productive resources (which are chiefly the time of their members) in ways that increased *both* the supply of market-orientated, money-earning activities *and* the demand for goods offered in the marketplace. Increased production specialization in the household gives access to augmented consumption choices in the marketplace.[14]

[11] See Table 4.1, p. 47. [12] See p. 91.
[13] De Vries, *The industrious revolution*, p. 86. [14] *Ibid.*, p. 10.

The advent of an 'industrious revolution' was a development which could in principle both increase the volume of consumer demand and change its character without necessarily resulting in a matching change in the real wage as conventionally measured. If the proportion of the total income of a household secured by the male breadwinner declined, the living standards and consumption patterns of the household might improve even though the income of the male breadwinner did not change. Indeed his income might fall while yet the income of the whole household was maintained or improved. De Vries noted that economists, while ready to treat supply and demand as paired forces in shaping market economies, nevertheless tended to explain growth largely in terms of 'supply-side' advances. The industrious revolution in his view came about because an increasingly large fraction of the population, ultimately the overwhelming majority, acquired a new appetite for a wide range of goods that were not necessities of life. To gain the means to satisfy their new desires, they were willing to work longer hours and to reorganise life within the household. Attention, he argued, should be paid also to 'demand-side' changes.

De Vries notes that contemporaries recognised that attitudes had changed. He quotes Sir Dudley North, who wrote that the appetite for non-essentials was 'the main spur to trade, or rather to industry and ingenuity', and that the prospect of acquiring such goods 'disposes [people] to work, when nothing else will incline them to it; for did men content themselves with bare necessities, we should have a poor world'. Or, as David Hume expressed the same thought: 'it is a violent method and in most cases impracticable, to oblige the labourer to toil in order to raise from the land more than what subsists himself and his family. Furnish him with manufactures and commodities and he will do it himself.'[15] The new attitudes were first visible in the material culture of the Dutch Republic in the seventeenth century but arose also in much of the rest of north-west Europe. In de Vries' view the reallocation of resources associated with the division of labour should not be regarded solely as a matter of work organisation at the level of the firm; rather it was 'achieved primarily at the level of the household, where it can be identified as the *simultaneous* rise in the percentage of household production sold to others and a rise in the percentage of household consumption purchased from others'.[16]

An industrious revolution, no less than an industrial revolution, meant a definitive abandonment of the world which Oliver Goldsmith depicted in his poem 'The Deserted Village', published in 1770, whose disappearance he regretted so bitterly:

[15] *Ibid.*, pp. 66–7. [16] *Ibid.*, p. 71.

A time there was, ere England's griefs began,
When every rood of ground maintained its man;
For him light labour spread her wholesome store,
Just gave what life required, but gave no more:
His blest companions, innocence and health;
And his best riches, ignorance of wealth.

The society and economy that Goldsmith described may never have borne a close resemblance to the reality of life in a peasant community but it serves to exemplify what is sometimes termed a *satisficer* concept of motive and action. If the conditions that represent a fulfilling and stable life can be achieved without constant effort, it makes good sense to enjoy the leisure that is then possible. If, on the contrary, a *maximiser* view is held, each ambition realised is to be regarded only as providing a stimulus to reach still higher.[17]

To the degree that the idea of an industrious revolution captures an aspect of the changes in train in the seventeenth and eighteenth centuries, its intrinsic nature suggests that relying on real wage data for individual occupations will cause the growth in consumption to be underestimated. There is good reason to suppose that the attitudinal changes that characterise the industrious revolution developed early and strongly in England. Once again the huge rise in the population of London and the pervasive influence of the capital on patterns of behaviour countrywide was of great importance. The steady rise in the percentages of the workforce engaged in secondary and tertiary employment, pronounced in both the seventeenth and in the eighteenth centuries, suggests the same, as does the evidence of probate inventories which are abundant from the later seventeenth and early eighteenth centuries, though much less so after the 1730s. They leave no doubt, that possession of the type of goods which might be expected to become more common with rising incomes – clocks, curtains, pictures, looking glasses, cooking utensils, furniture, bedding, and clothing – had become commonplace by the early and middle decades of the eighteenth century but had been far less widely owned half a century earlier.[18] Unfortunately, probate inventories provide information disproportionately about the possessions and life style of the middling sort and the wealthy. In this section of the community it seems clear that there was increasing prosperity and a matching change in life style. Houses became larger, more elaborately equipped

[17] There is an illuminating review of the range of constraints on choice and the degree of freedom of action in rural communities throughout pre-industrial Europe in Ogilvie, 'Choices and constraints'.

[18] Overton *et al.*, *Production and consumption*; Shammas, *The pre-industrial consumer*.

and furnished, and with a more specialised use of rooms. The increasing use of coal rather than wood for domestic heating led to warmer rooms and the construction of brick chimneys. The better sort, in short, could afford to live in greater comfort than their parents and grandparents.

Whether the lower orders benefited similarly is less certain, but it is increasingly difficult to view the plight of the working classes caught up in industrial and commercial cities in terms as stark as was once common. For example, the recent work of Emma Griffin, drawing upon the autobiographies of a large number of working men, provides much evidence of the benefits which contemporaries associated with moving from a rural area into a town or city. She takes issue with the Engels' view depicting the industrial revolution as resulting in the suffering and degradation of the working people caught up in it, a view which, she notes, has been echoed repeatedly in more recent times. She writes:

> It is my belief that the opportunities in the workplace were brighter for adult men in the late eighteenth and early nineteenth centuries than they had been at any other time in the eighteenth century or before. Work, and more particularly the wages that went with it, was a powerful tool for raising a man's status within his family and his community.[19]

In an extensive survey of the fortunes of scores of individual workers as recorded in their autobiographies she notes: 'repeatedly our writers tell us that work in cottage industry, factories, mines, warehouses, large cities and construction was better than the labour that had consumed their fathers' energies – and often their own early labours as well.'[20] Griffin's evidence refers to the later decades of the eighteenth century and the early decades of the nineteenth, but the pattern she describes may well hold good for much of the two preceding centuries. Earlier generations of men and women leaving the land to find employment in urban centres or in local handicraft and service employment may well have experienced similar good fortune. It was, of course, clearly not universally true that men and women arriving in urban areas experienced immediate benefit. Yet it is probable that the experience of the men whose lives and attitudes Griffin describes was true of many of their predecessors throughout the early modern period when moving from country to town.

Autobiographical evidence cannot be conclusive. If, for example, those who succeed in life are more likely to write an autobiography than those who are less fortunate, it is prudent to be wary of extrapolating from the experiences of the authors to other members of the communities in which they lived. But the apparent consensus among the writers on

[19] Griffin, *Liberty's dawn*, p. 26. [20] *Ibid.*, p. 46.

whose work Griffin draws is at least persuasive evidence of the benefits which often followed from moving from an original setting which was often agricultural.

Collective experience no less than personal reflection also calls in question too strong an insistence on the dark side of the industrial revolution. It should not be forgotten, for example, that urban mortality in England in the late eighteenth and early nineteenth centuries was substantially lower than it had been in earlier times, as shown by the fact that urban death rates before the later eighteenth century normally exceeded birth rates but the reverse was true thereafter. Moreover, when the conditions of urban life in early nineteenth-century England, as reflected in urban mortality levels, are compared with contemporary continental experience, there seems little reason to suppose that England was unfortunate; rather the reverse. The findings of Söderberg *et al.* are notable in this regard. They are described below but in summary they show that urban mortality in continental towns and cities was often higher and sometimes much higher than in Britain, and that in Britain mortality in industrial towns was closely similar to mortality in other towns.[21]

Although there are substantial problems in using real wage series as a guide to trends in the volume and structure of consumer demand in individual countries, inter-country comparisons can be illuminating. Allen has marshalled wage data for labourers in six large cities in Europe and Asia over the centuries from 1500 onwards. To simplify comparison, he converted the original information about wage levels into the grams of silver that the wage rate in question could purchase. When deflated by the cost of purchasing a basket of goods, this makes it possible to estimate real incomes and thus to simplify the measurement of change over time and also the comparison of real incomes of different places at the same time. Two baskets of goods were employed, one sufficient only for bare subsistence, the other reflecting the costs of a 'respectable' life style. Whichever of the two measures of real income were used in a comparison of six European and Asian cities, the same pattern of change is visible. In the high middle ages there were only relatively small differences in real incomes between the six cities, and all of them experienced a significant decline in income between the fifteenth and late sixteenth centuries, a time of rising population pressure in many regions. Thereafter the fortunes of the six cities varied markedly. Real incomes of labourers in four of the cities (Vienna, Florence, Delhi, and Beijing) continued to fall until the first quarter of the nineteenth century. At the end of this long period of decline incomes could barely cover the cost of the subsistence basket

[21] See pp. 93–5.

and would have covered only half the cost of achieving respectability. In sharp contrast in Amsterdam and London in the seventeenth and eighteenth centuries labourers' average incomes were always in excess of the cost of achieving respectability and in general lay at a level 25–50 per cent above it. Their incomes stood at three or four times above the subsistence level.[22]

Allen's estimates suggest that in London even labourers enjoyed an income that would allow a significant purchase of other goods and services after meeting the cost of securing basic necessities. A comparable calculation based on masons' wages reinforced this conclusion since from the late sixteenth century onwards their wages rose from *c.* 70 per cent above the respectability level *c.* 1600 to well over double that level by the end of the eighteenth century.[23] Many working class families would have been able to purchase 'comforts' as well as securing their basic necessities. Because their earnings were so far above bare subsistence, and given the character of income elasticity of demand for the products of primary, secondary, and tertiary products, this in turn would give rise to a surge in the demand for the products of the secondary and tertiary sectors. Since workers in other occupations were better paid than labourers, it is no surprise that in Table 5.2 the combined percentages of men in the secondary and tertiary sectors rose from 29.0 per cent in 1600 to 49.2 per cent in *c.* 1710. Wages in London were always higher than elsewhere in the country. Sometimes the difference between London and the provinces was substantial, but it tended to decrease over time. The implication of Allen's work, therefore, is that in the country as a whole the percentage increase in real incomes was greater than in London though their absolute level remained below the comparable level in the capital.

Hunt's investigation of the regional inequality of wage levels in Britain over the period from 1760 to 1914 shows very clearly the tendency of the wages of carpenters in towns at a distance from London to rise relative to wages in the metropolis. He also demonstrated the same pattern in agricultural wages that Allen later found. In industrial counties in the north, and notably in Lancashire, the wages of agricultural labourers advanced substantially. This finding suggests an aspect of wage trends that would strengthen further the evidence for improvement. To the degree that it was the case that wage rises were most marked in areas where population was rising faster than elsewhere, the degree of improvement visible in data for particular areas will tend to understate the scale of the overall rise. As Hunt remarked, 'when chronological wage analysis is supplemented by

[22] Allen, *The British industrial revolution*, Figure 2.2, p. 39, and Figure 2.3, p. 40.
[23] *Ibid.*, Figure 2.6, p. 45.

spatial analysis, each add weight to the more optimistic interpretations of the effect of industrialization upon workers' living standards'.[24]

As is widely recognised, and evident from the last few paragraphs, the attempt to measure living standards is both complex and controversial. The received wisdom has for long been that for the working class families a steady and continued rise in living standards began only in the second half of the nineteenth century. Feinstein undertook an exhaustive and sophisticated assessment of working class earnings and summarised his findings as follows:

> Wage earners' average real incomes were broadly stagnant for 50 years until the early 1830s, despite the fact that in many parts of the country they were starting from a very low level, having been falling in the second half of the eighteenth century. Some slight progress was made in the mid-1830s, but earnings then fell back again in the cyclical depression during 1838/42, and it was not until the mid-1840s that they at last started an ascent to a new height.[25]

More recently, Meredith and Oxley have produced an impressive survey of the literature on a related issue, nutrional levels in England in the eighteenth and nineteenth centuries. They conclude that food supply failed to keep pace with population growth, leading to the conclusion that 'The English population did not succumb to famine, yet they did suffer sickness, stunted growth, hunger and premature death, and they watched far too many of their babies die, in part for want of adequate nutrition'.[26]

The difficulty of arriving at a definitive conclusion about national trends in nutrition and living standards more generally deserves emphasis. It is evident from the wide-ranging and very detailed analysis of the fortunes of labourers made by Muldrew. In relation to nutrition, for example, changes in occupational structure have a bearing on what constitutes an adequate diet. Muldrew provides estimates of the daily calorific expenditure needed for different agricultural tasks. At one extreme, to carry out 8 hours of work when mowing with a scythe or cutting trees requires more than 6,500 calories; in contrast, grinding corn by hand requires only *c.* 5,000 calories.[27] The contrast is in a sense even greater, given that in both cases 2,100 calories of the total is expended in the basic metabolic rate and other essential activities. In the economy as a whole there would have been still greater differences by occupation. In the secondary sector there were many physically demanding activities, notably in coalmining, but there were also many men employed

24 Hunt, 'Industrialization and regional inequality', p. 960.
25 Feinstein, 'Pessimism perpetuated', p. 649.
26 Meredith and Oxley, 'Food and fodder', p. 213.
27 Muldrew, *Food, energy*, Table 3.8, p. 131.

in occupations which required a much more modest expenditure of energy, for example in shoemaking. There were almost 110,000 shoemakers in England in 1831. They were the largest occupation in the retail trade and handicraft category in the 1831 census. One man in thirty of all male workers in England at that date was a shoemaker.[28] In the tertiary sector clerical work was largely sedentary, and in most other tertiary sectors the level of energy expended was modest by the standards of agricultural work. Given the scale of occupational change between the mid seventeenth and mid nineteenth centuries, an unchanging average level of calorie intake would imply an improvement in the average nutritional level. It also suggests that a fall in the level of calorie intake did not necessarily mean worsening nutrition. And other changes probably had a similar implication. The increasing use of coal as a cheap source of domestic heating, *ceteris paribus*, will improve nutritional standards. The changing age structure of the population, with an increase in the proportion of children, also need to be taken into account.

In relation to the measurements of living standards, Muldrew illustrated how far trends measured by the income of individual labourers may diverge from trends measured by the families of the same labourers. In the first two-thirds of the eighteenth century, for example, a wife's average earnings from spinning tripled, rising more in absolute terms than male wages, leading Muldrew to remark that 'there is certainly evidence to support the part of de Vries' thesis which argues that increasingly family labour was adding income to family earnings'.[29] By the same token, the collapse of hand spinning when undercut by the introduction of factory production was an important source of the pressure on the real incomes of very many families at the end of the eighteenth century and the first quarter of the nineteenth.

Unambiguous evidence about trends in living standards may prove beyond reach, not least because the concept of a 'standard of living' is difficult to define in a fashion which commands universal assent, but indirect indicators of living standards such as the level of mortality, no less than reassessment of direct measures, suggest that a more optimistic conclusion than was once normal is justified.[30] There are comparable uncertainties and disagreements relating to nutrition. In relation to both questions it is helpful, and often illuminating, to attempt comparison between England and neighbouring countries as well as considering time trends in England taken in isolation.

28 See Table 8.1, p. 157.
29 Muldrew, *Food, energy*, p. 259; see also Table 5.19, p. 257 and associated discussion.
30 See pp. 93–5.

The changes in occupational structure and in the structure of consumer demand taking place in early modern England formed part of the wider changes then in train. To provide a background to these changes it is of interest to consider other aspects of the gradual transformation of the economy as a whole from Tudor times onwards, and in particular the centrality of London to developments in the first half of this period.

The scale of change over three centuries

At the time of the Great Exhibition in 1851, when the energy restriction experienced by all organic economies had been overcome in regard both to heat and to mechanical energy, and the scale of production of coal, iron, and cotton in Britain had far outstripped that of other countries, it was clear beyond doubt that, if only briefly, Britain had become the world's leading economy.[31] Three centuries earlier, in contrast, at the beginning of the period during which the English economy was progressively transformed, the country's relative position was the reverse of this. England lagged well behind her close neighbours on the continent. It is instructive to consider her state in the late Tudor period as a background to later developments.

The backwardness of the Tudor economy when compared with the more advanced areas of continental Europe has often been noted. Coleman, for example, wrote that, 'despite the shift to being an exporter of cloth rather than wool, industry in Tudor England remained technically backward in comparison with the best practices of continental Europe'. He added:

> Over a range of industries – paper, linen, silk, leather-working, hosiery, iron-founding, glass-making – English inferiority to French, Spanish, Italian, Flemish, or German products was manifest. In mining and metallurgy the Germans were the masters; in ship-building, first the Iberian powers and then the Dutch were well ahead of English methods. The import of continental skills and techniques, via immigrant labour and, in some cases, capital, is one of major themes of Tudor and Stuart industrial history.[32]

Coleman noted that in the second half of the seventeenth century the gap was closing. Industry made progress in part by importing better techniques from abroad, as in the case of silk-throwing and papermaking; but increasingly best practice was the result of local ingenuity and initiative rather than drawing upon continental expertise.

Clay in a similar wide-ranging review of economic and social change in England in the sixteenth and seventeenth centuries, also drew attention

[31] See pp. 182–5. [32] Coleman, *The economy of England*, p. 69.

to the many respects in which industrial achievement on the other side of the Channel far exceeded practice in England. It was 'an industrially backward country' in early Tudor times:

> All or most of the sail-cloth and canvas used in the country was imported, so were the hard-wearing linen–cotton fabrics known as fustians, all the paper, the window glass, the brass, steel, certain types of iron needed for specialist purposes and large quantities of a wide range of goods made from those metals, including knives, saws, wire, pins, needles, and hollow ware.[33]

In Clay's view, however, there were already some signs of change and improvement in the early seventeenth century. He suggested that new consumer goods industries were developing and that the home market was increasingly supplied by local production rather than by imports from abroad. He noted as an example that no window glass was home-produced in the mid sixteenth century but that by the 1590s window glass was almost exclusively supplied by local industry, and that the same became true of a wide range of other glass products in the early decades of the seventeenth century. He considered that what was true of glass production foreshadowed similar developments across a wide range of industries progressively during the seventeenth century.[34] In 1600, however, such changes lay predominantly in the future.

The backwardness of the English economy at the end of the sixteenth century is made manifest in evidence of a different type. New estimates of English county populations in 1600 have been made recently and it is therefore possible to calculate the population densities in each county.[35] The densities are revealing. The initial pattern derived from relating population totals to the gross area of each county conforms to what is probably the general expectation. The average population density of the ten northernmost counties in 1600 was 9.8 persons per 100 acres.[36] The average density in the rest of England (excluding Middlesex because of the presence of London) was 13.1 persons per 100 acres. The north of England, however, is much hillier than the south. The higher land is in the main unsuitable for agriculture, or at best of marginal value. To take account of this fact, if densities are recalculated by excluding land above 200 metres, the picture changes. The north–south difference disappears. The average density of the 10 northernmost English counties is 14.8 persons per 100 acres; that of the remaining 30 counties to the

[33] Clay, *Economic expansion and social change*, II, p. 6.

[34] *Ibid.*, II, pp. 36–8. [35] Wrigley, 'Rickman revisited'.

[36] The ten counties are Cheshire, Cumberland, Derbyshire, Durham, Lancashire, Northumberland, Westmorland, and the three Ridings of Yorkshire. For the county population totals: Wrigley, *The early English censuses*, Table A2.6, pp. 224–5.

south is 13.9 persons per 100 acres. Equally interesting is the fact that there was only a modest range of values among all 40 English counties (again excluding Middlesex). The standard deviation of the 40 counties is only 2.9. At a time when a very high proportion of the labour force worked on the land such notable similarity between the counties suggests, among other things, the possibility of similar agricultural practices and aims across the whole country, with a focus on local self-sufficiency rather than the specialisation which would have been possible only with the existence of regional and national markets.[37]

Ann Kussmaul's analysis of patterns of marriage seasonality suggests that this may have been the case. In her monograph on the rural economy of England in the early modern period Kussmaul made extensive use of parish registers. The relative monthly frequency of marriages recorded in the parish registers provides evidence of the character of the local agricultural economy. Kussmaul found that in the later sixteenth century a peak in marriage frequency in the autumn was common both to the traditionally 'arable' eastern counties and also to 'pastoral' counties in the west and north.[38] An autumn peak in marriages was characteristic of a farming year predominantly concerned with the harvesting of corn. In pastoral parishes the peak was in the late spring or early summer. In both farming types, the peak of marriages followed the season of the year in which the demand for labour had been at its height. In arable areas this occurred when the grain had been harvested, in pastoral areas when lambing and calving had taken place. Kussmaul depicts the population increase during the sixteenth century as having resulted in what Geertz termed 'agricultural involution'.[39] A rising population led to an increase in the price of grain, with the familiar result that the required increase in grain production was secured only at the cost of declining labour productivity in agriculture. During the seventeenth century the pattern changed. In northern and western areas the marriage seasonality associated with a focus primarily on pastoral products became the norm.[40] The new pattern was, she noted, 'the product of regional specialization in the use of land and labour', which in turn was the basis for the notable increase in agricultural productivity taking place over the seventeenth and eighteenth centuries.[41] It was increasingly the case that market-orientated farming was determining land use rather than a 'peasant' focus on local self-sufficiency. As a result, the notable similarity in the density of county

[37] For an indication of the scale of the change in the regional variation in agricultural employment, see Table 9.4, p. 193.

[38] Kussmaul, *A general view*, Figure 1.4, p. 12 and associated text.

[39] Geertz, *Agricultural involution*.

[40] Kussmaul, *A general view*, Chapter 8.

[41] *Ibid.*, p. 3.

population per 100 acres in 1600, at a time when a very large percentage of the labour force was employed in agriculture, gave way to marked regional differences in county agricultural employment densities in later centuries. In 1841, for example, the density was two-thirds higher in the eastern (south) region than in the northern region of England.[42]

This change may well have been greatly expedited by the very large acreage that passed from royal to private hands following the dissolution of the monasteries. Clay suggested that: 'If estates granted away to courtiers and royal servants in the mid-sixteenth century are also included, perhaps 25 per cent of the land of England had passed from royal into private hands by 1642.'[43] He considered that royal estates had been poorly managed. His conclusion is similar to that of Pollard when discussing events in Belgium after it became part of France in 1795. He noted that in Belgium the abolition without payment of seigneurial claims, restrictions, and obligations which had been instituted two years earlier in France made little difference in Belgium, but added that nonetheless, 'the confiscation of church lands and their sale to private persons gave a strong boost to capitalist agriculture in an area where church property had been particularly extensive'.[44]

In the later sixteenth century achieving local self-sufficiency was the prime concern. Corn crops were the mainstay of agricultural activity even in areas not well suited to arable agriculture. By the end of the seventeenth century, in contrast, 'large portions of England had stopped producing their own grain'.[45] In the earlier period, the low level of urbanisation and the primitive transport system meant that there was little incentive either to specialise or to increase output in excess of local need, except in the vicinity of London. Local self-sufficiency was a necessary imperative given the lack of access to wider markets and the opportunity to specialise that resulted. In late Tudor times on occasions when grain was moved between a producing and a receiving parish the average distance involved was much shorter than had become normal a century later.[46]

By the later sixteenth century rural England had already ceased to be a typically 'peasant' economy, at least in the sense that, in contrast with medieval times, in most parishes there was a wide spread in the size of landholdings with a small minority of farmers possessing holdings of 100 acres or more, and a much larger number of small proprietors with less than 20 acres.[47] Nevertheless, market conditions and modest real incomes enforced a focus on local self-sufficiency. Matters changed in

[42] Table 9.4, p. 193. [43] Clay, *Economic expansion and social change*, II, p. 263.
[44] Pollard, *Peaceful conquest*, p. 50.
[45] Kussmaul, *A general view*, p. 67. [46] *Ibid.*, pp. 98–9.
[47] Whittle, *The development of agrarian capitalism*, pp.190–6.

the seventeenth century. Growing urban demand, rising real incomes in the absence of any significant growth in the national population, and improved transport facilities created a novel situation. In the later sixteenth century arable parishes in which corn-growing was the principal focus of agricultural activity blanketed the country. In the next half-century there was rapid change. By the time the monarchy was restored following the civil war the familiar north-west/south-east pattern was well established with the pastoral/arable ratio high in the north and west.[48] Summarising the conclusions to be drawn from her earlier work Kussmaul wrote:

> At the start of the seventeenth century – Grain growing predominated in almost every area; it was fostered both by the continuation of rising grain prices in the first half of the century and by poor inter-regional connections and regional self-sufficiency in basic food-stuffs. By 1700, much the west of Britain had forsaken the production of grain, principally for the raising of sheep and cattle and for manufacturing.[49]

London's role in engendering change

By the end of the seventeenth century the English economy was greatly changed from its state at the century's beginning. In considering this remarkable advance, the central role played by London should be emphasised. Urban growth had often offered support for economic advance, while at the same time being dependent on economic development taking place in rural areas in the manner described by Adam Smith.[50] Urban growth implied an increasing agricultural surplus after meeting the food needs of the rural population, but also encouraged further specialisation by providing a market for the surplus, thus fostering a further increase in agricultural productivity. Positive feedback of this kind, of course, was normally reversed after a time in organic economies. A rising rural population would put pressure on local agriculture when seeking to meet the increased demand, and local agriculture was often able to meet this pressure only at the cost of falling output per head.[51] Yet during the seventeenth century the situation changed radically. The continued growth of London played a leading role in generating changes in the national

[48] Kussmaul, *A general view*, Table 3.3, p. 63; Figure 1.1, p. 2; Figure 1.4, p. 12.
[49] Kussmaul, 'The pattern of work', p. 1. [50] See p. 23.
[51] In relation to the livestock of medieval villagers in the thirteenth century, whose numbers were constrained by the quantity of available fodder, Postan remarked, 'the numbers of animals in our villages were exceedingly low. They were low in comparison with corresponding numbers at other dates and they were equally low in relation to the scale and needs of thirteenth-century husbandry.' Postan, 'Village livestock', p. 235.

economy that enabled the country to strike out along a new path of expansion. Much of the country was, so to speak, in London's backyard. Its influence was crucial in turning England from an essentially rural country, where a concentration on local self-sufficiency was characteristic of economic activity over large swathes of the country, into a market-orientated economy in which major gains in efficiency were possible, notably in agriculture and by providing incentives to improve transport facilities.

Although it was in the seventeenth century that the most dramatic change occurred, even in the sixteenth century London's centrality to national life was already clearly evident in some contexts. Rappaport's work on the granting of apprenticeships and admission of citizens by London livery companies showed that already in the middle of the sixteenth century in some contexts the links between the capital and the whole of the rest of the country were so close that distance from the capital was of little importance. Of the 1,028 men who became citizens by means of apprenticeship in 1551–3, 90 per cent had moved to London from elsewhere in the country: almost a third came from the six northernmost counties in England.[52] The comparable catchment areas for apprentices for towns other than London were modest in comparison.[53]

London was not merely a place to which people moved. It was a place in which there was much through traffic. Rappaport emphasised the scale of the migrant flow in both directions. Many of those who served an apprenticeship in London later left the city. Rappaport also provided a table comparing the daily wages of skilled and semi-skilled workmen in London with wages elsewhere in southern England for each decade from 1490–9 until 1600–9, showing that skilled wages were more than 30 per cent higher in the capital than in southern England; unskilled wages were also higher, but by a smaller margin of 26 per cent.[54] Although the comparative cost of living in the capital and elsewhere was not available for this period 'such a differential in wage rates may have driven many a man to seek work in London'.[55]

In the following century there is abundant evidence that as London's population increased its influence rose commensurately. The notes made by Richard Gough of Myddle, a village close to Shrewsbury, about his fellow parishioners in the later seventeenth century illustrate the frequency and routine nature of contact between Myddle and London, even though

[52] Rappaport, *Worlds within worlds*, pp. 76–7 and Figure 3.4, p. 79.

[53] Few apprentices travelled more than 20 miles to take up apprenticeships in cities such as Norwich, Worcester, Great Yarmouth, and York. *Ibid.*, p. 80.

[54] *Ibid.*, Table 3.6, p. 85. [55] *Ibid.*, p. 83.

the village was about 160 miles distant from the capital. Hey remarks in his introduction to an edition of Gough that, 'He frequently mentions London in passing as if it were commonplace that his neighbours should have been there. Men and women from all sections of his community went to the capital in search of fortune or excitement or to escape from trouble at home. Most of them kept in contact with their families, and further information about events in London and other parts of the country filtered back to Myddle through "the Gazet" and "our News letters".'[56]

As London's population surged in the seventeenth century its demography also became an important factor in increasing contact between the capital and its hinterland. The death rate in London was higher than the birth rate in the seventeenth century so that a large net immigrant flow was needed simply to avoid a reduction in numbers, but London was also increasing in size rapidly. A crude calculation intended to measure the combined effect of rapid growth and high mortality suggests that the survivors to adult years of roughly a sixth of all the births taking place in England would be living in London 20 years after a given cohort of children was born.[57] I argued that in these circumstances, 'it is probably fair to assume that this must have acted as a powerful solvent of the customs, prejudices and modes of action of traditional, rural England'.[58]

No less symbolic of the progressive reshaping of the English economy was the contrast between the seventeenth and eighteenth centuries. The growth of London in the seventeenth century and the stimulus it provided to induce change throughout the whole country might be described as exemplifying the scope for change within an organic economy. In the eighteenth century, however, the population of London grew no faster than that of the country as a whole. Urban growth elsewhere, and especially in the industrial and commercial centres in the north of England and the midlands, far outstripped that of the capital. A new type of stimulus, characteristic of an industrial revolution, was steadily increasing in importance.

Other aspects of urban life in England

Two further aspects of urban life in England before and during the industrial revolution deserve attention: urban mortality and levels of literacy.

Urban mortality

The death rate was on average higher than the birth rate in the majority of large towns and many smaller ones in early modern England

[56] Gough, *The history of Myddle*, p. 19. [57] Wrigley, 'A simple model', p. 137.
[58] *Ibid.*, p. 138.

and therefore a constant flow of in-migrants was needed to prevent population decline. If the urban population was increasing this implied a still higher level of inward movement. At some point if this situation prevails urban growth will cease because rural birth surpluses will no longer exceed the urban deficit. Interpretation of the implications of urban death rates exceeding birth rates is both complicated and controversial. This issue has been discussed at length by de Vries.[59] In relation to urban growth in England, however, it is probably sufficient to note that in the second half of the eighteenth century the balance between births and deaths in most towns and cities changed: there was local natural increase rather than decrease. Chambers' pathbreaking study of Nottingham in the eighteenth century showed that until the 1740s the number of deaths usually exceeded the number of births but that thereafter the reverse was normally the case, and that by the end of the century local natural increase was as important as immigration in contributing to the overall rise in population.[60] This pattern was typical of many provincial towns. The London bills of mortality and the parish registers of the capital present complex problems of interpretation, but Landers' painstaking and sophisticated use of the available evidence suggests that from the 1780s there was local natural increase in the capital whereas earlier in the century a substantial surplus of deaths was normal.[61] Ironically, the gloomy Dickensian view of urban sanitary conditions was penned at a time when urban growth was increasingly secured from urban birth surpluses.

Not only did the balance between urban births and deaths change markedly in England between the mid eighteenth and mid nineteenth centuries, but it is also the case that the work of Söderberg *et al.* suggests that English urban mortality in the early nineteenth century was substantially less severe than in many continental cities, and indeed that adult mortality levels in British industrial towns were no higher than in other towns which were growing far less rapidly. Söderberg *et al.* undertook their review as background to a discussion of the extraordinarily high mortality in Stockholm during this period. It was not until the 1850s that the crude death rate in Stockholm fell below the birth rate. Only Vienna displayed an equally severe regime, though Berlin was said to 'show many resemblances' to Stockholm and female age-specific mortality rates in Paris were broadly similar to those in the Swedish capital though male rates were far higher in Stockholm than in Paris. The massive excess of adult male over adult female death rates in Stockholm was

59 De Vries, *European urbanization*, pp. 179–98.
60 Chambers, 'Population change in a provincial town', Appendix, p. 122.
61 Landers, *Death and the metropolis*, Table 5.6, p. 175.

Table 5.4 *Age-specific mortality rates per 1,000 in England 1838–44*

	Industrial cities		**Non-industrial cities**		**Country districts**	
Age	Male	Female	Male	Female	Male	Female
25–34	10.5	11.2	11.5	9.5	9.1	11.4
35–44	13.6	14.6	15.5	12.5	10.4	12.4
45–54	21.3	18.6	21.8	14.4	14.1	14.1

Source: Söderberg *et al.*, *A stagnating metropolis*, Table 8.10, p. 199.

of special interest to Söderberg *et al.*, and they sought comparative data for cities elsewhere in Europe.

After first considering cities in continental Europe, Söderberg *et al.* turned their attention to Britain, showing, for example, that in 1821–5 male rates in Stockholm were much higher than in Glasgow, except for the 5–9 age group.[62] Having identified Liverpool, Manchester, Bristol, and Whitechapel as the 'three most disadvantaged English cities and the worst sub-district of London', they then compared male age-specific rates in Stockholm (1836–45) with the four English cities (1838–44).[63] Except in the age groups 5–9 and 10–14 the Stockholm rates were always higher than any of the English rates and in the age groups 15–24 to 45–54 more than twice as high as those in the English cities.[64] Their chief interest lay, however, in the extent of differences in age-specific rates for adult men and women since this was so striking and unusual in Stockholm, and they made further use of English data to examine the difference in sex-specific mortality rates in the three 10-year age groups 25–54 for a sample of English industrial cities, non-industrial cities, and country districts. The information in their table is reproduced in Table 5.4.

Male rates in industrial cities were lower than those in non-industrial cities in each of the three age groups but the reverse was true of female rates, while in country districts men experienced slightly lower death rates than in either of the two urban categories, and the same was true of female rates except in the 25–34 age group. Söderberg *et al.* did not provide listings of the cities and country districts on which the table is based, and both measuring English urban death rates using the material published by the Registrar General and attempting to establish their typicality presents complex difficulties.[65] Table 5.4 provides only adult rates

62 Söderberg *et al.*, *Stagnating metropolis*, Table 8.10, p. 177.
63 *Ibid.*, p. 178. 64 *Ibid.*, Table 8.6, p. 179.
65 See, for example, the description and discussion of these difficulties in Laxton and Williams, 'Urbanization and infant mortality'.

and further work may be needed to confirm that the rates in the table are representative of the three settlement types which they distinguished, and that rates earlier and later in life show a similar pattern. The table does, however, suggest the possibility, even the likelihood, both that mortality levels in the middle decades of life in the new, rapidly growing centres of industry were not greatly different from the levels prevailing generally in English towns and cities, and that any advantage enjoyed by rural areas was more modest than is sometimes assumed. The urban rate for a whole city represents, of course, a weighted average of the rates in its various districts. Mortality rates in the most unhealthy and overcrowded slum areas in English cities were much higher than in the more salubrious parts of those cities. It is clear and noteworthy, however, that urban mortality rates in the least healthy continental cities were substantially higher than was the case even in cities such as Liverpool and Glasgow in the first half of the nineteenth century.

Foreign visitors to England in the nineteenth century were often shocked by the environments and living conditions they found in the industrial cities of the north and midlands. Engels was specific and unrelenting in his condemnation of the suffering he described. Both his writings and the investigation of English urban mortality by Söderberg *et al.* reflect their particular interests. By providing a comparative setting for the cripplingly high death rates in Stockholm, however, the work of Söderberg *et al.* leaves no room for doubt that even the worst levels of urban mortality in England were well below those to be found in a number of continental countries. In assessing urban mortality in England in the period of the industrial revolution it is important to view the evidence in a comparative perspective.

If the negative balance between urban births and deaths, which was widespread in England in the seventeenth and early eighteenth centuries, had continued, it would not have been possible for the percentage of the population living in towns and cities to have risen above 50 per cent, as it did in the mid nineteenth century. It remains difficult adequately to account for the improvement in urban mortality which made possible continued urban growth, but its significance is unmistakable in making possible a situation in which eventually rural populations were massively outnumbered by the inhabitants of towns.

Literacy

It is widely considered that high levels of literacy, by increasing awareness of a wider world, facilitate change in living styles and tend to promote invention and innovation. It is also common to suppose that literacy levels were higher in towns than in the countryside. Evidence of literacy levels in England is intriguing, puzzling, and suggestive. In the *Preface* to the Occupation Abstract of the 1841 census there is a large table summarising the information presented in greater detail in the main tables of the census but also including summary data taken from the Registrar General's Annual Reports. The information about literacy shown in the section headed (1) of Table 5.5 was taken from the 1843 Annual Report and relates to the years 1839–44. In the columns headed M and F of section (1) are set out the percentages of men and women in each English county who were able to sign the marriage register rather than making a mark (in the 1841 census table the percentages recorded were those who made a mark but it is more relevant for present purposes to focus on those who could sign rather than those who could not). In sections (2) and (3) the counties are sorted by the percentages of men and women who were literate from highest to lowest, while in the final section (4) the same data are shown as ratios of male to female literacy, again sorted from highest to lowest.

The patterns in Table 5.5 display much of interest. Literacy levels for both men and women varied markedly in England in the mid nineteenth century, and in some cases the patterns revealed are perhaps little expected. It is no surprise in the male literacy column that Middlesex and Surrey are first and third (88 and 83 per cent). They reflect the situation in the capital where the tertiary sector provided the bulk of employment; but London men were barely more literate than those living in the north of England. Cumberland, Northumberland, and Westmorland were all at or above 80 per cent, and the East and North Ridings and Durham were close behind. The prime industrial counties, Warwickshire, the West Riding, Cheshire, and Lancashire, were quite close to one another in the middle of the table with male literacy rates ranging between 62 and 68 per cent, though Staffordshire was in the bottom quarter at 58 per cent. The last five counties were close neighbours. In Hertfordshire, Bedfordshire, Suffolk, Essex, and Cambridgeshire, the agricultural east, barely half of the grooms at marriage were able to sign.[66]

Female literacy did not always show a similar pattern to that of men. The London counties again had high rates of literacy with more than three-quarters of brides signing the register when marrying. And five of the six northern counties that figured prominently in male literacy followed suit in the female literacy list (the exception was Durham which had been eighth in the male list but was twenty-third in the female list).

66 These patterns were not a recent phenomenon, they were already evident in the later eighteenth century: Schofield, 'Dimensions of illiteracy', p. 444; Cressy, *Literacy and the social order*, Table 4.1, p. 73 and pp. 142–51.

Brides in industrial counties, however, did not parallel the positioning of their grooms. The three counties at the bottom of the female list were Cheshire, the West Riding, and Lancashire, with Lancashire some way below the other two. Staffordshire was also close to the bottom, though Warwickshire brides paralleled their grooms in the middle of the rankings.

It is tempting to suppose that the relatively low level of female literacy in Durham reflects the local prevalence of coal mining. The presence of mining may have produced the same tendency to depress female rates compared with male rates that is so evident in the leading industrial counties (though opportunities for female employment in mining areas were normally poor compared with, say, the cotton towns in Lancashire). This is an issue that should repay further attention.

The eastern agricultural counties that were at the bottom of the male list were also very low in the female list, though above the group of three industrial counties at the bottom.

Since the information relates to counties, it does not directly measure urban literacy levels. In the case of Middlesex and Surrey this does not present a significant problem since the population of the metropolis was a very large fraction of the total. In the industrial counties the urban pattern cannot be established so confidently. In Lancashire and the West Riding there were large rural tracts but the rural proportion of the county was in each case relatively small. Occupational data throw light on this point. In Lancashire in the 1841 census there were 403,954 men aged 20 and over with an occupation. Of these 257,537 were engaged in commerce, trade, and manufacture; 56,881 were labourers; and 41,696 were farmers, agricultural labourers, or gardeners and nurserymen (or 63.8, 14.1, and 10.3 per cent, respectively). In the West Riding, the situation was broadly similar: the comparable percentages were 64.8, 10.6, and 15.2 per cent.[67] Agriculture therefore occupied only about a tenth of the total in Lancashire and just over a seventh in the West Riding. Most people lived in an urban setting. The urban literacy level, however, was probably somewhat lower than the county level. Given the high levels of male literacy in the largely rural East and North Ridings, for example, it is probable that in the West Riding the urban level would be lower than the county figure for this reason, and the same may well have been true of Lancashire.

The information in Table 5.5 suggests many avenues of possible future research that might yield much of interest. For example, was the marked difference in literacy levels between the eastern agricultural counties and

[67] *1841 Census*, Occupation Abstract, part I, Preface, fold-out table between pp. 52 and 53.

Table 5.5 *Ability to sign 1839–44 (percentages)*

	(1) County percentages	M	F	(2) Male		(3) Female		(4) Male/female ratio	
1	Bedfordshire	51	38	Middlesex	88	Middlesex	77	Lancashire	1.88
2	Berkshire	59	56	Cumberland	84	Surrey	72	Yorkshire, W.R.	1.70
3	Buckinghamshire	60	50	Surrey	83	Westmorland	66	Cheshire	1.63
4	Cambridgeshire	53	44	Northumberland	82	Cumberland	64	Durham	1.45
5	Cheshire	62	38	Westmorland	80	Rutland	64	Cornwall	1.44
6	Cornwall	65	45	Yorkshire, E.R.	79	Dorset	62	Staffordshire	1.41
7	Cumberland	84	64	Yorkshire, N.R.	78	Northumberland	62	Worcestershire	1.35
8	Derbyshire	70	52	Durham	74	Yorkshire, E.R.	62	Derbyshire	1.35
9	Devon	72	60	Devon	72	Yorkshire, N.R.	62	Bedfordshire	1.34
10	Dorset	70	62	Gloucestershire	72	Kent	61	Nottinghamshire	1.34
11	Durham	74	51	Sussex	72	Sussex	61	Northumberland	1.32
12	Essex	53	47	Kent	71	Devon	60	Cumberland	1.31
13	Gloucestershire	72	59	Derbyshire	70	Gloucestershire	59	Lincolnshire	1.28
14	Hampshire	68	59	Dorset	70	Hampshire	59	Warwickshire	1.28
15	Herefordshire	62	56	Hampshire	68	Berkshire	56	Yorkshire, E.R.	1.27
16	Hertfordshire	50	44	Leicestershire	68	Herefordshire	56	Wiltshire	1.27
17	Huntingdonshire	56	48	Lincolnshire	68	Leicestershire	55	Northamptonshire	1.27
18	Kent	71	61	Warwickshire	68	Oxfordshire	54	Yorkshire, N.R.	1.26
19	Lancashire	62	33	Nottinghamshire	67	Lincolnshire	53	Leicestershire	1.24
20	Leicestershire	68	55	Cornwall	65	Warwickshire	53	Somerset	1.24
21	Lincolnshire	68	53	Oxfordshire	65	Derbyshire	52	Shropshire	1.23

22	Middlesex	88	77	Somerset	63	Norfolk	52	Gloucestershire	1.22
23	Norfolk	58	52	Yorkshire, W.R.	63	Durham	51	Westmorlamd	1.21
24	Northamptonshire	62	49	Cheshire	62	Somerset	51	Cambridgeshire	1.20
25	Northumberland	82	62	Herefordshire	62	Buckinghamshire	50	Oxfordshire	1.20
26	Nottinghamshire	67	50	Lancashire	62	Nottinghamshire	50	Buckinghamshire	1.20
27	Oxfordshire	65	54	Northamptonshire	62	Northamptonshire	49	Devon	1.20
28	Rutland	60	64	Buckinghamshire	60	Huntingdonshire	48	Sussex	1.18
29	Shropshire	59	48	Rutland	60	Shropshire	48	Huntingdonshire	1.17
30	Somerset	63	51	Berkshire	59	Suffolk	48	Kent	1.16
31	Staffordshire	58	41	Shropshire	59	Essex	47	Surrey	1.15
32	Suffolk	53	48	Norfolk	58	Cornwall	45	Hampshire	1.15
33	Surrey	83	72	Staffordshire	58	Wiltshire	45	Middlesex	1.14
34	Sussex	72	61	Wiltshire	57	Cambridgeshire	44	Hertfordshire	1.14
35	Warwickshire	68	53	Huntingdonshire	56	Hertfordshire	44	Dorset	1.13
36	Westmorland	80	66	Worcestershire	54	Staffordshire	41	Essex	1.13
37	Wiltshire	57	45	Cambridgeshire	53	Worcestershire	40	Norfolk	1.12
38	Worcestershire	54	40	Essex	53	Bedfordshire	38	Herefordshire	1.11
39	Yorkshire, E.R.	79	62	Suffolk	53	Cheshire	38	Suffolk	1.10
40	Yorkshire, N.R.	78	62	Bedfordshire	51	Yorkshire, W.R.	37	Berkshire	1.05
41	Yorkshire, W.R.	63	37	Hertfordshire	50	Lancashire	33	Rutland	0.94

Source: *1841 Census*, Occupation Abstract, part I, Preface, pp. 10–11.

agricultural counties in the north of England, such as the North Riding, a reflection of the much higher ratio of agricultural labourers to farmers in eastern counties compared with northern counties, or were rural parts of the north different for other reasons?[68] But the question at issue at present is more limited. The high levels of literacy in London suggests that where much employment was in commercial and service industries literacy levels were relatively high, but that the urban growth brought about by the inception of an industrial revolution was associated with lower literacy and that this was much more clearly marked with brides than with grooms. The clumsiness of the county as measurement unit is clear. Future research may resolve some of the uncertainties attendant upon relying on county data, but it seems safe to recognise that there was no simple link between urban life and high literacy levels in England at the time of the industrial revolution. In the new industrial centres there was only a moderate level of literacy in the male population and the level in the female population was very low compared with rural areas in the north of England.

In Chapter 4 urban growth was explicitly one of the subjects under study. In this chapter, although it does not figure in the chapter's title, its importance when considering the gradual transformation of the economy and society of early modern England is unmistakable. All the major changes which were in train, however, were interlinked so that it is arbitrary to assign primacy to any one of them, a point illustrated by the subject matter of Chapter 6, which discusses the significance of the west European marriage system in helping to preserve a relatively favourable balance between population and production. It is a topic that was first brought into focus by Malthus. He is sometimes portrayed as a prophet of gloom, understandably so if only the text of his *Essay on population* is considered, but as he became conscious of the importance of the distinction between the positive check and the preventive check in relation to prevailing living standards, the implications of his analysis changed radically. Even in a purely organic economy Malthus' later work suggested that it was possible for the prevailing standard of living of the bulk of the population to be maintained well clear of the 'Malthusian' precipice. In early modern England the sensitivity of nuptiality to economic circumstances brought substantial benefit.

68 The scale of the contrast between southern and eastern England and the northern counties is vividly apparent in Burnette, 'Agriculture', Figure 3.1, p. 94.

6 Demography and the economy

The demographic characteristics of a society may have an important bearing on its prevailing standard of living and economic growth prospects. This was an issue explored by Hajnal in his remarkable essay on marriage in western and eastern Europe, published in 1965. He was intent on exploring the nature and significance of the west European marriage system. Table 6.1 reproduces the table that appeared on the first page of his essay.

The differences between the two marriage systems are striking. They are especially pronounced in the case of women. In the western pattern, approaching half of the women in the age group 25–29 are unmarried, and this remains true of roughly a sixth of women even in the 45–49 age group. In eastern Europe in both these age groups the proportion of women who had never married was negligible. Hajnal provided evidence that what was true of eastern Europe was true of almost all societies elsewhere in the world for which he had reliable data. The difference in proportions ever married in the two systems clearly implies wide differences in the average age at first marriage. Hajnal noted, for example, that in Serbia, in 1896–1905, the decade centred on the year for which Table 6.1 shows percentages single, the mean age at first marriage for women was 19.7 years.[1] In the west European marriage system the average female age at first marriage, though it varied considerably, was three to eight years later in life.

Hajnal noted that: 'There was a widespread conviction among eighteenth-century authors that European conditions were fundamentally different not only in marriage, birth and death rates, but above all in standards of living, from those obtaining elsewhere in the world.'[2] He was, however, very conscious of the lack of empirical evidence to enable the issue to be explored effectively, not least because reliable demographic evidence for earlier centuries was so slender. Since his essay was published much new research on the west European marriage system has

[1] Hajnal, 'European marriage patterns', p. 109. [2] *Ibid.*, p. 131.

Table 6.1 *Hajnal's table of percentages single at selected ages in four European countries in 1900*

	Men			Women		
	20–24	*25–29*	*45–49*	*20–24*	*25–29*	*45–49*
West European pattern						
Belgium	85	50	16	71	41	17
Sweden	92	61	13	80	52	19
East European pattern						
Bulgaria	58	23	3	24	3	1
Serbia	50	18	3	16	2	1

Note: Hajnal described Belgium and Sweden simply as a 'European pattern', but it seemed preferable to use the term that has become conventional in naming them.
Source: Hajnal, 'European marriage patterns', Table 1, p. 101.

been carried out. It has become clear that the system had existed for centuries in some countries rather than being of recent origin, as Hajnal supposed.[3] Even though exponential growth was physically impossible in organic economies, the prevailing standard of living was not foredoomed to be depressed close to bare subsistence for the mass of the population in societies in which the west European marriage system had become established. In drawing attention to this fact, exemplified in the economic history of countries in north-west Europe, Hajnal emphasised that he was essentially re-expressing views which Malthus had propounded as a mature thinker.[4]

Malthus suggested that output growth could at best be expected to behave like an arithmetic progression, whereas population if unchecked characteristically experienced geometric growth. The *Essay on population* was a counter-polemic. He was anxious to counter the views of Condorcet, Godwin, and others who considered that society could be reconstructed in ways which promised to give rise to steady progress across the whole spectrum of individual and social life. His argument proved hard to dismiss when first published, and has remained influential ever since. The later versions of the *Essay on population* reflect the fact that, on further reflection and with a far wider acquaintance with the available

[3] I have attempted to describe the impact of Hajnal's work on the research carried out by historical demographers since its publication in Wrigley, 'European marriage patterns and their implications'.

[4] He wrote: 'The main theme of this paper is not new. It is one of the main topics of Malthus' *Essay* and indeed implicit in its very structure (especially in the revised version of the second edition).' Hajnal, 'European marriage patterns', p. 130.

information about populations all over the world, Malthus had come to adopt a substantially different stance. Crucially, he became aware that there were important differences between the demographic characteristics of western European countries and countries in other parts of the world. In particular, he recognised that the 'preventive check' might make it possible for a society to avoid the danger of being driven towards a 'Malthusian' precipice. Given the character of the west European marriage system, a favourable balance between production and population was not necessarily a temporary episode, but might be sustained over an indefinite period. Nuptiality played a very important role in determining population trends, influencing both fertility levels and, indirectly, also mortality levels. Population growth might cease well short of the point at which most families were living close to the point of bare subsistence. He also became conscious of the fact that the economic–demographic process was subject to long-term 'oscillations' during which living standards might move for substantial periods of time in either direction. What might happen towards the end of the period of increasing general prosperity?

> From high real wages, or the power of commanding a large portion of the necessaries of life, two very different results may follow; one, that of a rapid increase in population, in which case the high wages are chiefly spent in the maintenance of large and frequent families; and the other, that of a decided improvement in the modes of subsistence, and the conveniences and comforts enjoyed, without a proportionate acceleration in the rate of increase.[5]

The conclusions of the mature Malthus were very different from the view that Adam Smith had expressed, a view that foreshadowed Malthus' argument in the *Essay on population* so closely that it suggests the possibility that the young Malthus was paraphrasing and extending it.[6] Figure 6.1 illustrates the range of possibilities for an organic economy that Malthus came to recognise as his thinking developed. It is helpful in illustrating that where the 'west European' marriage system existed it was not inevitable that the bulk of the population must live close to a bare subsistence level.

The upper half of Figure 6.1 shows the points at which population growth ceases on different assumptions about fertility and mortality behaviour. In the lower half the connection between population size and real incomes is illustrated. In an organic economy, if fertility is high and invariant (F_1), the population will continue to rise until the increasing pressure on resources and the accompanying fall in living standards causes mortality to rise to the same level as fertility. The bulk of the

[5] Malthus, *Principles of political economy*, p. 183. [6] See p. 24.

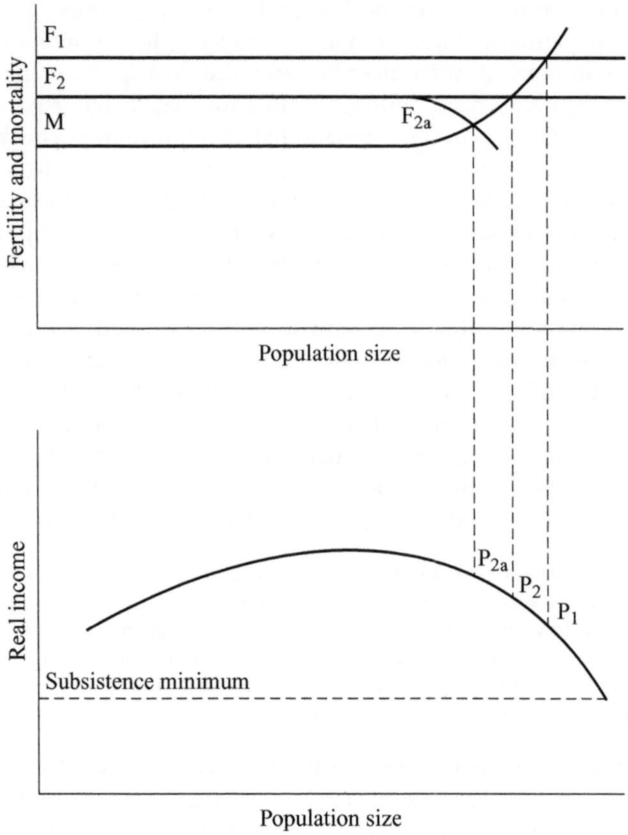

Figure 6.1 Fertility, mortality, and living standards

population will live close to the Malthusian precipice (P_1). If fertility is also invariant but at a lower level (F_2), because the average age at marriage is higher and a proportion of each rising generation remains single for life, population growth will cease at a lower level than in the case of F_1 and real incomes will be somewhat higher (P_2). However, if fertility is not invariant but declines as living standards fall (F_{2a}), population growth will cease at a point where living standards are well clear of deep poverty (P_{2a}). The figure illustrates both the position produced if population growth is arrested solely by the operation of the positive check and the range of possibilities that he came to recognise as he extended his knowledge of the marriage systems to be found in much of western Europe, and their contrast with the marriage systems found elsewhere. The F_1 possibility always remained, but once it was clear that decisions to marry might themselves be influenced by economic circumstances, causing fertility as well as mortality to change as conditions worsened or improved, it was no longer necessary to suppose that the bulk of any population must live close to bare subsistence. In short, F_1 represents a 'high-pressure' demographic system; F_{2a} represents a 'low-pressure' alternative. In the first case the standard of living will be significantly lower than in the alternative.

In summary, in an organic economy population growth is limited by its productive capacity and is determined by the interplay of fertility and mortality. If fertility is high and invariant growth will continue until mortality rises to the same level, and living standards will be severely depressed. In this situation, the level of mortality is largely determined by the level of fertility. If the prevailing fertility level is somewhat lower, because marriage takes place later in life and a proportion of each generation remains single, and if marriage decisions are influenced by prevailing economic conditions – in short, if fertility as well as mortality is sensitive to the level and trend of living standards – a different outcome is readily possible. Although in any organic economy living standards may vary over time in sympathy with fluctuations in population growth rates, where the 'preventive check' exists the rise in numbers may stop well short of the edge of a 'Malthusian' precipice. Given the nature of organic economies, the potential disadvantages of a society in which fertility is high and invariant are clear. The poor will indeed always be with you. But this is only a limiting possibility. There were many circumstances that might cause fertility to fall well short of the highest level attainable. Clearly this will be true where, as in the west European marriage system, there is a high average age at marriage for women and conventions that lead to a proportion of each rising generation of women never marrying. Other practices, of course, such as prolonged breastfeeding, abstinence from intercourse, or separation could result in relatively long birth intervals and therefore reduce the fertility level. Given its nature, however, the west European marriage system was more likely to produce a relatively favourable balance between numbers and resources in organic societies than other demographic systems.

The range of possible relationships between social, economic, and demographic characteristics of a society in the context of the west European system is admirably summarised in an essay by Schofield. As he noted, and described with clarity and coherence, 'a particular historical configuration of the components of demographic structure has considerable implications for the social and economic aspects of that society', and having set out a series of six models to illustrate this point, he concluded:

What is remarkable about the populations of pre-industrial western Europe is that they not only evolved a set of social rules, which effectively linked their rate of family formation with changes in their environment, but also managed to secure such low fertility that they achieved both a demographically efficient replacement of their population, and an age-structure which was economically more advantageous than the age-structures generally to be found among non-industrial societies today.[7]

The west European marriage system

If fertility was not only held to a relatively low level by late marriage and frequent celibacy but was also sensitive to prevailing economic circumstances, the 'preventive check' could substantially relieve the pressure on resources which attended its absence. Conventions governing marriage decisions in organic economies varied widely, with widely differing implications for living standards. At one extreme there were societies in which every woman was married at or close to the age of arriving at sexual maturity unless she was seriously handicapped physically or mentally. The timing of marriage for women was determined by physiological change. At the other extreme in the west European marriage system, economic circumstances played a major role in influencing the timing and frequency of marriage. The social convention that brought this about lay in the expectation that on marriage the newly married couple would set up a new household rather than joining an existing household as was the norm in many other organic societies. This created an economic hurdle to be surmounted before a marriage could take place. In the case of the female partner, rather than the timing of marriage being governed by reaching or approaching sexual maturity, it was strongly influenced by the time spent by the couple in securing an adequate sum in advance of marriage to enable them to create a new household. This meant that the average age at marriage for women was characteristically in the mid 20s rather the mid and late teens. Family sizes were therefore significantly smaller. With a mean birth interval of 30 months, for example, marriage at 25 rather than 18 would reduce completed family size by 2.8 children on average. If the economic barrier to be surmounted was severe, or saving was difficult and parents were unable or unwilling to assist, it also meant that a proportion of both sexes would never marry because they had failed to assemble the wherewithal to do so. In peasant communities, for example, the ability to marry might depend upon gaining

[7] Schofield, 'The relationship between demographic structure and environment', pp. 147 and 160.

access to a holding. If holdings were not subdivided this would result in an unchanging number of married couples.

Nuptiality decisions in the west European system were sensitive to both short-term economic circumstances and to secular trends. In the short term, the timing of marriages was influenced by price movements. When living costs rose because a bad harvest caused grain prices to soar, marriages were delayed.[8] Long-term economic trends that affected living standards might also influence the timing and extent of marriage. Worsening economic circumstances tended to produce a rise in the proportion of men and women remaining single; and those who did marry would do so later in life. There were no automatic responses of this type, evident wherever a west European marriage system existed. Many marriages in western Europe were made 'imprudently' but the existence of the conventions associated with the west European system increased the likelihood that fertility levels would fall short of the levels found elsewhere, and that marriage decisions would reflect both immediate circumstances and longer-term economic trends.

In early modern England a comparatively benign relationship between economic circumstances, nuptiality, and fertility existed, producing a relatively favourable balance between population and production. The information contained in Figure 6.2 is suggestive in this regard. It traces crude first marriage rates, female age at first marriage, and real wage trends over three centuries. Over this long period changes in the three variables paralleled each other closely. During the late sixteenth and early seventeenth centuries when population was rising rapidly, from 3.1 million in 1551 to 5.1 million in 1636, real wages were in decline. The fall in living standards was paralleled by a reduction in nuptiality that gradually arrested population growth. Nevertheless, in this period the fall in living standards at times produced the 'classic' effects characteristic of organic economies. The poor harvests and high grain prices of the late 1590s, for example, caused a sharp rise in the number of deaths between the late autumn of 1596 and the late spring of 1598.[9] But this proved to be the last occasion when a sharp rise in prices caused a mortality crisis in the country as a whole. Other countries were less fortunate. A century later in the 1690s harvest failure caused a steep rise in the price of cereals across much of Europe. There was crisis mortality in parts of France and Scotland in this decade. In the Beauvaisis, for example, poor harvests caused a sharp increase in the price of food grains. In

[8] Lee, 'Short-term variation'.

[9] Between November 1596 and May 1598: Wrigley and Schofield, *The population history of England*, Table A2.4, p. 512.

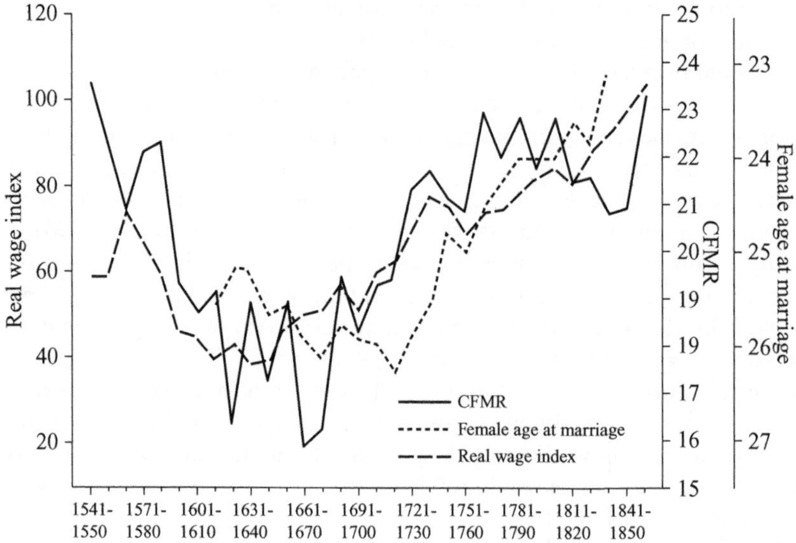

Figure 6.2 Crude first marriage rates (CFMR), female age at marriage, and real wage trends in England from 1541–50 to 1841–50

The CFMR was calculated by relating first marriages to a weighted average of the population in the four five-year age groups in the span of years 15–34. It is expressed as a rate per 1,000. Further details may be found in the source quoted below. The female age at marriage was calculated from bachelor/spinster marriages.

Sources: CFMR and real wage index: Wrigley, 'British population during the "long" eighteenth century', Figure 3.7, p. 78. Age at marriage: Wrigley *et al.*, *English population history*, Table 5.3, p. 134.

1693–4 this resulted in a surge in mortality throughout the region, which reached extreme levels in parishes such as Breteuil and Mouy.[10] The price of consumables was also high in England in the 1690s, causing a sharp contraction in real wages, but there was no parallel rise in the number of deaths.[11] During the decade as a whole the total of deaths was substantially lower than in the 1680s and very similar to the total in the 1700s.[12] Assisted by the operation of the old poor law in relieving want, the English economy had developed to a point which conferred

10 Goubert., *Beauvais*, II, pp. 56–7, 78–9.

11 The Exeter wheat price series averaged 30.9 shillings per quarter over the 11 years 1680–90, but then rose sharply to average 42.3 shillings in the next nine years 1691–9, before returning to a lower level in 1700–7 when it averaged 28.6 shillings. In the two years 1696–7 when prices peaked the average was 56.5 shillings. Mitchell, *British historical statistics*, Chapter 14, Table 16, pp. 752–5.

12 Wrigley *et al.*, *Population history of England*, Appendix 2, pp. 498–9.

increasing immunity from the pressures which in past centuries had often led to increased mortality.

The relative immunity of early modern England from the worst effects of harvest failure from the seventeenth century onwards was not, of course, due solely to the functioning of the relationship between economic and demographic fluctuations visible in Figure 6.2. The remarkable advances in agricultural productivity in the seventeenth century, which have already been described, was a background factor of great importance in cushioning the impact of poor harvests; and the existence of the old poor law was a vital source of support both generally and in particular when the price of bread shot up in the wake of a bad harvest. But the close parallelism in the movement of the three variables shown in Figure 6.2 is illuminating nonetheless. During the period of declining real wages in the sixteenth and early seventeenth centuries the crude first marriage rate fell from *c.* 23 per 1,000 to *c.* 18 per 1,000, but had reverted to its earlier level in the later eighteenth century. Female age at first marriage varied in a similar fashion. It had risen to 26 years by the middle decades of the seventeenth century but fell to 23 years early in the nineteenth century. Changes in the proportion of women never marrying are more difficult to establish from family reconstitution data but it seems likely that this proportion rose markedly in the last decades of the Tudor period and in the early decades of the seventeenth century, reaching a peak of about 20 per cent in the middle of the century, but halving to about 10 per cent by the beginning of the eighteenth century and thereafter changing little.[13] As a result of the changes in marriage behaviour, fertility levels changed in sympathy. The gross reproduction rate had averaged 2.58 in the quarter-century 1541–65 but fell to 1.82 in the quarter century 1651–76, a fall of 29 per cent. Thereafter it rose strongly, reaching a peak of 2.75 in the first quarter of the nineteenth century, 1801–26.[14] The relative importance of changes in marriage age and celibacy in influencing overall fertility rates varied over time, but their combined effect was to cause these rates to vary in sympathy with secular economic change, as reflected in an index of the real wage.

The functioning of the nuptiality valve made it easier to achieve a more favourable ratio between population totals and their means of support than would have been possible otherwise. It is intriguing to note that, despite the large rise in the proportion of women who were single in the age groups in which fecundity is at its height, the proportion of all births which occurred outside marriage was very low in the last quarter of the

[13] Wrigley *et al.*, *English population history*, p. 195.
[14] *Ibid.*, Table A9.1, pp. 614–15.

seventeenth century, comprising only 1.8 per cent of all births. It was substantially higher at the end of the eighteenth century even though age at marriage had fallen by three years and the proportion of women who never married was much lower: in 1775–99 5.9 per cent of all births were illegitimate, in 1800–24 6.2 per cent.[15] A much smaller proportion of women in the fertile age groups were single but they had a far higher fertility level. The fertility *rate* among single women increased much more steeply than the illegitimacy *percentage*. In the decades when the illegitimacy percentage was high *c.* 1800, about a quarter of all first births were illegitimate and a further quarter were conceived before marriage.[16] Social attitudes to extra-marital intercourse appear to have changed in parallel with nuptiality decisions. When marriage was early and almost universal, illegitimacy did not give rise to severe sanctions, but the reverse was the case when marriage was late and a higher proportion of women never married. The relative importance of changes in marriage age and celibacy in influencing overall fertility rates varied over time, but their combined effect was to cause fertility to vary in sympathy with secular economic change, as reflected in real wages.

The significance of the west European marriage system, emphasised by Malthus and later by Hajnal, has continued to attract widespread attention in recent years. In particular, the prospect that it afforded of a more favourable balance between population and production has been widely explored. There are, however, also other features associated with it which have received less attention but should be borne in mind in considering the history of countries where marriage practice reflected some or all of the characteristics of the west European system. Two in particular should be noted.

Where fertility levels were relatively low and the population was either broadly stationary or growing slowly mortality levels would also be low.[17] If infant and child mortality rates are modest, the proportion of each new birth cohort reaching an age at which its members can contribute positively to output rather than being an economic burden upon those of working age will be higher than where birth and death rates are both high. Model life tables are helpful in clarifying the scale of the advantage enjoyed by countries in which mortality was low by the standards prevailing in most organic economies. The model North life tables produced by Coale and Demeny show that at level 9, where expectation of life at birth for the sexes combined is approximately 38.5 years, about

[15] *Ibid.*, Table 6.2, p. 219.
[16] Wrigley, 'Marriage, fertility and population growth', p. 162.
[17] Wrigley, 'No death without birth'.

65 per cent of each birth cohort will reach the age of 15 years. At level 6 where the comparable expectation of life is approximately 31.0 years, only 56 per cent of the birth cohort will reach age 15.[18] In early modern England expectation of life varied over time but was chiefly in the range from 32 to 40 years. The comparable ranges in much of Europe were substantially less favourable. In France, for example, life expectancy fluctuated between 25 and 31 years (decadal averages) between 1740 and 1800.[19] Even in the nineteenth century in parts of Europe mortality levels were as unfavourable as in the most unhealthy decades in early modern England. Over the period 1821–81 life expectancy in Italy averaged 33 years.[20] During the half-century in which mortality was highest in early modern England, 1651–1700, expectation of life at birth over ten successive quinquennia averaged 35 years.[21] An implication of relatively high mortality is that fertility must also be high if the population is not to decline. This in turn implies that, *ceteris paribus*, age at marriage will be lower and celibacy less common than in countries where a 'low-pressure' rather than a 'high-pressure' demographic system exists.

A second distinctive feature attaching to the west European marriage system may also have benefited average earnings. Late marriage and the fact that a significant proportion of women remained single affected the composition of the labour force. In England unmarried women normally entered the labour force. A single woman is usually regarded as contributing more to national output than a married woman. This is a complex issue with many uncertainties. It is true that a single woman contributed more than a married woman to that part of total output that is captured by the conventional statistics of a market economy, but a substantial proportion of all the goods and services produced in early modern England did not involve a market sale. Home produced beer, for example, escaped measurement in this way but was no doubt drunk as readily as beer sold in an inn. Again, woollen textiles were produced in many households and married women formed part of the production unit in question. Much, though not all, household production of woollen products gave rise to a market sale, but what fraction of the sum involved should be counted as part of the output of married women is difficult to establish. However, a notional exercise can illustrate the potential economic significance of late marriage and high celibacy.

[18] Coale and Demeny, *Regional model life tables*, pp. 225, 228.

[19] Livi-Bacci, *The population of Europe*, p. 90.

[20] Malanima, *L'economia italiana*, Table 2.5, p. 54.

[21] Wrigley *et al.*, *English population history*, Table A9.1, pp. 614–15.

Assume that labour force participation begins at age 16; that in one population the average age at marriage for women is 20 and in another population 25; and that in the former 5 per cent never marry and the latter 15 per cent. Assume further that the output of a single woman is 75 per cent of that of a man, but that for a married woman the comparable figure is 25 per cent. On these assumptions the production of 100 women all of whom lived to the age of 65 (when production is assumed to cease) would be 29 per cent higher in the second population than in the first. The output of 100 men who began work at age 16 and ceased to be productive at age 65 is straightforward to calculate. Combining the output of 100 women and 100 men suggests that in the second population the combined output of both sexes would be 7 per cent larger than in the first population. Needless to say, such an exercise embodies dubious assumptions and is ludicrously oversimplified. If the effect of mortality during the working life is taken into account, for example, the resultant percentage differences would change. And the calculation implicitly relates primarily to production that passes through the market. The scale of household production that does not involve a market transaction might alter the picture. An alternative calculation taking this into account would produce a different result. Nevertheless, this consideration enhances the probability that the existence of the west European marriage system benefited living standards. To the degree that this illustrative calculation captures a feature of the west European marriage system, it suggests a further economic benefit.

It is salutary to be aware of the potential importance of these characteristics of the west European marriage system in influencing living standards. Superficially minor differences appear substantially more important if the income elasticity of demand for the products of the secondary and tertiary sectors relative to primary sector products is taken into account. A small rise in average family income can create a disproportionate rise in demand for products other than the basic necessities, as suggested by the simple calculation made earlier to illustrate this point.[22] In short, the nature of the range of the different demographic systems found in organic economies played a significant role in accounting for the variation in living standards that existed between them.

Schofield concluded his survey of the range of different feedback relationships between nuptiality decisions, social custom, and the economic circumstances to be found in western Europe before the industrial revolution, by remarking:

22 See p. 75.

What is remarkable about the populations of pre-industrial western Europe is that they not only evolved a set of social rules, which effectively linked their rate of family formation with changes in their environment, but also managed to secure such low fertility that they achieved – a demographically efficient replacement of their population.[23]

The old poor law

In considering the distinctive features of English society that helped in keeping the population some distance from the Malthusian precipice, mention should be made of the contribution of the old poor law.

Even though the west European marriage system helped to make possible a ratio between productive capacity and population size which served to keep the poor above bare subsistence in an average year, they were still vulnerable when a severe harvest failure or a run of years with below-average harvests caused the price of grain to rise to the point where many families had little to eat. In England, however, the old poor law helped to minimise the impact of high grain prices on the living standards of the most vulnerable in a parish. The poor law administration was parish based and the sums disbursed were raised from local taxes. In his reconstruction of English national accounts for 1688 primarily based on data collected by Gregory King, Richard Stone used an estimate made by Davenant to assess the scale of poor relief as £600,000 per annum, representing 1.4 per cent of national income, and a sum almost a third as large as all expenditure by central government.[24]

In the period of the Napoleonic wars, when at times cereal prices rose far above their pre-war level, poor law expenditure per inhabitant in a sample of parishes, both in those where the population was rising rapidly and in those where there was only slow growth, rose in close sympathy with the price of bread, thus shielding the poor from the miseries which often ensued following poor harvests.[25] Much the same had been true of the period of high prices in the 1690s when high grain prices caused severe mortality in many European countries, but, though prices were also high in England, there was no corresponding rise in the death rate.[26]

23 Schofield, 'The relationship between demographic structure and environment', p. 160.
24 Stone, *Some British empiricists*, p. 106 and Table 3.7, p. 98.
25 In the 1780s and early 1790s the price of wheat per quarter fluctuated between 40 shillings and 55 shillings but then rose steeply and in 1800 and 1801 reached 113 shillings and 119 shillings, respectively. Mitchell, *British historical statistics*, Chapter 14, pp. 756–7. The parish expenditures in the sample parishes is described in Wrigley, 'Coping with rapid population growth', pp. 44–8.
26 See pp. 107–9.

This issue caught Malthus' attention and he gave a lucid explanation of the value of the Poor Law in difficult times. In 1800, he published an essay entitled *An investigation of the cause of the present high price of provisions*. Despite his wish to see the Poor Law abolished because of its supposed encouragement to improvident marriage, it is striking evidence of his open-mindedness that he recognised its significance in enabling England to escape from paying the penalty often exacted by harvest failure. In the second half of 1799 he had paid a lengthy visit to Scandinavia and when he returned to England he found that there was much discussion and complaint about the high price of bread. In his essay, he described how in the summer of 1799 he had travelled through the province Värmland in western Sweden where the inhabitants were reduced to eating dried sorrel and the inner bark of fir because of the failure of the rye harvest. He touched on an issue that has also attracted the attention of Amartya Sen, and he drew a similar conclusion.[27] He was struck by the fact that when he returned to England the increase in the price of bread was greater than in the areas of Sweden worst affected by famine. He reiterated his opposition to the Poor Law but added:

> I am inclined to think that their operation in the present scarcity has been advantageous to the country. The principal benefit which they have produced is exactly that which is most bitterly complained of – the high price of all the necessities of life. The poor cry out loudly at this price; but, in so doing, they are very little aware of what they are about; for it has undoubtedly been owing to this price that a much greater number of them has not been starved.
>
> It was calculated that there were only two thirds of an average crop last year. Probably even with the aid of all that we imported, the deficiency still remained a fifth or a sixth. Supposing ten millions of people in the island; the whole of this deficiency, had things been left to their natural course, would have fallen almost exclusively on two, or perhaps three millions of the poorest inhabitants, a very considerable number of whom must in consequence have starved. The operation of the parish allowances, by raising the price of provisions so high, caused the distress to be divided among five or six millions, perhaps, instead of two or three, and to be by no means unfelt even by the remainder of the population.[28]

The transfer of increased purchasing power to the poor produced the superficially paradoxical result that the price of bread was increased, but all continued to be able to buy a sufficiency. In Sweden the price of rye increased less dramatically precisely because the poor had not the means

27 Sen, *Poverty and famines*. The similarity between Malthus' views and those of Sen is discussed in Wrigley, 'Corn and crisis', pp. 209–10.

28 Malthus, *An investigation*, pp. 13–14.

to enter the market for bread. The price of rye in western Sweden 'had not risen above double its usual average' but in England wheat had risen to 'above three times its former price'.[29]

Some years later Malthus clarified further his views on the poor laws. In a letter written in 1807 to Samuel Whitbread, an MP, concerning his proposed bill on the amendment of the poor laws, he made it very clear that his concern about the availability of poor law support was that it tended to encourage improvident marriages and so, by raising the fertility level, indirectly to depress living standards among the poor. He did not object in any way to taxing the rich to improve the lot of the poor. He wrote:

> With regard to the large sum which is collected from the higher classes of society for the support of the poor, I can safely say, that in the discussion of the question it has always been with me a most subordinate consideration.

He then referred to his concern that the present operation of the poor laws had 'the fatal and unavoidable consequence of continually increasing their number', but added:

> Were it possible to fix the number of the poor and to avoid the further depression of the independent labourer, I should be the first to propose that those who were actually in want should be most liberally relieved, and that they should receive it as a right, and not as a bounty.[30]

What changed in the industrial revolution

This section calls attention to an aspect of the industrial revolution which emerges with unusual clarity by making use of demographic data, because it identifies the period in the eighteenth century when one of the most fundamental relationships between production and population which was common to all organic economies disappeared, reflecting the ability, by drawing upon new energy sources, to produce on a scale not previously possible. Figure 6.2 showed that some aspects of the relationship between economic circumstances and demographic behaviour remained largely unchanging during the three centuries when there were nonetheless profound changes in the character of the English economy culminating in what is conventionally termed an industrial revolution. Figure 6.3 throws light on one of its most important concomitants, the arrival of the possibility of sustaining and even improving the standard of living of the mass of the population even though the population was growing rapidly.

[29] *Ibid.*, p. 6. [30] Malthus, 'The amendment of the poor laws', p. 9.

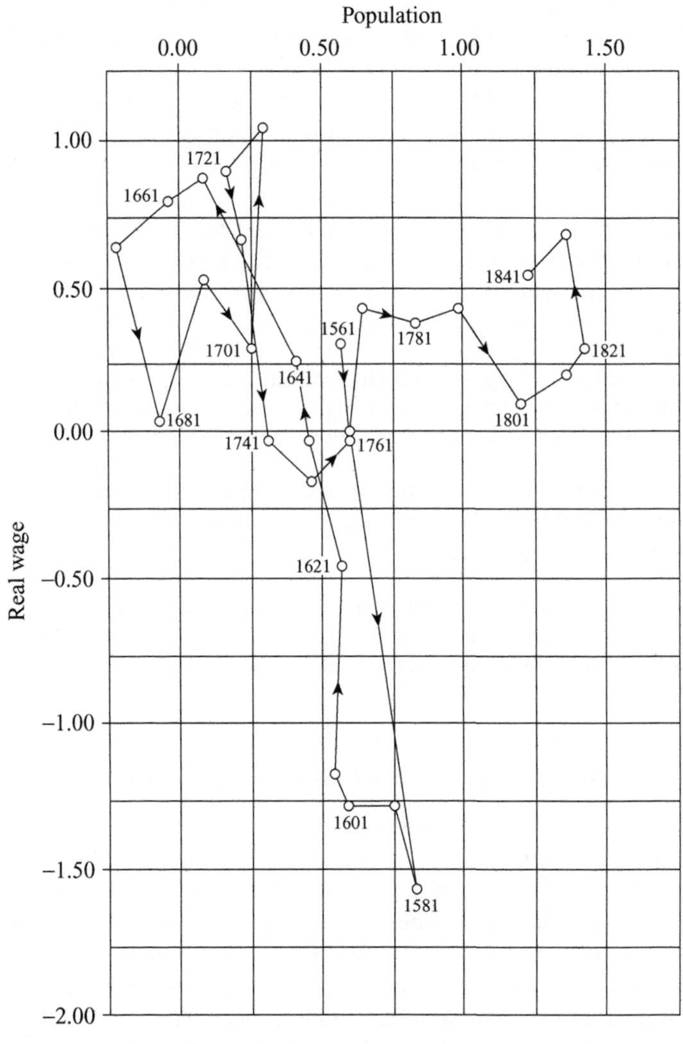

Figure 6.3 Real wage change and population growth rates 1561–1841 (percentage change per annum)
Note: The points on the graph are ten years apart and each point represents the annual rate of change over a 30-year period centring on the date shown.
Sources: Population: Wrigley *et al.*, *English population history*, Table A9.1, pp. 614–15. The real wage series is that used in Wrigley, 'British population during the "long" eighteenth century', Figure 3.7, p. 78.

In England from the late sixteenth century until the middle of the eighteenth century the 'classic' relationship to be expected where the west European marriage system prevailed is evident. If the population was increasing and living standards were falling, nuptiality declined, inducing a fall in fertility sufficient to arrest the reduction in living standards. For a time living standards would then improve and nuptiality and fertility would rise, causing numbers also to increase, eventually inducing a reversion to the situation first described, thus producing a cyclical pattern of behaviour. The fluctuations were slow. Both periods of increasing and of declining prosperity might last several decades, but this was a 'low-pressure' system in which even at the bottom of the cycle living standards were maintained above a subsistence minimum. Figure 6.3 suggests that until the mid eighteenth century the economy could support a rate of 0.25 to 0.50 per cent per annum without experiencing a decline in living standards. Any rate above this level induced a sharp fall in living standards. If population was increasing very slowly, stationary, or declining, as in the later seventeenth and early eighteenth centuries, living standards rose.

In the second half of the eighteenth century, however, a very different relationship between real wages and population growth rates arose. The population growth rate rose to a record level, reaching almost 1.5 per cent per annum but, instead of plunging, the real wage was maintained and even tended upwards. A radically different situation had arisen. There was a profound change in the relationship between population growth rates and real wage trends. Rapid population growth no longer resulted in a sharply falling standard of living. Always previously the pattern to be expected in any organic economy was visible: when the rate of growth of population was high the real wage fell; when it was low or negative the real wage rose. In the second half of the eighteenth century, however, this was no longer the case. The rate of population growth rose to unprecedented heights, peaking in the early decades of the nineteenth century. On past expectation this should have caused a dramatic fall in the real wage but instead of plunging abysmally it did not even turn negative, instead maintaining an average rate of growth a little below 0.5 per cent per annum. Moreover, for reasons explored in Chapter 5, there is good reason to suspect that real wage measurement will conceal or understate improvement in living standards in a period when the occupational structure of the population is changing and the proportion of the workforce engaged in secondary and tertiary activities is rising.

Figure 6.3 in a sense revives the view that the industrial revolution took place in the later eighteenth century. Something had occurred to release England from a constraint which had from time immemorial made a prolonged and uninterrupted rise in living standards an idle dream. The graph symbolises the achievement of the capacity not only to sustain a rapidly rising population but even to produce goods and services on a scale to offer the prospect of rising living standards at the same time. The lesson suggested by Figure 6.3 should be taken in conjunction with the absence of change shown in Figure 6.2. The relationship between marriage, fertility, and real wage trends continued without significant change throughout the eighteenth and the early decades of the nineteenth century. The major change that had taken place lay in the absence of a sharp fall in living standards following a population surge. Figure 6.3 shows the inception of a period in which exponential growth in the economy could be sustained.

It was critical to achieving this state that rates of population growth in areas with differing economic structures should parallel the differing growth possibilities that they offered. It has recently proved possible to estimate the populations of English hundreds at decadal intervals from 1761 to 1851. At one extreme, if growth had been broadly uniform throughout the country, populations in rural agricultural areas would have experienced rapid growth and would have suffered widespread unemployment or underemployment, as happened in the later decades of the sixteenth century. It would imply that growth elsewhere was not proceeding fast enough to provide alternative employment in industry and service occupations. At the other extreme, population growth rates in deeply rural areas might have remained close to zero balanced by a dramatic increase in places where there was a rapid expansion in secondary and tertiary activities. If the very rapid rise in the national population is broken down into population growth rates for groups of hundreds the nature of the changes taking place in England become vividly clear, supporting the view that the exceptionally rapid rate of population growth was accommodated relatively easily.

Hundredal population growth rates

It will be recalled that during the seventeenth and eighteenth centuries the rates of increase of non-urban populations in England and on the continent were virtually the same, but that there was a massive difference in the rate of growth of urban populations, which accounted for almost all the difference in overall growth rates between England and her neighbours (Table 4.3). The national growth rate continued to be much higher in England than on the continent in the early decades of the nineteenth century and the rapid rise in the proportion of the population living in towns and cities continued. In the mid century England became the first country anywhere, as far as is known, in which more than half the population was living in towns. Table 6.2 shows the growth

Table 6.2 *Population totals of selected European countries 1750–1850*

	England	The six continental countries combined	The Netherlands	France	Germany	Sweden	Italy	Spain
			Population (million)					
1750	5.9	69.7	1.9	24.6	17.0	1.8	15.8	8.6
1800	8.7	87.2	2.1	29.3	24.5	2.4	18.3	10.6
1850	16.7	117.8	3.1	36.3	35.4	3.5	24.7	14.8
			Percentage annual growth rates					
1750–1800	0.77	0.45	0.20	0.35	0.73	0.56	0.29	0.42
1800–1850	1.32	0.60	0.78	0.43	0.76	0.79	0.60	0.67
			Relative size of populations (England = 100)					
1750	100	1181	32	416	287	30	267	145
1800	100	1002	24	338	283	27	211	122
1850	100	705	19	217	212	21	148	88

Sources: England: Wrigley and Schofield, *The population history of England*, Table A9.1, pp. 614–15. Other countries: Livi-Bacci, *The population of Europe*, Table 1.1, pp. 8–9.

rates of six continental countries between 1750 and 1850. In this period, the combined population of the six countries increased from 69.7 to 117.8 million, or by 69 per cent. Over the same period the English population increased from 5.9 to 16.7 million, an increase of 183 per cent. Although rates of increase in the other countries varied, all were substantially lower than the English rate. In 1750, the combined population of these six countries was almost twelve times larger than that of England. One hundred years later their combined population was seven times that of England, a remarkably pronounced and swift change. What was happening in England to account for such a dramatic contrast? The availability of hundredal population data clarifies the nature of the changes taking place between 1750 and 1850, bringing into focus several aspects of the fundamental changes taking place in the English economy as the industrial revolution gradually approached completion.

Table 6.3 is in two halves. In the top section, the criterion by which the hundreds are divided is the absolute scale of the increase taking place over the ninety-year period. In the bottom section, the hundreds are divided according to their population growth rates, taken as the ratio between the population totals in 1761 and 1851.[31] Thus in the bottom

[31] The starting date is 1761 rather than 1751 because it is only possible to estimate hundredal populations with confidence from this date: Wrigley, *The early English censuses*, pp. 112–17.

Table 6.3 *Population growth in 610 English hundreds 1761–1851*

	Population in 1761 (1)	Population in 1851 (2)	Population increase 1761–1851 (3)	Share of population 1761 (4)	Share of population 1851 (5)	Share of growth 1761–1851 (6)	Average population per hundred in 1761 (7)	Ratio of population 1851/1761 (8)	Percentage growth p.a. 1761–1851 (9)
			Criterion: scale of increase of population of the hundred						
Top 10 per cent	2,043,341	9,080,630	7,037,289	32.4	53.3	65.7	33,497	4.44	1.67
1st quarter	3,314,974	12,066,612	8,751,638	52.5	70.9	81.7	21,666	3.64	1.45
2nd quarter	1,339,062	2,506,722	1,167,660	21.2	14.7	10.9	8,810	1.87	0.70
3rd quarter	953,989	1,526,091	572,102	15.1	9.0	5.3	6,235	1.60	0.52
4th quarter	702,315	928,055	225,740	11.1	5.5	2.1	4,620	1.32	0.31
Top half	4,654,036	14,573,334	9,919,298	73.8	85.6	92.6	15,259	3.13	1.28
Bottom half	1,656,304	2,454,146	797,842	26.2	14.4	7.4	5,431	1.48	0.44
			Criterion: rate of growth of population of the hundred						
Top 10 per cent	1,298,856	7,311,648	6,012,792	20.6	42.9	56.1	21,293	5.63	1.94
1st quarter	2,308,594	10,198,961	7,890,367	36.6	59.9	73.6	15,089	4.42	1.66
2nd quarter	1,428,201	3,031,355	1,603,154	22.6	17.8	15.0	9,396	2.12	0.83
3rd quarter	1,286,156	2,126,103	839,947	20.4	12.5	7.8	8,406	1.65	0.58
4th quarter	1,287,389	1,671,061	383,672	20.4	9.8	3.6	8,470	1.30	0.29
Top half	3,736,795	13,230,316	9,493,521	59.2	77.7	88.6	12,252	3.54	1.41
Bottom half	2,573,545	3,797,164	1,223,619	40.8	22.3	11.4	8,438	1.48	0.43
England	**6,310,340**	**17,027,480**	**10,717,140**				**10,345**	**2.70**	**1.11**

Source: Wrigley, *The early English censuses*, Table A2.7, pp. 226–53.

section of the table a hundred in which the population rose from 1,000 to 5,000 would rank higher than a hundred whose population was 10,000 in 1761 and 20,000 in 1851 because its population increased five-fold over the period whereas population of the other hundred only doubled, but their positions would be reversed in the top section of the table since the population increase in the first hundred is only 4,000 compared to 10,000 in the second hundred. In both sections the 610 hundreds are split into seven groups. There are groups for each of the four quarters, ordered by their speed of growth; two groups consisting of the top and bottom halves of the hundreds; and a top 10 per cent group in which comparable information for the 61 fastest-growing hundreds is given.

The upper section Table 6.3 leaves no doubt that population growth was highly concentrated in the late eighteenth and early nineteenth centuries. Of the overall growth between 1761 and 1851, 66 per cent took place in the top 10 per cent of the hundreds, 82 per cent in the top quarter, and 93 per cent in the top half. In contrast, only 7 per cent of the increase occurred in the 305 hundreds in the bottom half of the distribution; in the bottom quarter only 2 per cent (column (6)). The population of the top 10 per cent of the hundreds was almost four-and-a-half times as large in 1851 as had been in 1761, whereas the population of the bottom half rose by less than a half (column (8)). The underlying totals perhaps bring out the scale of the contrast more starkly. In 1761, the population of the top 10 per cent of hundreds was 2.04 million; that of the bottom half of hundreds 1.66 million. At this date, therefore, the difference between the two was modest; the population of the bottom half was more than 80 per cent as large as that of the top 10 per cent. In 1851, the comparable totals were 7.04 and 2.45 million, and the latter total was only 35 per cent of the former. The population growth rate in the top 10 per cent would cause a population to double in *c.* 40 years; the comparable period for the hundreds in the bottom half is *c.* 160 years (column (9)). It may be of interest to note that the growth rate in the bottom half of hundreds is closely similar to the rate of growth which was consonant with broadly maintaining the current standard of living in the period when England was still essentially an organic economy (Figure 6.2).

The lower section of Table 6.3 parallels the exercise carried out in creating the upper section, but whereas the criterion by which each hundred was categorised in the upper section was the absolute size of population increase between 1761 and 1851, the criterion used in forming the lower section was the rate of growth. Changing the criterion necessarily produces different patterns. For example, the ratios in column (8) in the bottom section are more widely spread; those in column (6) are closer together. Equally predictable is the change in the ordering of the individual hundreds when comparing the same group in the two sections of the table. For example, the first two hundreds in the top 10 per cent list when ordered by scale of growth are Salford and Ossulstone, Tower, symbolising the vigour of Lancastrian industry and the continued expansion of the capital. Intriguingly, the first two hundreds ordered by rate of growth are Brighton and Cheltenham, symbolising perhaps wealth, leisure, retirement, and entertainment.

Table 6.3 shows that there was a very wide spread of growth rates in England in the industrial revolution period. In the lower section, where rate of growth is the criterion used to classify the hundreds, the third and fourth quarters contained 40.8 per cent of the national population in 1761, but in 1851 their share had shrunk to only 22.3 per cent. During this period only 11.4 per cent of the increase in the national population took place in the bottom half hundreds. Column (7) in the lower section brings to light an interesting fact about population growth rates. Except in the first quarter the average populations of the hundreds in 1761 were very similar, indeed in the third and fourth quarters virtually identical. This represents a sharp contrast with the comparable average populations in the upper section where the average population declines steadily and substantially from the first to the fourth quarter. The pattern in the upper section is predictable. The larger the initial population, the smaller the percentage increase needed to produce any given absolute rise in the population total. The pattern in the lower section is perhaps less predictable. It shows that in the second, third, and fourth quarters the initial population size and the growth rate in the following century are not significantly correlated. The average size of the starting population of a hundred is much the same although the growth rate in the second quarter is almost three times as great as in the fourth quarter. A hundred with a small population in 1761 is no more and no less likely to grow rapidly than hundreds with larger populations.

Although there are instructive contrasts between the two sections of Table 6.3 there are also closer similarities than might have been expected. For example, the percentage rate of growth per annum (column (9)) in the bottom half of the two sections is virtually identical (0.44 and 0.43), and in the top half of the two sections the rate in the upper section is only slightly below the comparable rate in the lower section (1.28 and 1.41). These similarities are linked to the fact that the starting population in the top half in the upper section of the table is larger than in the top half of the bottom section, while the reverse is true in the bottom halves of the two sections (the ratios in question are 1.25 and 0.64).

Agriculture was the dominant occupation of the hundreds in the third and fourth quarters of the lower section of Table 6.3, in which rate of population growth between 1761 and 1851 was the criterion used to order the data. Table 6.4 sets out some relevant data taken from the 1831 census. In 1831 agriculture employed 53.7 per cent of the workforce in the bottom half of the hundreds when ordered by rate of population growth, compared to 22.7 per cent in the top half (column (3)). Figure 6.2 showed that the acceleration in the rate of population growth that began in the middle decades of the eighteenth century did not produce the misery that had previously attended rapid growth. Real wages held steady or increased slightly between the mid eighteenth and mid nineteenth centuries. Table 6.4 suggests that the reason for the absence of the pressures which had normally accompanied rising numbers lay in the fact that the population in hundreds in which agriculture was the dominant employer did not experience a rapid increase in numbers even though the country as a whole was experiencing an unprecedented population surge. Columns (5) and (6) are also instructive in this regard. Agricultural employment per 100 acres in 1831 varied very little between the top and bottom halves of the distribution. The density was slightly lower in the fourth quarter than in the third, but again the difference was modest. Since the total of men employed in agriculture changed very little during this period, it is probable that densities per 100 acres were also broadly constant. The increase in population in rural areas was principally the result of increasing employment in handicrafts, trades, and services rather than employment on the land.

As a footnote to the percentages in column (3) of Table 6.4, it should be noted that they are somewhat misleading as a guide to the level of agricultural employment in rural areas. The criterion for the inclusion of a hundred in a given group in the table was the rate of growth of its population. A substantial proportion of the hundreds in the third and fourth quarters were slow-growing but far from agricultural. Hundreds such as Alnwick in the Coquetdale hundred in Northumberland, or Wotton-under-Edge in the hundred of Berkeley in Gloucestershire had only a modest percentage of their labour forces working on the land. Alnwick was a market centre with almost half of its manpower engaged in retail trade or handicrafts serving the local market. In Wotton-under-Edge, of the 1,288 men aged 20 and over 491 were employed in manufacture and 365 in retail trade and handicrafts. There were many similar hundreds. Even a conservative adjustment to remove such hundreds in estimating agricultural employment percentages shows that the percentages in the table substantially understate the proportion of the workforce employed in agriculture in truly 'rural' hundreds. If the fourth-quarter totals are

Table 6.4 *Agricultural employment in English hundreds in 1831 and population growth rates 1761–1851*

	Men aged 20 and over (1)	**Employed in agriculture** (2)	**Per cent in agriculture** (3)	**Per cent of agricultural total** (4)	**Acreage** (5)	**Agricultural employment per 100 acres** (6)	**Population growth rate: per cent p.a. 1761–1851** (7)
3rd quarter	455,002	242,471	53.3	24.9	7,537,766	3.22	0.58
4th quarter	357,952	194,470	54.3	20.0	6,950,700	2.80	0.29
Bottom half	812,954	436,941	53.7	44.9	14,488,466	3.02	0.43
Top half	2,360,096	536,165	22.7	55.1	16,956,682	3.16	1.41
England	**3,173,050**	**973,106**	**30.7**	**100.0**	**31,445,148**	**3.09**	**1.11**

Sources: Agricultural employment: *1831 Census*, Enumeration Abstract, I and II. Population growth: Wrigley, *The early English censuses*, Table A2.7, pp. 226–53.

adjusted to exclude both parishes with 2,000 or more inhabitants that had a low percentage of agricultural employment and also parishes that, though smaller, were boroughs with little agricultural employment, the agricultural percentage of the fourth quarter rises from 54.3 to 60.9 per cent. A more searching adjustment removing also parishes with smaller populations that were clearly not agricultural would probably raise this percentage to *c.* 65 per cent.

Internal migration

Table 6.3 shows that hundredal growth rates varied dramatically in England between the mid eighteenth and mid nineteenth centuries, implying that there was a high level of internal migration from bottom-half hundreds to hundreds whose populations were expanding rapidly. The size of the net migratory flow is a function of the difference between the level of the local natural increase and the scale of the overall rise or fall in the size of the population over the same time period. At one extreme, in seventeenth-century London the scale of the inflow was considerably greater than the rise in the population of the capital because the death rate was higher than the birth rate, so that a net inflow was needed even to avoid population decline. At the other extreme the rate of population increase in many agricultural areas was slow, even though there were substantial surpluses of births over deaths.

National registration of births and deaths in England began in 1837. Given the deficiencies of baptism and burial registration before the inception of civil registration, an account of the evolution of hundredal birth and death rates over the ninety-year period from 1761 to 1851 is unfortunately not feasible. The early years of civil registration, however, provide data that suggest that with one exception the rates of natural increase were broadly similar across the country and that therefore the widely differing rates of population growth in the groups of hundreds in Table 6.3 were indeed largely due to internal migration rather than differing rates of local natural increase.

Table 6.5 sets out birth rates, death rates, and rates of natural increase for four groups of counties with contrasting economic constitutions, and for the country as a whole. The birth rate in the industrial group was higher than in the other three groups but, with the exception of the metropolitan group, the rates of natural increase in the four groups in both periods were virtually identical. The difference in crude death rates among the groups mirrored those in the crude birth rates, resulting in closely similar rates of natural increase, again apart for the metropolitan group. If the rates in Table 6.5 were a reliable guide to the preceding

Table 6.5 *Rates of natural increase per 1,000 population in England in county groups 1849–53*

	1849–53		
	CBR	**CDR**	**RNI**
Industrial	38.0	24.8	13.2
Metropolitan	33.9	23.3	10.5
Agricultural	33.2	19.9	13.3
Mixed	35.2	21.9	13.3
England	**35.2**	**22.4**	**12.8**

Notes: CBR = crude birth rate; CDR = crude death rate; RNI = rate of natural increase. The agricultural counties comprise all those in which in 1831 the percentage of the labour force working in agriculture was 44 per cent or higher. The counties in each group were as follows. *Industrial*: Cheshire, Lancashire, Staffordshire, Warwickshire, Yorkshire, W.R. *Metropolitan:* Middlesex, Surrey. *Agricultural*: Bedfordshire, Berkshire, Buckinghamshire, Cambridgeshire, Devon, Dorset, Essex, Herefordshire, Hertfordshire, Huntingdonshire, Lincolnshire, Norfolk, Northamptonshire, Oxfordshire, Rutland, Suffolk, Sussex, Westmorland, Wiltshire, Yorkshire, N.R. *Mixed*: Cornwall, Cumberland, Derbyshire, Durham, Gloucestershire, Hampshire, Kent, Leicestershire, Northumberland, Nottinghamshire, Shropshire, Somerset, Worcestershire, Yorkshire, E.R.

Source: Annual Reports of Registrar General. The recorded totals of births and deaths have been corrected for under-registration: Wrigley and Schofield, *The population history of England*, Table A8.5, p. 636.

century they would suggest that differences in crude rates of natural increase played only a modest role in accounting for the differing rates of population growth that are so notable in Table 6.3. Clearly it is questionable whether any safe inferences of this kind can be drawn from the rates in Table 6.5. It is highly probable, for example, that in London, and therefore in the metropolitan group, the rate of natural increase in the later eighteenth century, and to a lesser degree in the early nineteenth century, was much lower than suggested by Table 6.5 because of high mortality. Population growth in the metropolis was more heavily dependent on migration in the early decades of the nineteenth century than in the mid century. Moreover, because the units in the two tables, hundreds and counties, were different, this fact alone must make any inferences tentative.

What follows is essentially a *ballon d'essai* prompted by the fact that the estimates of birth rates, death rates, and rates of natural increase for 1841–50 in Table 6.6, estimated using inverse projection, are almost

Table 6.6 *England: crude birth, death, and natural increase rates per 1,000*

	CBR	CDR	CRNI
1801–10	37.8	23.9	13.9
1811–20	39.3	23.4	15.9
1821–30	38.8	23.1	15.7
1831–40	35.7	22.5	13.2
1841–50	35.3	22.7	12.7

Source: Wrigley *et al.*, *English population history*, Table A9.1, pp. 614–15.

identical to the rates in Table 6.5 which were taken from the Registrar General's annual reports corrected for under-registration. Table 6.6 lists the decennial birth, death, and natural increase rates for each decade in the first half of the nineteenth century. If we assume that in this half-century the rate of natural increase in the four county groups preserved the same pattern relative to the national rate as is found in the 1841–50 decade, it is possible to generate estimates of net migration in each group, and these are set out in Table 6.7. For example, the rate of natural increase in the industrial group in 1849–53 (Table 6.5) was higher than the national rate in the ratio 1.0313. The national crude rate of natural increase was 12.7 per 1,000 in 1841–50, suggesting that the rate in the industrial group was 13.1 per 1,000. Over a ten-year period an annual growth rate at this level would increase the population by 13.9 per cent. The population of the industrial group in 1841 was 4.252 million. Multiplying this total by 1.139 suggests that in the absence of any migration the population in 1851 would have been 4.843 million, which in turn implies a net in-migration total of 177,000. Using this logic for each decade in the first half of the nineteenth century results in the net migration estimates set out in Table 6.7.

In Table 6.7, for each group and for England as a whole, there are three lines of information. The top line gives the population at each of the first six censuses. The second line shows the population total that would have been reached if the natural increase over the preceding decade had alone determined the total. The third line shows the scale of the net migration during the decade that these two totals imply. Table 6.8 summarises net migration over the half-century as a whole.

The summary information in Table 6.8 suggests that in the industrial group net migration provided 22.9 per cent of the population increase taking place over the half-century (the population increased by 3,016,210 and net migration totalled 690,727). In the metropolitan group the

Table 6.7 *Natural increase and implied migration in England and in four county groups in each decade 1801–51*

		1801	1811	1821	1831	1841	1851
Industrial	Census	2,004,204	2,368,084	2,855,920	3,512,522	4,252,335	5,020,414
	Total from natural increase		2,310,847	2,789.603	3,352,850	4,021,838	4,843,410
	Implied migration		57,237	66,317	159,672	230,497	177,004
	Census	1,142,326	1,338,504	1,590,392	1,894,092	2,208,960	2,621,145
Metropolitan							
	Total from natural increase		1,279,405	1,524,556	1,808,276	2,110,018	3,449,737
	Implied migration		59,099	65,836	85,816	98,942	171,408
	Census	2,852,083	3,126,300	3,565,661	3,946,781	4,271,651	4,575,366
Agricultural							
	Total from natural increase		3,291,304	3,685,908	4,193,217	4,523,011	4,869,682
	Implied migration		−165,004	−120,247	−246,436	−251,360	−294,316
Mixed	Census	2,657,485	3,014,889	3,427,216	3,880,171	4,357,337	4,787,218
	Total from natural increase		3,066,738	3,554,554	4,030,406	4,446,676	4,967,364
	Implied migration		−51,849	−127,338	−150,235	−89,339	−180,146
England	Census	8,656,098	9,847,777	11,439,189	13,233,566	15,090,283	17,004,143
	Total from natural increase		9,937,201	11,531,747	13,372,412	15,086,265	17,127,471
	Implied migration		−89,424	−92,558	−138,846	4,018	−123,328

Source: Population totals: Wrigley *et al.*, *English population history*, Table A9.1, pp. 614–15.

Table 6.8 *Natural increase and implied migration during the half-century 1801–51*

	Industrial counties	Metropolitan counties	Agricultural counties	Mixed counties	England
Population 1801	2,004,204	1,142,326	2,852,083	2,657,485	8,656,098
Population 1851	5,020,414	2,621,145	4,575,366	4,787,218	17,004,143
Increase 1801–51	3,016,210	1,478,819	1,723,283	2,129,733	8,348,045
Net migration 1801–51	690,727	481,101	−1,077,363	−598,907	440,138
Net migration as percentage of increase	22.9	32.5	−62.5	−28.1	−5.3

Source: Table 6.7.

corresponding percentage is 32.5 per cent while in the agricultural group net migration reduced the increase that would otherwise have occurred by 62.5 per cent, and in the mixed group the corresponding reduction was 28.1 per cent. Population change in the agricultural group, therefore, was affected more severely by net migration than the other three groups. The cumulative total of net out-migrants from the agricultural group over the half-century was 1.077 million. Net movements in the other three groups were all substantially smaller. For England as a whole, emigration reduced the population increase which would otherwise have occurred by 5.3 per cent over the half-century. The cumulative total of net emigration over the half-century was 440,138, a relatively modest total, perhaps explained in part by the movement to England from the other three countries in the British Isles. The estimate, however, accords well with that made by Baines, who suggested that there were ‘more than 500,000 net English emigrants between 1815 and 1850’.[32]

There are good reasons to treat with reserve the result of an exercise that incorporates so many assumptions that are open to question. It is certain, for example, that although net movement into London in 1841–50 may be fairly accurately measured since the assumptions underlying the calculation are probably appropriate, over the half-century as a whole the scale of net movement is substantially underestimated since the rate of natural increase in the early decades of the century will be overestimated.

32 Baines, *Migration in a mature economy*, p. 58.

This in turn will mean that the net out-migration from other groups will be underestimated. Nevertheless, the exercise appears capable of throwing light on the relative scale of movement in and out of the county groups. For example, the counties in the industrial group form a large block of territory (they were contiguous with one another). In the first half of the nineteenth century less than a quarter of the population increase taking place was the result of net in-migration. In this period the industrial group was growing faster than any other group including the London group (the population of the industrial group rose by 150 per cent; the metropolitan group by 129 per cent). In these circumstances, therefore, it may be reason for surprise at first sight that the net in-migration percentage in the industrial group was not higher. It was only a third as high as the level of net out-migration from agricultural counties. It may simply reflect, however, the high level of migratory movement that took place within the boundaries of the industrial group of counties. There were, of course, extensive tracts of land in the industrial counties where the workforce was largely agricultural and where the scale of out-migration probably mirrored that in the agricultural counties. The fact that in agricultural counties the level of net out-migration was high reflected a different scenario. Job opportunities were to be found only by moving to an area with a different economic base. If the same was true of the extensive tracts within the industrial counties which were rural in character with agriculture as the main source of local employment, job opportunities would have been available without leaving the industrial county group, and would result in a relatively modest level of net in-migration in the group as whole.

Given the very wide range in population growth rates at the hundredal level shown in Table 6.3, it is inescapably clear that in the later eighteenth and early nineteenth centuries a high proportion of each generation left the place in which they were born, and in so doing reflected the fundamental reshaping of the country's economy. To the degree that the results contained in Tables 6.7 and 6.8 are justified they suggest, not surprisingly, that much of the migration taking place, especially in the industrial and mixed counties, did not involve movement between the different county groups. It might prove illuminating to investigate the feasibility of employing the same method of estimating net migration to estimate movement for smaller units – for example, at the level of the individual county – but it is beyond the scope of this chapter to attempt this.

Conclusion

There is much to support a remark which Chambers made in assessing the social and economic implications of the English demographic system in the centuries preceding the industrial revolution: 'The combination of high age at marriage, the existence of various social and institutional obstacles to high nuptiality, and at the same time a quite remarkable degree of geographical mobility laid the groundwork for a competitive and acquisitive society in which the ratio of resources to population was thereby kept in a favourable balance.'[33]

The relative importance of the many inter-related changes in train in England as it gradually ceased to be an organic economy cannot be established with any certainty. It is essentially meaningless, for example, to speculate about whether the absence of the west European marriage system would have ruled out the possibility of England escaping from the constraints attaching to all organic economies. It is clear, however, that its presence was a contributory factor in facilitating the changes that took place. The nature of the marriage system in England in the seventeenth and eighteenth centuries meant that the level of fertility no less than the level of mortality was sensitive to prevailing economic circumstances and trends, and that this was conducive to preserving a standard of living substantially above bare subsistence. Since even marginal differences in prevailing real incomes can give rise to significant differences in the structure of aggregate demand, this fact contributed to the changing occupational structure of the country and its increasing urbanisation.

[33] Chambers, *Population, economy, and society*, p. 50.

7 Transport

Von Thünen's *The isolated state* provides a telling analysis of the constraints imposed by transport costs on economic activity in an organic economy. Von Thünen had personal experience of these constraints since as a young man he bought the estate of Tellow in Mecklenburg. He describes, for example, the transfer of a load of grain weighing 2,400 pounds by a wagon drawn by four horses from the estate to the town of Rostock, a distance of 23 miles. In hauling the wagon to Rostock the horses consumed 150 pounds of grain so that only 2,250 pounds of grain was delivered.[1] The energy needed to transfer the product reduced its value by 6 per cent, illustrating the way in which the energy consumed in effecting a transfer gradually reduced the net value of the goods delivered. The heavier and bulkier the product, the more severely the accessible market area was limited.

One of the central issues examined in *The isolated state* is the way in which transport cost strongly influenced land use in an area surrounding a town. In approaching this topic, von Thünen was influenced by his reading of *The wealth of nations*. Adam Smith stressed the significance of transport costs in relation to the size of an accessible market. In an assessment of the importance of good transport facilities, he asserted that: 'Good roads, canals, and navigable rivers, by diminishing the expence of carriage, put the remote parts of the country more nearly upon a level with those in the neighbourhood of the town. They are upon that account the greatest of all improvements. They encourage the cultivation of the remote, which must always be the most extensive circle of the country.'[2]

[1] Von Thünen, *The isolated state*, pp. xv, 13.

[2] Smith, *The wealth of nations*, I, p. 165. On occasion, his belief in the high significance of transport costs led him to make some intriguing assertions. In seeking to explain why it was that 'Egypt seems to have been the first [country] in which either agriculture or manufactures were cultivated and improved to any considerable degree', he attributed this to the fact that the Nile provided 'communication by water carriage, not only between all the great towns, but between all the considerable villages', and ended by remarking that 'The extent and easiness of inland navigation was probably one of the principal causes of the early improvement of Egypt'. *Ibid.*, I, p. 24.

Von Thünen's book is an examination of the characteristic pattern of land use in the countryside surrounding a market town in an organic economy. To simplify his exposition he assumed that the surrounding countryside was a uniform flat plain. In these circumstances, the type of crop that will be found in any given area will be a function of its value to weight ratio and its distance from the town. Jointly, these two factors will give rise to a series of concentric bands of land use providing the food and fuel needs of the town.

In the band closest to the town the land is devoted to market gardening, fruit-growing, and milk production (perishability rather than transport cost determines this usage). The next band illustrates vividly the restrictive nature of high transport cost. It is forest land from which the town meets its fuel needs both for domestic heating and for local industry. Access to timber is also vital for other purposes, notably for the construction industry. Because of its bulk and weight timber has to be grown close to the town. Its price rapidly becomes prohibitive as the length of the journey to market increases. Sieferle echoed von Thünen's thinking when he remarked: 'The supply of wood was as important to the agricultural economy as was that of other plant products. The forest must be understood as an integral component of agriculture, rather than as an alternative to it.'[3]

The outermost circle is devoted to pasture since, for example, beef cattle can provide their own transport by walking to market at a relatively low cost, and sheep's wool is both light, durable, and of relatively high value per unit weight. In von Thünen's model the outermost circle is the sixth band. The three bands between the timber and pastoral bands are devoted to cereal growing.

High transport costs operate rather like tariff barriers. Most local industries are, in effect, protected in much the same way that a tariff would provide protection. Competition is restricted, except in regard to products of high value per unit weight. In contrast, if transport costs are low an efficient producer will be able to sell at a profit over a larger area, and the consumer will benefit. Hence Adam Smith's insistence that transport improvements are 'the greatest of all improvements'. Von Thünen emphasised the same point when he introduced a river that crossed his uniform plain, passing through the market town at its centre. The strips of land on either side of the river distort the original simple pattern

[3] Sieferle, *The subterranean forest*, p. 52. This was also a basic theme of Galloway *et al.* in their analysis of the needs of medieval London. They noted that 'Of all the constraints upon the growth of pre-industrial cities, perhaps none was more crucial than the fuel supply': Galloway *et al.* 'Fuelling the city', p. 447.

of concentric bands of land use. The bands are extended outwards on either side of the river because close to the river the cost of transporting a crop or other produce to the town might be no higher at, say, three times the distance from the town at which the same cost is incurred if the product is moved over land. Szostak, in assessing the benefits derived from declining transport costs, noted that: 'as the cost of obtaining raw materials falls, the cost of the final goods falls. Thus it is possible to shift the supply curve without any change in the methods of production and widen the market intensively by moving along the existing demand curve.'[4]

The fact that von Thünen's model is helpful in exploring many aspects of the provision of transport facilities in England in the seventeenth and eighteenth centuries points to a feature of the history of transport provision in this period which distinguishes it from other major sectors of productive activity. Until the advent of the railway, transport continued to be entirely an 'organic economy' activity. In contrast with other major branches of the economy, the energy used in transport was exclusively mechanical energy and until the middle decades of the nineteenth century this continued to be provided, as in the past, by animal muscle on land and by the wind at sea. Only with the development of an effective method of converting heat energy into mechanical energy did this change.

The change began at the very end of the seventeenth century with the Savery engine, soon followed by the Newcomen engine. The first Newcomen engine, which came to be widely employed in mine drainage, was erected in 1712. Newcomen engines, though of great value to the coalmining industry, converted only a tiny fraction of the energy in the coal they consumed into useful work, and given the high cost per ton-mile of transporting coal, their low efficiency meant that they were principally used to drain coal mines since at the pithead no transport cost was incurred. Each improvement in the efficiency of steam engines, however, enabled them to be employed at a greater distance from the pithead. Watt achieved an important advance with his introduction of a separate condenser to enable the cylinder to remain permanently hot rather than being reheated before each stroke of the piston. In the Newcomen engine, cold water was injected into the cylinder to create a vacuum, which meant that much heat was wasted. Watt's engine, which had proved its potential by the mid 1770s, represented a major advance. It was significantly more economical than those of Savery or Newcomen and the pace of advance did not slacken thereafter.

[4] Szostak, *The role of transportation*, p. 11.

The later work of Watt, and especially his invention in 1781 of sun and planet gearing to enable the steam engine to provide rotary motion, laid the foundations for the far wider use of steam engines as a source of mechanical power. For example, they could supply the power to work forge hammers and rolling and slitting machinery, which in turn meant that the iron industry was no longer dependent on water power and could relocate on or close to coalfields. The telling contributions of Smeaton and Trevithick in further improving the efficiency of the steam engine allowed it to be employed in a steadily increasing range of industrial activities. The efficiency gains were cumulatively substantial. In the 1720s Newcomen pumping engines used about 45 lb of coal to generate 1 horsepower-hour. By 1760 this figure had fallen to 30 lb. Smeaton was able to construct engines using as little as 17.6 lb by the 1770s. In 1778, however, he measured the consumption of a Watt engine and found that it was twice as efficient, consuming only 8.8 lb per horsepower-hour, while by the 1830s Cornish engines more than halved this figure, averaging only 3.5 lb per horsepower-hour.[5]

The stage was set for perhaps the most striking single advance resulting from the improvements that had been achieved. The increasing efficiency of the steam engine culminated in the development of a railway engine which was both much more powerful and much speedier than any earlier form of land transport. Rail networks were soon constructed. Inland transport was no longer subject to the limitations inherent in an organic economy. Much had been done in the seventeenth and eighteenth centuries to advance the efficiency with which the mechanical energy derived from animal muscle was converted into useful work, but the limitations of this power base remained. The maximum speed of transport movement was set by the physique of the horse on both roads and canals, and maximum loads were similarly determined.

Before considering the changes in transport provision which were achieved in the seventeenth and eighteenth centuries, it is convenient to review one of the features of organic economies which tended to limit the extent of improvements to the transport networks which could be undertaken, and to note how the transport requirements of the new era substantially modified the situation: or, to express this more succinctly, the difference between dendritic and linear transport systems.

[5] Allen has provided an excellent description of the development of the steam engine, from an initial period when its very low efficiency greatly restricted its use to the period in the mid nineteenth century when it became the universal workhorse of industry and transport: Allen, *The British industrial revolution*, Chapter 7.

Areal and punctiform

In considering transport in an organic economy it is important to bear in mind the fact that since the land was the source of all food and most raw materials, production was *areal*. This was reflected in Tudor England in the distribution of the population across the face of the land. Agriculture was by far the largest source of employment; probably more than 70 per cent of the workforce laboured on the land. There was also much related employment in rural crafts – smiths, carpenters, masons, millers, ale house keepers, etc. The urban percentage was modest. London grew rapidly during the sixteenth century. In 1520 its population was *c.* 60,000 and this figure had risen three-fold to *c.* 200,000 by 1600, but at this date the population of other towns with 5,000 or more inhabitants was only 135,000.[6] The combined total of the urban population in 1600, 335,000, was only 8 per cent of the national total. The overall distribution of population, therefore, was closely linked to the area of farmland. As already noted, in 1600 overall population densities were higher in the south than in the north, but if land above 200 metres is excluded they were remarkably similar throughout the whole of England. Excluding Middlesex because it included most of London, the average density per 100 acres was 14.1 persons, with a modest standard deviation of 2.9 persons.[7]

If production is *areal* the associated transport system will be *dendritic*. Much of the agricultural production takes place towards the periphery of the farmland surrounding a town and is therefore transported to the town from the outermost twigs of the system. In order to reach an urban market the grain must journey first along the twigs to reach the small branches and then the larger boughs before reaching a main trunk of the system. Similarly, for urban products to reach rural markets they must journey through the dendritic system in the opposite direction. The volume of traffic along any given stretch of road will be modest except on the roads close to the main market. In organic economies this meant that it was difficult to secure an adequate return on road improvement since the resulting saving in reduced transport cost could seldom justify the initial expenditure. Large volumes of traffic were only to be found on roads close to the largest towns. In von Thünen's world the presence of a town engendered traffic flows because towns needed food and fuel from the surrounding countryside. In the absence of urban demand local self-sufficiency was the norm and traffic volumes were very low. Given that

[6] Wrigley, 'Urban growth and agricultural change', Table 7.2, p. 162.

[7] See pp. 87–8 for more detail on county population densities in 1600.

early Tudor England was one of the least urbanised countries in Europe this implied modest traffic volumes on most roads. Jackman summarised the situation:

> From what we are able to learn as to the roads in the country and in the towns, it may be stated that they were in accord with the comparatively meagre demands of agriculture and industry, which were then on a small scale. The population was mainly agricultural; the community tended to be self-sufficing, and to have but little business relations with outside communities; and the roads were of such a character as merely to satisfy the demands of the great majority of the people.[8]

One of the key features fostering change as an industrial revolution gradually took shape was a major change in the incentive to invest in improved transport systems. This occurred chiefly because of two inter-related developments in the country's economy during the seventeenth and eighteenth centuries. One of them increased the proportion of production and consumption which was *punctiform* in character and which therefore also increased the proportion of transport that was *linear* rather than dendritic in character. The other increased traffic volumes even where the traffic movement was essentially dendritic. Both contributed to increasing the volume of traffic throughout the whole system, and therefore enhanced the incentive to invest in transport improvements.

The first was linked to the increasing use of coal rather than wood as the source of heat energy. This was a general phenomenon but occurred earlier and progressed more rapidly in towns than in the countryside. Both towns and coalmines may be regarded as notional points and traffic between them was linear in character. There was both rapid urban growth and a steady replacement of wood by coal as a fuel in towns. As a result the volume of movement sometimes became sufficient to justify the construction of an artificial waterway, a canal, which greatly reduced the price of coal in places along its course. The cost of constructing a canal between a mining centre and a large town or an industrial centre was many times greater than improving the road between them, but the reduction in the cost of coal and other products which followed its construction often provided a strong incentive to undertake it. And as towns increased in size and industry expanded, the incentive increased commensurately. The huge rise in the volume of coal production, and therefore of the scale of coal movement, steadily strengthened this incentive. Already in the mid eighteenth century the tonnage of coal mined

[8] Jackman, *The development of transportation*, p. 14.

equalled the weight of the cereal harvest, and by the end of the century it was almost three times greater.[9]

The second change occurred because of the notable advance in agricultural productivity in early modern England. The net yield of grain per acre almost tripled from 6.3 to 17.6 bushels per acre.[10] The area needed to provide bread grain for a town whose population did not change would therefore shrink commensurately, but the volume of traffic along the roads in this reduced area would rise sharply to reflect the new situation. Equally, if the town tripled in size the matching rise in traffic volumes would occur throughout an unchanging urban 'footprint'. The urban population of England increased greatly between 1600 and 1800. The combined population of towns with 5,000 or more inhabitants rose from 335,000 to 2,380,000 over the period. The combined effect of rising net output per acre and the massive increase in urban population gave rise to a great increase in the movement of grain and other agricultural products along the country's roads. In this case the movement was dendritic, affecting the road system as a whole rather than linear routes within it. Road surfaces became subject to far greater wear and tear but there was a matching incentive to maintain and improve them given the importance of the traffic to the local economies that were served. Large numbers of turnpike trusts were created for this reason. The transport system that carried this increased volume remained dendritic rather than linear but, to use the appropriate metaphor, the twigs swelled in size to small branches, and the branches became as thick as the boughs had been in the past.

Canals

Movement of goods over water was much cheaper than over land, a fact that was common knowledge in early modern times. In 1675 Sir Robert Southwell suggested that transport by 'wheel carriage' was twenty times as expensive as carriage by sea, and twelve times as expensive as inland water transport.[11] Location on a navigable river was widely recognised as a major advantage for any town. John Taylor in the mid seventeenth century remarked: 'There is not any town or city which hath a navigable river at it, that is poore, nor scarce any that are rich, which want a river, with the benefits of boats.'[12] River navigation posed greater difficulties

9 See p. 42. 10 See pp. 52–3.

11 Willan, *The inland trade*, p. 1. It is of interest that Southwell considered that in his day 60 per cent of all land carriage was by packhorse even though this was a third dearer than carriage by wagon.

12 Turnbull, 'Canals, coal and regional growth', p. 538.

than movement by canal. This was so even on big rivers like the Severn. Bagwell noted that, at one extreme, it was known to rise 18 feet in five hours, while at the other extreme Thomas Telford once reported that the water depth was less than 16 inches. Indeed in 1796 the river was navigable for only two months in twelve.[13] Canals, of course, were not immune to such difficulties. Their still waters froze readily and the operation of a series of locks was dependent on an adequate inflow of water. Prolonged dry weather could therefore also cause disruption but canals brought great benefit where point-to-point traffic volumes were high. The value of access to water transport, whether by river, canal, or through a coastal harbour, was clear. It was vividly exemplified in the mutual advantages enjoyed by London and Tyneside arising from the movement of 'seacoal' by coastal shipping down the east coast.[14]

Comparison of movement costs per ton-mile by road and by canal have produced a range of estimates since movement costs on both forms of transport varied substantially, but the existence of a marked difference is not in doubt. Freeman, in a wide-ranging review of transport in the industrial revolution, supported Jackman's conclusion that 'the cost of canal conveyance was from one-fourth to one-half of the cost of carriage by road'.[15] Canals were very well suited to the transport of heavy and bulky commodities of low value per unit weight from point to point, but before the large-scale production of coal other commodities did not meet these requirements. As Duckham remarked: 'The easier conveyance of coal was, of course, the primary motive behind the creation of most canals, and cheaper fuel prices were among the first benefits of the canal age to be enjoyed by contemporaries.'[16] Their construction could only repay the investment required if traffic volumes were high and reduced the unit costs of movement sufficiently to justify the initial investment. They were not well suited to the transport of agricultural products. Agricultural production was areal and required a dendritic transport system that typically involved moving small volumes over a system whose total mileage was large.

Canal construction began in earnest only from the 1760s. In this and the following decade there were fifty-two Acts of Parliament concerning

13 Bagwell, *The transport revolution*, p. 14.

14 As Beier and Finlay noted: 'London was almost unique in Europe in combining the role of capital city and great port': Beier and Finlay, *London*, p. 14.

15 Jackman, *The development of transportation*, p. 729. It is of interest that, after noting Jackman's view, Freeman added that 'Coastwise transport, meanwhile, could be cheaper than inland water by an equivalent proportion': Freeman, 'Introduction', p. 12.

16 Duckham, 'Canals and river navigations', p. 130.

inland navigation, of which more than half were for new schemes, and for the first time the proposals included some for long trunk canals such as the Trent and Mersey in 1766 and the Leeds and Liverpool in 1770.[17] The rising scale of coal production in the later eighteenth century spurred much of the heightened interest in canal building. As with many other aspects of change as the industrial revolution took shape, the connection between canal construction and rising coal production was one of positive feedback. An increase in the demand for coal encouraged making provision for its cheaper transport. The resulting fall in the price of coal in markets served by canal led to further increases in demand. By the mid nineteenth century, when canal construction had produced something approaching a national network and before rail competition had brought about a severe contraction in canal activity, there were 25,000 barges on British inland waterways and barges were home to perhaps 50,000 people.[18]

The value of canals was well understood by contemporaries. The intimate connection between canal construction, reliable access to affordable coal, and industrial success was repeatedly emphasised by Aikin in his survey of a wide tract of territory centred on Manchester that included most of Lancashire and Cheshire, and also parts of Derbyshire, Staffordshire, and the West Riding. He described both the construction and the operation of many canals and discussed the probable benefits to be expected from the completion of canals currently under construction. He admired especially the achievements of 'that wonderful self-instructed genius *James Brindley*', even including in his book a print of Barton bridge which carried the Bridgwater canal over the Irwell, and noting that 'those who had at first ridiculed the attempt, as equivalent to building a castle in the air, were obliged to join in admiration of the wonderful abilities of the engineer'.[19] He summarised his admiration for what had been achieved and its promise for the future (his book was published in 1795) as follows:

> Meantime, the prodigious additions made within a few years to the system of inland navigation, now extended to almost every corner of the kingdom, cannot but impress the mind with magnificent ideas of the opulence, the spirit, and the enlarged views which characterize the commercial interest of this country. Nothing seems too bold for it to undertake, too difficult for it to atchieve; and should not external changes produce a durable check to national prosperity, its future progress is beyond the reach of calculation.[20]

[17] *Ibid.*, pp. 101–3. [18] Bagwell, *The transport revolution*, p. 33.
[19] Aikin, *The country round Manchester*, pp. 112, 114. [20] *Ibid.*, p. 136.

What Aikin described in the Manchester region was paralleled in other industrial regions. The Birmingham area was poorly endowed with navigable rivers and had many industries that needed heat energy. Coal was used from an early date. Court noted that it was carried as much as ten to fifteen miles by road and that this fact enabled Birmingham to secure coal from the Black Country in the seventeenth and eighteenth centuries, but he emphasised the importance of the change brought about by canal construction: 'The express intention of the Birmingham canal was to facilitate the transport of coal into Birmingham from the Black Country.'[21] An Act was obtained in 1767 and the first boat-load of coal from Wednesbury reached Birmingham in November 1769. The price of coal dropped from 13s. a ton to 7s. 6d.[22] As a result, the consumption of coal in the Birmingham area rose steeply, matched by the 'advance of colliery business under the stimulus of the new transport'.[23] The creation of links from collieries to industrial centres and major towns was the archetypal reason for canal construction, though the canal boats also moved large tonnages of other heavy, bulky goods of low unit value, such as limestone, salt, bricks, and timber. Like the Birmingham area, the Potteries were heavily handicapped by high transport costs before the construction of canals. It is not surprising that Josiah Wedgwood urged strongly in favour of the construction of the Trent and Mersey canal. The local roads were so poor that they appear even to have discouraged wheeled transport. The existing system was said to consist of 'pack-horses and asses heavily laden with coal, – tubs full of ground flint from the mills, crates of ware or panniers of clay' and the animals were described as 'floundering knee-deep' through the local muddy roads.[24]

In agricultural districts, because production was areal and traffic networks dendritic, canals were unlikely to succeed. Clapham in his discussion of unsuccessful canal construction remarked: 'It is clear – that canal-building across the watersheds of southern England – it might almost be said, canal-building in the South – had not been a paying enterprise.'[25] Successful canals away from the coalfield areas were characteristically those connecting major urban centres that afforded large flows of point-to-point traffic, such as the Grand Junction canal between London and Birmingham.

Although water transport was much cheaper per ton-mile than overland transport, the balance of advantage between the two forms of

21 Court, *The rise of the Midland industries*, p. 164.
22 *Ibid.*, p. 165. 23 *Ibid.*, p. 165.
24 Jackman, *The development of transportation in modern England*, p. 304.
25 Clapham, *An economic history of modern Britain*, I, p. 82.

transport could tip either way. From point to point canals could offer much lower transport costs but since the canal network was far less dense than the road network, delivery point to point was feasible by canal only for a limited number of places, and when transhipment from water to land transport was necessary to deliver goods from A to B it was sometimes no more expensive, and frequently more convenient, to make use of road transport alone.

Turnpike roads

Canal construction on a large scale began only in the later eighteenth century. Significant road improvements began earlier. The administrative framework for identifying promising opportunities for road improvement and transforming promise into reality was the turnpike trust. The first trust set up in the form that was thereafter standard was created in 1706 and this form became normal from 1714 onwards.[26] The trustees were empowered to erect gates, collect tolls, and borrow money. The trusts were locally based which helped to limit opposition to the payment of tolls to finance repairs. As with canal construction, road improvements were a response to the increase in traffic volumes outlined above.

Given the difference between dendritic and linear transport systems, road improvement was the dominant form of transport investment in the south and east of England, with canal construction more prominent in the coalfield and industrial centres in the north and midlands. The period in which by far the largest number of Turnpike Acts was passed was the 1750s and 1760s. In the first half of the eighteenth century the bulk of the mileage of turnpike roads was focused on London, reflecting the density of traffic flows over a dendritic network where traffic volumes become progressively larger with decreasing distance to an urban market. A market as large as London resulted in substantial traffic volumes even at some distance from the capital. In the second half of the century turnpiking was pursued vigorously country-wide, blanketing the whole country. By 1770 turnpike road coverage was denser in the industrial north and midlands than in the vicinity of London.[27] In the later stages of turnpike legislation in the half-century from the 1790s to the 1830s Lancashire and Yorkshire accounted for almost a third of all the new Acts.[28] Road improvement in these areas was sometimes supplementary

[26] My description of the nature of the turnpike trust system depends heavily on Albert, 'The turnpike trusts'.

[27] *Ibid.*, Figure 5, p. 40 and Figure 6, p. 43.

[28] Freeman, 'Introduction', p. 39.

to canal construction since the delivery of coal to its final consumer often meant movement over land to complete it.

Turnpike trusts succeeded in providing a substantial improvement in road surfaces with consequent reductions in journey times and movement costs. The volume of passenger traffic in and out of London, for example, increased markedly during the eighteenth century. The number of passenger services available each week from London to a selection of provincial towns increased ten-fold between 1715 and 1796 from 158 to 1,596 and the number of passenger-miles performed weekly by these services between the same dates rose even more dramatically from 67,000 to 1,040,000 over the same period. There was a further rise in passenger-miles in the early nineteenth century; in 1840 the total stood at 2,369,000. The weekly service total rose much less steeply in the early decades of the nineteenth century, standing at 1,765 in 1840.[29]

It is little wonder that Arthur Young was so struck by the contrast between London and Paris in the volume of traffic on the roads approaching each capital. He wrote: 'The road to Orleans is one the greatest that leads from Paris, I expected, therefore, to have my former impression of the little traffic near the city removed; but on the contrary it was confirmed; it is a desert compared with those around London. In ten miles we met not one stage or diligence; only two messageries, and very few chaises; not a tenth of what would have been met had we been leaving London at the same hour.'[30]

Freight traffic to and from London by road also rose very substantially during the eighteenth century. Between the capital and a selection of provincial towns traffic in 1715 has been estimated at 13,279 ton-miles, rising to 135,996 ton-miles in 1796 and to 458,516 ton-miles in 1840.[31]

More generally, Gerhold assessed changes in the productivity of road transport between the late seventeenth century and the mid nineteenth century, and concluded that productivity in long-distance freight traffic more than doubled and may have tripled in this period, and that the comparable increase in the productivity of stage coach traffic rose four-fold.[32] In both cases, the increase was calculated without taking into account the reduction in journey times. It is clear that if the benefit of shorter journey times could be incorporated into the overall picture it would raise the productivity figure significantly. Gerhold later provided evidence that London stage coach service speeds more than doubled between 1750

29 Chartres and Turnbull, 'Road transport', Table 3, p. 69.

30 Young, *Travels in France*, p. 16. The former impression to which he referred is recorded on p. 13 and he returned to the same theme on p. 75.

31 Chartres and Turnbull, 'Road transport', Table 7, p. 85.

32 Gerhold, 'Productivity change', p. 511.

and 1840 from less than 4 to more then 8 miles per hour.[33] Even at its maximum *c.* 1840, however, the speed at which passenger traffic moved, though greatly improved, and much higher than was normal on the continent, was only a fraction of the speed achieved on the railways later in the century. Much could be achieved within the framework of an organic economy but only access to mechanical energy from a new source not subject to the limitations of old could bring transport into line with the other parts of the economy where the use of fossil fuel had freed them from ancient restrictions.

In the eighteenth century the English economy benefited from substantial improvements to transport facilities for both passengers and freight. The two most important sources of this improvement were the result of the construction of canals and the activities of the turnpike trusts. Their relative importance in facilitating growth in the economy generally is difficult to establish, not least because they were as much complementary as competitive, but it is of interest to note that an attempt to measure the sums spent on creating, improving, and maintaining canals and turnpike roads over the century from 1750 to 1850 suggests that both the absolute amounts spent and the trends over time in these expenditures were very similar. In both cases the sums involved grew rapidly down to about the second decade of the nineteenth century but thereafter were flat for a quarter of a century before declining in the 1840s.[34]

One further factor that played an important role in increasing the volume of traffic on English roads and canals in the eighteenth century should be borne in mind. During the century the English population increased by two-thirds, from 5.21 to 8.67 million. Even in the absence of all the other changes that gave rise to an increased volume of movement of passengers and goods, the population increase might be expected to have increased traffic volumes proportionately. The rise in agricultural output per acre, the growth of urban population, the rapid growth in coal production, and the increase in population in combination transformed the scale of traffic movement and thereby provided a strong incentive to invest in improving roads and building canals.

The railway

A decade after the publication of Deane and Cole's pathbreaking application of the technique of national income accounting to the analysis of change before and during the industrial revolution, Phyllis Deane offered

[33] Gerhold, 'The development of stage coaching', Figure 1, p. 825.
[34] Hawke and Higgins, 'Transport and social overhead capital', Figure 12.1, p. 229.

her further reflections on the nature of the industrial revolution in a lengthy essay. Describing the situation of the economy in the immediate aftermath of the Napoleonic wars, she remarked:

> Essentially, however, Great Britain was still a pre-industrial economy in which the state of the harvest was the most significant determinant of the change in national income between one year and the next. Possibly it was merely a matter of time before the balance between manufacturing industry and agriculture would have shifted finally in favour of the former and a fully fledged industrial state, in which growth was the normal condition, would have emerged as a natural matter of course. The next major discontinuity in the process of development however coincided with the coming of the steam railways and, in the event, it was this that ensured the completion of industrialisation.[35]

Deane's first sentence might be paraphrased as the judgement that England was still an organic economy in the decades immediately following the war period, but that the construction of the railway network symbolised the achievement of a definitive release from the constraints that had always limited growth possibilities in organic economies. There is good reason to consider that her selection of the symbolic significance of the railway as epitomising the arrival of the new era is justified. Her judgement might be expressed as reflecting what became possible when the access to heat energy without the restrictions inherent in organic economies, which had been gained during the seventeenth and eighteenth centuries, was paralleled by comparable access to mechanical energy in the nineteenth century.

If a date were to be selected to represent the symbolic beginning of the railway age it might well be 1830. In 1829 the directors of the Liverpool and Manchester Railway offered a prize of £500 to the designers of a locomotive which did not exceed 6 tons in weight and could pull a load at least three times its weight at no less than 10 miles an hour. The trials were held at Rainhill, about 10 miles east of Liverpool, in October 1829. They provided Robert Stephenson with the opportunity to demonstrate the superiority of the *Rocket* over the rival locomotives. Although some of the other locomotives provided a serious challenge, the *Rocket*, which achieved a speed in excess of 30 miles per hour, won the day.[36]

The Liverpool and Manchester Railway opened on 15 September 1830. The Liverpool and Manchester line was not the first line designed for steam traction. The first such line was the Stockton and Darlington line which was opened in 1825 but, as Deane noted, 'Horsedrawn coaches continued to be used for passenger traffic on this line for some

[35] Deane, 'The industrial revolution in Great Britain', pp. 208–9.
[36] Bagwell, *The transport revolution*, pp. 91–2.

years yet and contemporaries remained dubious of the steam locomotive until well into the 1830s'.[37] Jackman emphasized the importance of the opening of the Liverpool and Manchester line. Earlier lines had been built for limited and specific purposes as adjuncts to particular enterprises:

> With the Liverpool and Manchester line, the railway era really began. It was the first railway that was constructed for the express purpose of carrying passengers as well as freight; and no other power was ever used on it but that of locomotive engines. Up to this time, all others, except the Surrey Iron Railway, had contemplated the carriage of one commodity (usually coal, iron or stone) and were operated as adjuncts to a colliery, quarry, or the like –.
>
> The Liverpool and Manchester, on the contrary, was constructed for the public welfare, rather than for private profit, as we can readily judge by the fact that no person could subscribe for more than ten shares.

Profits were limited by Act of Parliament to 10 per cent, 'and the undertakers were so anxious to encourage industry and commerce that they declared they would be satisfied with even five per cent'.[38]

The success of the Liverpool and Manchester Railway was reflected in the heavy investment in new lines in the 1830s and 1840s, which meant that at the time of the Great Exhibition in 1851 an embryonic national rail network with over 6,000 miles of track had been constructed.

With the creation of a national rail network both passenger fares and the cost of moving goods declined sharply. Moreover, speed of movement by rail far outstripped that by road, symbolised by the adoption countrywide of a 'railway clock'. Railway timetables embodied this innovation. Midday in Bristol occurred at the same moment as in London, rather than being determined by the zenith of the sun. It was the reduction in time in travelling from A to B which for the first time made it possible for newspapers to achieve national same-day circulation, and meat, milk, fruit, and vegetables to arrive fresh at market after travelling across the country rather than being drawn from the immediate surroundings of the town. The stage coach had greatly expanded the volume of passenger travel by road in the late eighteenth and early nineteenth centuries and had reduced journey time very substantially. The number of people travelling by stage coach rose roughly fifteen-fold over the half-century preceding the 1830s, and journey times were halved. Bogart has assembled data on the average speed of journeys which suggest that it rose from 2.61 miles per hour *c.* 1750 to 7.96 miles per hour *c.* 1820.[39] There

[37] Deane, 'The industrial revolution in Great Britain', p. 209.
[38] Jackman, *The development of transportation*, p. 526.
[39] Bogart, 'The transport revolution', Table 13.1, p. 379.

were, in short, very substantial advances in road transport in the era when animal muscle remained the exclusive energy source. But these achievements were dwarfed by what followed when rail travel was available. Whereas the number of individual stage coach journeys was of the order of 10 million in the 1830s, passenger journeys by rail already numbered 30 million by 1845 and by 1870 had risen to 336 million.[40] It is indicative of the superiority of rail travel to older forms of transport for both passengers and goods that within a few decades of the creation of the rail network the turnpike trusts had disappeared and the canal system was in terminal decline. Many canals passed into the ownership of rail companies.

The railway was the most striking single example of the transformative effect of gaining freedom from the constraints on the availability of mechanical energy that had inhibited growth in all organic economies. The advent of steam power produced its most dramatic effect in the transport industry. Other industrial sectors had already gained partial freedom from the constraints limiting growth in organic economies. Their heat energy requirements had been increasingly met from burning coal rather than wood, but they too benefited greatly from the increasing use of steam engines to provide the mechanical power needed to drive machinery of all types. The energy released by burning coal could now be used with equal facility to provide both heat and mechanical energy. The progressive gains in the efficiency of the steam engine steadily reduced the advantage of a coalfield location. Less coal was needed to provide any given quantity of mechanical energy, while the development of railway networks also reduced the cost of transporting coal. The English economy ceased to be organic; an industrial revolution had been accomplished. The transport sector played a major role in facilitating the changes that occurred. Between 1700 and 1860 Bogart's estimates suggests that average annual rate of total factor productivity in all forms of overland transport was *c.* 2 per cent in freight haulage and *c.* 1 per cent in passenger movement. He also calculated that over the whole period from 1700 to 1860 the average annual level of total factor productivity (TFP) growth for freight transport was as high as that for cotton textiles between 1780 and 1860.[41]

It is worth adding that although the construction of a rail network symbolised the end of the dominance of human and animal muscle as the prime source of the mechanical energy used in the transport of both goods

40 Bagwell, *The transport revolution*, p. 43.

41 Bogart, 'The transport revolution', Table 13.5, p. 385. The TFP calculation is on the same page.

and people, it certainly did not lead to a decline in the employment of horses in the transport industry. On the contrary, the nineteenth century might be regarded as the golden age of the horse in both country and town. Both the construction of canals and railways produced an increase in the demand for horse transport. Before embarking on a canal boat or railway train it was frequently necessary to use coach or cart to move people or goods from their original point of departure to the canal or railway. Equally, arrival at a wharf, a railway station, or rail siding was frequently followed by resort to horse-drawn transport to reach the final destinations of the passengers or loads of goods. Between 1811 and 1901 Thompson estimated that the number of horses employed in transferring goods, and in pulling buses, trams, and stage and hackney carriages increased from 251,000 to 1,166,000 and that horses 'used in agriculture' rose from 800,000 to 1,089,000. There were also major increases in horses in private usage.[42] Greene, writing about horse usage in the United States, notes that the average density of horses in the forty-six largest cities in the country when urban horse usage peaked in 1900 was 426 horses per square mile. She estimates that in Philadelphia, where the density was *c*. 400 per square mile, there were more than 50,000 horses in the city as a whole.[43]

The pressure on horse supply had long been apparent at the local level. It was felt, for example, in the eighteenth century by coal mines when a mine was at some distance from the nearest navigable water. Langton, describing this problem in Lancashire, wrote: 'At Haydock in 1756, just before the Sankey was opened, coal sales stopped when ploughing began and in 1769, when the canal was presumably the colliery's main market, sales dipped during haytime as agriculture took its prime claim on the available horses.'[44] Horses had, of course, long been employed in large numbers in moving coal over short distances. It is said that 20,000 horses were employed in the Newcastle coal trade in 1696.[45] Musson noted that horses were still widely used as a source of power in the classic period of the industrial revolution: 'They had long worked drainage pumps and winding whims for mines and were commonly employed to drive grinding wheels in potteries and glassworks (flint-mills), in tanneries (bark-mills), in lime-kilns for grinding chalk and in brickworks for mixing clay (pug-mills); they also came to be used frequently to drive carding, scribbling and spinning machinery in early textile horse-mills.'[46] With the increasing

[42] Thompson, 'Nineteenth-century horse sense', Appendix, p. 80.
[43] Greene, *Horses at work*, pp. 171–2. [44] Langton, *Geographical change*, p. 174.
[45] Bagwell, *The transport revolution*, p. 89.
[46] Musson, *The growth of British industry*, p. 109.

employment of steam engines as the main source of mechanical energy in industry, horses became redundant in the settings that Musson listed but remained very widely employed in both personal and goods traffic until the era of the bus and the motor car. It is, of course, indicative of their importance that when they were in many contexts supplanted by steam engines, the capacity of the steam engine to perform work was still measured in 'horse-power'.

It is tempting to focus on the railway engine as the most conspicuous embodiment of success in enabling transport to gain access to the stock of energy present in fossil fuel rather than depending on the annual flow of energy provided from plant photosynthesis, but it should not be overlooked that steam engines were transforming movement over water as well as over land. During the seventeenth and eighteenth centuries there had been a massive increase in the use of wind power at sea. For example, the steady rise in coal shipments from the Tyne to the Thames involved both a big increase in the tonnage of vessels engaged in the trade and a marked increase in manpower productivity. Wilson noted that the collier fleet had grown from 400 small open boats in 1600 to 1,400 large square-rigged colliers in 1700, and that the average cargo had risen by a factor of four or five over the century. At the beginning of the century it took twenty men to handle a 100 ton vessel but by 1660 ten men could manage a 250 ton collier.[47] There was a massive expansion in the merchant fleet generally in the early modern period with the great increase in long-distance oceanic trade, which involved a steep rise in the use of energy derived from wind. Table 3.2 shows that the consumption of wind energy per head of population increased from 59 to 1,282 megajoules between 1561–70 and 1800–9 and that this was the only energy source, other than coal, which increased its share of overall energy consumption over the period, while admittedly remaining only a small element of the national total throughout (it increased from 0.3 to 2.4 per cent of the national total). But once coal could provide mechanical as well as heat energy, the steam engine gradually replaced sail to drive ships across the oceans. In the middle and later decades of the nineteenth century, paddle wheels and screw propellers replaced masts and sails. Transport costs for goods and passengers fell and trade volumes increased further. Changes in wind direction no longer made for uncertain journey times. The days were ended when London suffered and shivered because adverse winds prevented sailing vessels laden with Tyneside coal from entering the Thames.

[47] Wilson, *England's apprenticeship*, p. 45.

Conclusion

Levasseur, the French economist and demographer, writing in the 1880s and reviewing the change in energy availability in France over the previous forty years, found a vivid metaphor to express the scale of the change that had taken place. He noted that it was estimated that 1 steam horse power produced the equivalent of the energy output of 21 men. In 1840 French industry and commerce had had at its disposal the equivalent of just over 1 million men from this new energy source. They were he suggested 'true slaves, the most sober, docile, and tireless that could be imagined'. Less than half a century later in 1885–7 their number had risen to 98 million, 'two-and-a-half slaves for each inhabitant of France'.[48]

The timing of change in England differed from that in France, and the energy quantities involved were very different but Levasseur's flight of fancy is just as applicable to England as to France. Over a longer period the use of fossil fuel as the prime energy source also produced vast numbers of 'slaves' in England. The timing of the transfer to the new energy source varied across the industrial sectors, and because transport used only mechanical energy it could not move into the new era until fossil fuel could be used to provide mechanical as well as heat energy. Once this had happened the whole economy was freed from the constraints that had seemed insurmountable to the classical economists. The country was finally able to escape from the 'laborious poverty of early times'. The building of a rail network in England symbolised the fact that mechanical energy no less than heat energy could be secured as required from coal. The transport sector had joined other sectors of the economy in escaping from the restrictions of an organic economy.

[48] Levasseur, *La population française*, III, p. 74.

8 England in 1831

In 1831 England was entering the last phase of the long process of change that came to be termed an 'industrial revolution'. Following the invention and steady improvement of the efficiency of the steam engine, coal was able to transform the supply of mechanical energy as it had already transformed the supply of heat energy, but this second advance was in its early stages in 1831. Land transport, for example, still remained almost exclusively dependent on the traditional sources of energy in organic economies, but in 1830 the dawn of a new transport era was symbolised by the opening of the first commercially successful railway line between Liverpool and Manchester, providing both passenger and freight facilities, and depending exclusively on the traction power of the steam engine. The country was on the eve of the construction of a railway network on which the steam engine could transport both goods and passengers on a scale and at a speed that greatly exceeded anything previously achieved. In the following year the fourth national census was taken. It provides a revealing insight into several aspects of the English economy as it was about to enter the period when the supply of mechanical energy was transformed in a fashion that paralleled what had happened earlier with heat energy. During the middle decades of the nineteenth century, roughly between the 1830s and 1870s, the use of steam engines as the source of mechanical energy became general in all branches of industrial production.[1] With the supply of both energy types freed from dependence on plant photosynthesis, a prolonged period of exponential growth became possible – an industrial revolution.

[1] For instance, in the very rapidly expanding cotton industry, Deane in a later essay, basing her comment on von Tunzelman's exhaustive study of the use of steam power in the period down to 1860, remarked: 'It was not until the 1840s and 1850s, when the development and diffusion of high-pressure steam engines appreciably reduced the costs of using steam, that textile industries generally began to find it the most economical source of power': Deane, 'The British industrial revolution', p. 18.

The unusual character of the 1831 census

The 1831 census was the fourth and last census that Rickman directed. Like all earlier and later censuses it provided counts of the totals of men and women alive at the time but it had a number of features which distinguish it from other censuses, features which are at once frustrating in that there is often no directly comparable information in later censuses and illuminating in that it provides an insight into aspects of the structure of the economy which might otherwise have remained largely invisible.

Two of the features that set the 1831 census apart from other censuses were especially important in determining the type of description and analysis which is possible. The first is the fact that with very few exceptions the same information about occupation was provided about all the units for which data were collected, from the country as a whole at one extreme down to the individual parish or township at the other. This feature of the 1831 census makes it possible to undertake some types of analysis that are not possible with other censuses. It is normal in censuses to provide more detailed information for the larger units than for the smaller ones. If, for example, information is provided about the number of men and women employed in scores of different occupations at the level of the whole country, it is idle to expect comparably detailed information for very small units comprising only a few hundred people rather than many millions. Therefore, if the same level of detail about occupations is provided for all units from the smallest to the whole country, as was the case in 1831, only a strictly limited number of occupational categories can be included, but there are countervailing advantages of great value.

The second distinctive feature of the census, presumably reflecting a decision taken by Rickman personally, was the decision to distinguish between those industries and occupations providing goods and services to a local market and those serving a wider national or international market. That this was Rickman's intention is far from obvious at first glance. The totals in these two occupational groupings were displayed in adjacent columns headed respectively: 'Employed in manufacture or in making manufacturing machinery' and 'Employed in retail, trade, or in handicraft as masters or workmen'. In the section in the Preface that lists the questions addressed to the overseers in England and schoolmasters in Scotland who were responsible for collecting the information needed for the census, these two categories are more fully defined, though still without specifying explicitly what Rickman had in mind. The eighth and ninth questions addressed to enumerators ran as follows:

How many males upwards of twenty years old are employed in manufacture or in making manufacturing machinery: but not including labourers in warehouses, porters, messengers, etc.; who are to be included in a subsequent class?

and

How many males upwards of twenty years old are employed in retail trade or handicraft, as masters, shopmen, journeymen, apprentices, or in any capacity requiring skill in the business; but not including labourers, porters, messengers, etc., who are to be included in a subsequent class?[2]

[The subsequent class in question was the eleventh in which was to be included 'miners, fishermen, boatmen, excavators of canals, roadmakers, toll collectors, or labourers employed by persons of the three preceding classes'. The three preceding classes were the two just listed and the tenth class consisting of 'wholesale merchants, bankers, capitalists, professional persons, artists, architects, teachers, clerks, surveyors and educated men'.]

It should be noted that all the totals provided for each occupational category in the 1831 census relate to men aged 20 and over. There were no parallel occupational data for women, unlike the following census in 1841 which treated the sexes equally in this regard and included totals for men and women in employment who were under 20 as well as for those who were 20 years old and above.[3]

Neither in the titles of the 'manufacture' and 'retail trade or handicraft' occupational categories, nor in the phrasing of the questions for which the overseers were required to provide answers, was there any direct reference to the distinction between serving a local market and selling more widely, but there is much incidental comment in the body of the returns to show that the importance of this distinction was understood and observed at all levels of the census operation. It should first be noted that as a guide to enable the overseers to conform to Rickman's view of the character of 'retail trade or handicraft', a list was issued with each census schedule naming the one hundred occupations 'of the most usual denominations of retail, trade and handicraft'. Further, at the end of each county section in the census there is a detailed breakdown of the overall total of men employed in the retail trade and handicraft category, specifying the number of men in every occupation, even if the occupation gave employment to only one man. The lists do not include any textile employment, nor employment in the iron industry, in most types of metal

2 *1831 Census*, Enumeration Abstract, I, Preface, p. vi.

3 There were two minor exceptions to this summary, both relating to servants. Totals were recorded in the 1831 census for male servants under the age of 20 as well as for male servants aged 20 and above; and totals of female servants were given without division by age.

working, in pottery and earthenware, and in glass and glass products. Such employments were clearly presumed not to be serving purely local markets; they were manufactures not trades.[4]

The census also includes incidental comments which support the presumption that the enumerators were conscious of the distinction between those producing for a local market and those distributing their products more widely. In a footnote beneath the pages listing the numbers employed in each individual occupation in the retail trade and handicraft category in Northamptonshire there is a slightly shame-faced example of this: 'The shoemakers upwards of twenty years of age in the towns of Northampton, Wellingborough and Irthlingborough, in so far as they may appear to exceed the usual number of shoemakers in places of similar population, and therefore produce an article consumed elsewhere, may be deemed manufacturers –; but for the sake of conformity, they appear in the above specification of trades and handicrafts.'[5]

The attempt to divide production for a local market from that for national and international markets is, of course, somewhat artificial since many men did not fit simply into one of the two alternative categories, but it is clear that the attempt to conform to the distinction was in the forefront of the minds of those involved, and that Rickman believed that the distinction was observed. He remarked that:

> the technical difficulty of precise distinction between manufacture and the handicraft has produced many questions, to which answer has been made, that he who works for a consumer of an article in the place where both parties reside is to be deemed handicraft; he who works for an intermediate dealer (for what may be termed export) is a manufacturer. But this kind of doubt is too infrequent to produce any material uncertainty in the aggregate.[6]

Except for retail trade and handicraft, in the 'Summaries' printed at the end of each county section, there were simply totals for each of the occupational categories used in the census for the county as a whole and for each hundred in the county. There is, however, one exception to this generalisation. A footnote was provided to the column for manufacture for each county providing rough estimates of the totals of men employed in the main industries in the county. This was not provided for any of the other occupational categories. The footnote to the manufacture column

4 It was not, of course, intended that the returns should be restricted to the 100 occupations that were listed, and in the event a total of 426 different occupations figured in the returns made in this class recorded in the census.

5 *1831 Census*, Enumeration Abstract, I, pp. 446–7. Gatley drew attention to a similar problem with boatbuilders: Gatley, *An introduction to the 1831 census*, p. 8.

6 *1831 Census*, Comparative Account of the Population of Great Britain, pp. 6–7. I am grateful to Professor Eddy Higgs for drawing my attention to this passage.

in Gloucestershire illustrates the kind of information provided in these footnotes. Approximately 7 per cent of the workforce in Gloucestershire was in manufacture, a total of 5,992 men. The footnote to this total remarked that 'the manufactures of Gloucestershire are numerous and important' as indicated by the 4,500 men employed as clothiers. There were also 600 hatmakers, and 300 in stockingmaking and framemaking. Smaller approximate totals were provided for lacemaking, pinmaking, tinplate manufacture, and edge toolmaking. Reference is also made to glass bottle manufacture; the production of articles made of linen; and brass, iron, soap, and vinegar manufacture but without estimated totals of the number of men employed. In most cases the places that were prominent in the manufacture of the named product are mentioned.[7] The county manufacturing footnotes can therefore provide helpful information about the size and location of industry in a county, though only rough estimates of employment totals, and then only for the more important industries. The character of the industries listed in these county footnotes and the totals involved confirms the fact that they were not serving simply a local market.

There were a total of only six occupational categories for which returns of the totals of men aged 20 and above were required: agriculture; manufacture; retail trade and handicraft; finance and the professions; labourers and a rather motley collection of other occupations, most of which involved bodily labour; and servants. But there was also a seventh category, which again sets the 1831 census apart from most later censuses, providing totals for men aged 20 and over who were unable to work because of retirement, old age, disease, or bodily disablement. Later censuses, with the partial exception of the 1841 census, did not continue this practice.[8] In later censuses the recorded totals of men employed in a given occupation are misleadingly high since they include many men well above working age. For example, in 1851 the total of carpenters and joiners in England and Wales was recorded as 133,675 of whom 6,906 were aged 60–64; 4,418 aged 65–69; 3,235 aged 70–74; 2,019 aged 75–79; 788 aged 80–84; and 338 aged 85 and above.[9] If each successive total from 65–69 upwards is expressed as a ratio to the total in 60–64 the ratios are 64, 47, 29, 11, and 5. If the same exercise is carried out for the

[7] *1831 Census*, Enumeration Abstract, I, pp. 226–7.

[8] The 1841 census, while not explicitly following the practice of the 1831 census in identifying men who were unable to work by reason of age or infirmity, recorded what it termed the 'residue of population'. The size of this total, when expressed as a percentage of the total of men who had an occupation, is closely similar to the 1831 percentage of men who were aged or infirm, which suggests that the same convention was followed.

[9] *1851 Census*, Population tables, II, vol. 1, Table XXV.

male population in these age groups for England and Wales as a whole the ratios are 67, 50, 29, 14, and 6; a very similar set of ratios. There can be no doubt, therefore, that in the case of the 1851 census, including all those given an occupation who were aged 20 and over causes a substantial exaggeration of the number of men actively engaged in that occupation.[10]

Evidence of the success of Rickman's new categorisation of occupations

Table 8.1 summarises data on retail trade and handicraft for England as a whole and for the same four groups of counties as figured in Table 6.5. It both suggests that Rickman was successful in his innovatory attempt to distinguish the two types of employment that he was intent on examining, and provides a useful background to the later tables based on hundredal rather than county data.

Table 8.1 gives totals of employment in the ten occupations that employed the largest number of men in England as a whole in the retail trade and handicraft category in 1831. These are shown in descending order of size in the column headed 'England'. The largest occupation was shoemaking, which employed 109,390 men. Approximately 1 man in 30 in the entire English male workforce was a shoemaker. The four occupations employing the largest number of men (shoemakers, carpenters, tailors, and publicans) provided work for a total of 304,486 men, roughly matching the entire workforce engaged in manufacture (310,813). The top ten occupations accounted for more than half of the total employment in retail trade and handicraft as a whole (495,091 and 957,569).

In the columns for the four county groups in Table 8.1 the totals on each line are those relating to the list of occupations in the first column. In many cases, however the rank order by size differs from the national pattern. The number in the column to the left of each employment total shows the rank order of the occupation in that occupational group. For example, in the industrial group shoemakers and carpenters were first and second in size, conforming to the national pattern, and they therefore have 1 and 2 in this column, but tailors, the third largest occupation in the retail and handicraft group nationally, were outnumbered by publicans and therefore have 4 in the column showing rank order, while publicans,

[10] The same characteristic is evident in the 1861 and 1871 censuses. If in the age groups 65–74 and 75 and over the total of men who are allotted an occupation is expressed as a percentage of all males in the same age group, in 1861 the percentages are 95.4 and 88.7 per cent and in 1871 94.0 and 84.8 per cent.

Table 8.1 *The retail trade and handicraft category in the 1831 census (men aged 20 and above)*

		England (1)		**Industrial counties** (2)		**Metropolitan counties** (3)		**Agricultural counties** (4)		**Other counties** (5)
Shoe and boot maker or mender	**1**	**109,390**	1	24,857	1	19,205	1	33,939	1	31,389
Carpenter	**2**	**83,206**	2	15,170	2	16,289	2	27,390	2	24,357
Tailor, breeches maker	**3**	**59,828**	4	13,343	3	15,848	4	15,073	4	15,564
Publican, hotel or innkeeper, retailer of beer	**4**	**52,062**	3	14,018	6	6,383	3	16,244	5	15,417
Blacksmith, horseshoes	**5**	**44,889**	5	9,502	10	4,612	5	15,054	3	15,721
Mason or waller	**6**	**31,220**	7	8,904			9	8,505	6	11,807
Shopkeeper	**7**	**30,968**	6	8,954			8	9,023	8	8,817
Butcher, flesher	**8**	**30,854**	8	6,843	8	5,190	7	9,210	7	9,611
Bricklayer	**9**	**29,010**	9	5,741	5	6,555	6	9,598	9	7,116
Baker, gingerbread, fancy	**10**	**23,664**			4	6,766	10	7,950	10	6,370
Grocer, greengrocer	**11**				9	5,010				
Cabinet maker	**12**		10	4,465	7	5,656				
Total of the above		**495,091**		**111,797**		**91,514**		**151,986**		**146,169**
Total as percentage of males 20 plus		**15.6**		**13.8**		**19.1**		**15.8**		**15.8**
Retail and handicraft		**957,569**		**225,667**		**207,359**		**259,597**		**264,905**
Retail and handicraft as percentage of males 20 plus		**30.2**		**27.9**		**43.4**		**27.0**		**28.6**
Males 20 plus		**3,173,074**		**808,574**		**478,086**		**959,896**		**926,518**

Notes: The county groups. *Industrial*: Cheshire, Lancashire, Staffordshire, Warwickshire, Yorkshire, W.R. *Metropolitan*: Middlesex, Surrey. *Agricultural*: Bedfordshire, Berkshire, Buckinghamshire, Cambridgeshire, Devon, Dorset, Essex, Herefordshire, Hertfordshire, Huntingdonshire, Lincolnshire, Norfolk, Northamptonshire, Oxfordshire, Rutland, Suffolk, Sussex, Westmorland, Wiltshire, Yorkshire, N.R. *Other*: Cornwall, Cumberland, Derbyshire, Durham, Gloucestershire, Hampshire, Kent, Leicestershire, Northumberland, Nottinghamshire, Shropshire, Somerset, Worcestershire, Yorkshire, E.R.
Source: *1831 Census*, Enumeration Abstract, I and II.

the fourth largest occupation nationally, have 3 in the rank order column. It is notable that in two of the four groups, 'agricultural counties' and 'other counties', the ten largest occupations in the retail trade and handicraft sector were the same as in England as a whole, though with some differences in rank order. In the industrial counties group cabinetmakers fell outside the national top ten list. In the metropolitan counties there were two similar cases, cabinet makers and grocers, the seventh and ninth largest of the top ten occupations in that group. Their inclusion was at the expense of masons and shopkeepers, as is clear from the blank spaces in the column. Grocer and greengrocer (a combined category) and cabinet maker were the eleventh and twelfth largest occupations nationally, as indicated in the appropriate column. The absence of mason from the top ten list for the metropolitan counties is partially accounted for by the fact that bricklayer was the fifth largest occupation, compared to ninth in the list for England. Mason and bricklayer were both engaged in meeting the need for accommodation, which was universal. If one was unusually prominent the other occupation would necessarily be under-represented.

The fact that the occupations employing the largest number of men in the retail trade and handicraft category were closely similar in all the county groups, and that they catered for basic human needs which were everywhere the same and that could for the most part only be satisfied locally – the supply of food, drink, clothing and footwear, and accommodation – lends further support to the supposition that inclusion in the retail trade and handicraft category was restricted to employment in occupations serving a local market and that the overseers were successful in discriminating between those employed in serving a local market and others. This conclusion is reinforced by the information in the two rows in the lower half of the table showing the percentages of the male workforce employed in the top ten trades and in the retail trade and handicraft sector as a whole. The overall percentages in retail trade and handicraft in the industrial, agricultural, and other counties groups are closely similar to those for England as a whole; and the same is also true of the percentages in the top ten occupations. Once again, this conforms to the assumption that they were meeting local needs. The overall employment structures in the three groups differed substantially, of course, but the imperative requirement to make provision locally for a range of basic human needs produced similarity in the scale of employment in the occupations devoted to meeting these needs, when expressed as a fraction of the total labour force. The metropolitan counties group, effectively London, has higher percentages on both measures, as is to be expected given the fact that the population was largely urban. This point is discussed more fully in the next section, in which hundredal data are used.

Occupational analysis of the English hundreds

County data can bring to light much else of interest about England in 1831. For example, it is immediately clear from the county summaries that employment in manufacture, that is in industries that served national and international markets, was very heavily concentrated. Nation-wide manufacture employed 310,813 men aged 20 and above. The five industrial counties (Warwickshire, Staffordshire, Cheshire, Lancashire, and the West Riding) accounted for 70 per cent of this total (217,621). In the remaining 36 counties only 93,192 men were similarly employed. In Lancashire and the West Riding alone there were 172,186 men engaged in manufacture (97,517 and 74,669, respectively), approaching twice the number in the thirty-six agricultural, metropolitan, and other counties.

Counties, however, were themselves composed of widely differing local economies. Even in Lancashire and the West Riding there were large areas that were dominantly agricultural. In 1831 England was divided into 41 counties, 641 hundreds, and 14,350 parishes, chapelries, and townships. Much of interest is obscured or blurred unless description and analysis are based on a smaller unit than the county. The hundred is helpful in this regard. The next section is devoted to the description of some features of the English economy in 1831 that can be depicted more effectively using hundredal data, though far more could be covered using such data than is attempted here. The value of what follows may lie as much in what it suggests for future work as in what there is space to cover immediately. Ideally, of course, it would be desirable to bring description and analysis down to the level of the parish and township, since the same level of detail is available for them as for the larger units, but to do so is beyond the scope of this chapter.

Tables 8.2 and 8.3 should be read in conjunction with each other. The first is primarily given over to absolute totals; the second converts these totals into percentage distributions. Each table is divided between groups of three types of hundred: those where either agriculture, manufacture, or retail trade and handicraft were especially prominent. Each occupational group consists of the hundreds that were most heavily engaged in that branch of the economy. There were 339 agricultural hundreds; 24 manufacturing hundeds; and 90 retail trade and handicraft hundreds. The minimum percentage required for inclusion in each group varied considerably: in the agricultural group it was 55 per cent; in the retail trade and handicraft group 45 per cent; in the industrial group 30 per cent. As well

Table 8.2 *Occupational specialisation in English hundreds in 1831: employment totals*

(1) Per cent of labour force	(2) No. of hundreds	(3) Acreage (000)	(4) Population	(5) Males 20 plus	(6) Active males	(7) Agriculture	(8) Manufacture	(9) Retail trade, handicraft	(10) Finance and the professions	(11) Labourers not in agriculture	(12) Servants	(13) Other males
						Agricultural hundreds						
In agricultural employment												
70 plus	103	4,253	765,495	192,822	183,504	135,447	293	34,676	3,752	6,419	2,917	9,318
60–9	164	7,961	1,682,303	421,657	398,159	259,146	3,013	91,610	11,160	25,301	7,929	23,498
55–9	72	4,742	1,079,939	267,025	251,158	144,256	4,515	66,606	8,808	21,917	5,056	15,867
Total	**339**	**16,956**	**3,527,737**	**881,504**	**832,821**	**538,849**	**7,821**	**192,892**	**23,720**	**53,637**	**15,902**	**48,683**
Per cent of national total	52.9	53.9	27.1	27.7	27.9	55.3	2.5	20.1	13.2	10.9	22.5	25.8
						Manufacturing hundreds						
In manufacturing employment												
40 plus	12	862	1,231,528	284,715	274,483	29,686	128,173	59,915	9,830	44,733	2,146	10,232
30–39	12	618	794,786	194,019	185,806	19,943	65,686	59,704	8,872	29,924	1,677	8,213
Total	**24**	**1,480**	**2,026,314**	**478,734**	**460,289**	**49,629**	**193,859**	**119,619**	**18,702**	**74,657**	**3,823**	**18,445**
Per cent of national total	3.7	4.7	15.6	15.1	15.4	5.1	62.4	12.5	10.4	15.1	5.4	9.8

						Retail trade and handicraft hundreds						
In retail, handicraft employment												
60 plus	19	35	319,495	77,543	71,114	2,315	1,223	45,197	7,098	13,319	1,962	6,429
50–9	52	186	1,090,722	257,919	228,346	11,681	8,275	126,836	24,217	51,015	6,322	29,573
45–9	19	108	1,425,912	368,571	349,729	6,839	16,063	167,802	47,640	93,187	18,198	18,842
Total	**90**	**329**	**2,836,129**	**704,033**	**649,189**	**20,835**	**25,561**	**339,835**	**78,955**	**157,521**	**26,482**	**56,844**
Per cent of national total	14.0	1.0	21.8	22.2	21.8	2.1	8.2	35.5	44.1	31.9	37.7	30.2
3 groups above combined	453	18,765	8,390,180	2,064,271	1,942,299	609,313	227,241	652,346	121,377	285,815	46,207	121,972
Per cent of national total	70.7	59.7	64.6	65.1	65.1	62.6	73.1	68.1	67.7	57.9	65.7	64.8
Rest of England	188	12,686	4,598,042	1,108,779	1,042,382	363,793	83,572	305,223	57,801	207,912	24,081	66,397
Per cent of national total	29.3	40.3	35.4	34.9	34.9	37.4	26.9	31.9	32.3	42.1	34.3	35.2
England	641	31,450	12,988,222	3,173,050	2,984,681	973,106	310,813	957,569	179,178	493,727	70,288	188,369

Notes: The census definitions of the occupational groups in columns (7) to (13) were as follows (excluding the introductory phrase in each definition that stated that it referred to men 'upwards of twenty years old'):

Agriculture: 'employed in agriculture, including graziers, cowkeepers, shepherds, and other farm servants, gardeners (not taxed or taxable as male servants), and nurserymen.'

Manufacture: 'employed in manufacture or in making manufacturing machinery; but not including labourers in warehouses, porters, messengers, etc.'

Retail trade and handicraft: 'employed in retail trade or in handicraft, as masters, shopmen, journeymen, apprentices, or in any capacity requiring skill in the business; but not including labourers, porters, messengers, etc.'

Capitalists: 'wholesale merchants, bankers, capitalists, professional persons, artists, architects, teachers, clerks, surveyors, and other educated men.'

Labourers not in agriculture: 'miners, fishermen, boatmen, excavators of canals, roadmakers, toll collectors, or labourers employed by persons of the three preceding classes, or otherwise employed in any kind of bodily labour, excepting in agriculture.'

Other males: 'retired tradesmen, superannuated labourers, and males diseased or disabled in body or mind.'

Male servants: 'household servants – also waiters and attendants at inns.'

Source: *1831 Census*, Enumeration Abstract, I and II.

as showing totals of employment in each group as a whole, the groups are subdivided to show the relative importance of hundreds that specialised particularly strongly in the occupation which defined membership of the group in question and those which were somewhat less specialised. For example, there were 103 hundreds in which more than 70 per cent of the workforce was engaged in agriculture, a high degree of specialisation (in the most 'agricultural' of the hundreds, Hormer in Berkshire, the percentage reached 84.9 per cent). The next subgroup, consisting of 164 hundreds in which 60–9 per cent of the labour force worked on the land, was much larger than the first subgroup in both population and in the size of the agricultural workforce. The third subgroup consists of 72 hundreds in which 55–9 per cent of the workforce was in agriculture. The headings of each column are largely self-explanatory. The occupational categories in columns (7) to (12) in Table 8.2 are those employed by the census. To provide extra clarity the census definitions of their content are set out in the notes to Table 8.2. The totals of 'Active males' in column (6) were obtained by deducting the 'Other males' from the total of males aged 20 or more in column (5). As already noted, 'Other males' were those men who were not in the active workforce because they were elderly, retired, crippled, or otherwise severely handicapped and unable to work. All the percentages of the size of the labour force in each occupational group in Table 8.3 are the result of relating the totals in that group in Table 8.2 to the total of *active* males in the table. It should be noted that in the 1831 census many boroughs and towns were treated as if they were hundreds and are included in the summary table at the end of each county. The same details are given for them as for conventional hundreds.[11]

With two exceptions all the 453 hundreds which qualified for inclusion in one of the three groups and for which details are provided in Table 8.2 qualified only for the group in which they were included. The two exceptions were Norwich city and the town of Kendal in Westmorland, which each qualified both for the retail trade and handicraft and for the manufacturing groups. In both cases, the percentage of the labour force employed in retail trade and handicraft was much larger than the percentage in manufacturing, and these two towns were included in the former group.

[11] In the Preface to the census in reporting this practice the following statement was made. 'For this there is a better reason than at first sight appears: corporate towns and some other places have a peculiar jurisdiction and really are not in any hundred. – Hence the strict propriety of placing many cities and towns at the end of the respective counties: and for the sake of comparison, other towns, which have risen in importance since the disuse of granting charters and immunities, are placed with the rest.' *1831 Census*, Enumeration Abstract, I, Preface, p. xvi.

Table 8.3 *Occupational specialisation in English hundreds in 1831: percentages*

Per cent of labour force (1)	No. of hundreds (2)	Per cent in agriculture (3)	Per cent in manufacture (4)	Per cent in retail trade, handicraft (5)	Per cent finance and the professions (6)	Per cent labourers not in agriculture (7)	Per cent servants (8)	Agricultural employment per 100 acres (9)	M/F ratio (10)	Average acreage (11)	Average population (12)
				Agricultural hundreds							
In agricultural employment											
70 plus	103	73.8	0.2	18.9	2.0	3.5	1.6	3.2	102.4	41,287	7,432
60–9	164	65.1	0.8	23.0	2.8	6.4	2.0	3.3	100.7	48,543	10,258
55–9	72	57.4	1.8	26.5	3.5	8.7	2.0	3.0	98.7	65,586	14,999
Total	**339**	**64.7**	**0.9**	**23.2**	**2.8**	**6.4**	**1.9**	**3.2**	**100.4**	**50,017**	**10,406**
				Manufacturing hundreds							
In manufacturing employment											
40 plus	12	10.8	46.7	21.8	3.6	16.3	0.8	3.4	97.7	71,836	102,627
30–9	12	10.7	35.4	32.1	4.8	16.1	0.9	3.2	95.0	51,514	66,232
Total	**24**	**10.8**	**42.1**	**26.0**	**4.1**	**16.2**	**0.8**	**3.4**	**96.6**	**61,675**	**84,430**
				Retail trade, handicraft hundreds							
In retail, handicraft employment											
60 plus	19	3.3	1.7	63.6	10.0	18.7	2.8	6.7	86.5	1,831	16,816
50–9	52	5.1	3.6	55.5	10.6	22.3	2.8	6.3	86.5	3,581	20,975
45–9	19	2.0	4.6	48.0	13.6	26.6	5.2	6.3	85.8	5,670	75,048
Total	**90**	**3.2**	**3.9**	**52.3**	**12.2**	**24.3**	**4.1**	**6.3**	**86.1**	**3,653**	**31,513**
3 groups above	**453**	**31.4**	**11.7**	**33.6**	**6.2**	**14.7**	**2.4**	**3.2**	**94.5**	**41,423**	**18,521**
Rest of England	**188**	**34.9**	**8.0**	**29.3**	**5.5**	**19.9**	**2.3**	**2.9**	**95.4**	**67,480**	**24,458**
England	**641**	**32.6**	**10.4**	**32.1**	**6.0**	**16.5**	**2.4**	**3.1**	**94.8**	**49,065**	**20,262**

Source: As for Table 8.2.

A preliminary point to note in reviewing Tables 8.2 and 8.3 is that the average area of the 'hundreds' in the retail trade and handicraft group was far smaller than in the agricultural and manufacturing groups (column (11), Table 8.3). They were towns that, because of the conventions observed by the census, were treated as hundreds. The average size of the hundreds in the retail trade and handicraft group was 3,700 acres, compared to 50,000 acres in the agricultural group and 61,700 acres in the manufacturing group. This necessarily limited the scale of agricultural employment in the retail group, though many of the towns included parishes that were far from 'urban' in character. For example, the town of Colchester consisted of sixteen parishes and covered 11,264 acres. Four of the parishes, Bere Church, Greenstead, Lexden, and St Michael Mile End, covered 8,136 acres, 72 per cent of the total area, and of their combined labour force of 611 men, 358, 59 per cent of the total, were agriculturally employed, a high enough percentage, if they had been a small separate hundred, to have caused them to be included in the agricultural group of hundreds. And there were many other towns within whose boundaries there were parishes that were rural rather than urban. At first sight, it might appear paradoxical that agricultural employment per 100 acres was twice as high in the retail group as in the other two groups where the density of agricultural employment mirrored the national average. The reason may probably be found in the definition of the composition of 'agricultural employment', which included gardeners and nurserymen, who were frequently located close to urban markets, and who made a living from much smaller plots than farmers.

The retail trade and handicraft group was also very different from the other groups in that the male/female ratio was much lower than elsewhere. There were only 86.1 men per 100 women in this group. The 1831 census records the number of men aged 20 and over as well as the overall total of males but for women only provides overall totals. This prevents examination of the sex ratio by age group. An unusually low ratio is usually the product of differential migration and it might therefore be expected that the sex ratio for adults would be more unbalanced than for the population as a whole. Although this cannot to demonstrated directly from the 1831 census data, its existence and probable scale can be determined by turning to the 1841 census which records totals of those under 20 and 20 and over for both men and women. The information was provided only for counties and for a selection of cities and towns within each county. The ninety 'hundreds' in the retail trade and handicraft group in Table 8.3 were all towns, and for sixty-four of them the 1841 census provides the sex ratio breakdown required. The overall sex ratio for the sixty-four towns in 1841 was 88.8. For the same towns in 1831 it had been 86.2. Because the required age split was provided for both sexes in 1841, it reveals that the sex ratio for those under 20 was 95.0 and for adults above 20 it was 84.7. The ratio for adults was 4.1 lower than for the population as a whole. Assuming a similar difference ten years earlier the adult sex ratio in 1831 was approximately 82 men per 100 women. There was, of course, substantial variation according to the nature of the town's economy. In centres which provided accommodation and entertainment for the wealthy the ratio was much lower than in urban settings generally. In Bath and Brighton, for example, the overall ratios in 1841 were 70.6 and 76.1, and ratio for those aged 20 and over 61.1 and 67.7.

Low urban sex ratios were not a recent phenomenon. They were pronounced already in the later seventeenth century. They are sometimes thought to have been chiefly the product of the demand for female servants in urban settings. Souden, however, taking advantage of the excellent quality of many returns made under the Marriage Duty Act of 1695, showed that even if the sex ratio is calculated after removing servants from the totals the ratio was only slightly altered.[12] Other employment opportunities for women existed in 'washing, sewing, spinning, charring, lodgings keeping', and Souden added that 'Expansion of the tertiary sector is very likely to produce widening scope for the employment of females'.[13] Dividing his material into three classes, villages, small towns, and large towns, he showed clear evidence that the sex ratio declined as the population of the unit increased, from 100 or higher in villages to the low 80s in large towns.[14] Urban growth and rising urban incomes had broadened the demand for services other than living-in service, and this increased female employment.

The percentages in each column of Table 8.3 contain much of interest. Between them the three groups in Table 8.2 (agriculture, manufacture, and retail and handicraft) employed 65.1 per cent of the active male labour force in England (column (5)). On the line recording for each successive column how large a percentage of the national total lay in the three groups combined, there are entries for the six occupational groups used in the census (columns (7)–(12)). Four of the six percentages in these columns are in the mid 60s. The two exceptions are in 'manufacture' and 'labourers not in agriculture' (columns (8) and (11)), whose respective percentages are 73.1 and 57.9. In the case of 'manufacture' this underlines the exceptional extent to which this activity was concentrated in a remarkably small group of hundreds: 62.4 per cent of the manufacturing labour force lived in a mere 24 hundreds, a higher

[12] Souden, 'Migrants and the population structure', Table 18, p. 153.
[13] *Ibid.*, pp. 159–60. [14] *Ibid.*, Table 17, p. 150.

Table 8.4 *The 24 industrial hundreds*

County	**Hundred**	**County**	**Hundred**
Cheshire	Macclesfield	Staffordshire	Newcastle-under-Lyme Borough
Cheshire	Macclesfield Town	Staffordshire	Stafford Borough
Cumberland	Carlisle City	Warwickshire	Coventry City
Lancashire	Blackburn	Warwickshire	Coventry County
Lancashire	Leyland	Wiltshire	Melksham
Lancashire	Manchester	Wiltshire	Westbury
Lancashire	Salford	Worcestershire	Kidderminster Town
Lancashire	Wigan Borough	Yorkshire, W.R.	Agbrigg
Leicestershire	Guthlaxton	Yorkshire, W.R.	Leeds Town
Leicestershire	Leicester Borough	Yorkshire, W.R.	Morley
Nottinghamshire	Broxtow	Yorkshire, W.R.	Staincross
Nottinghamshire	Nottingham Town	Yorkshire, W.R.	Strafforth & Tickhill

Source: As for Table 8.2.

percentage than the comparable figure for the agriculture group, where 55.3 per cent of the national total of men working on the land were spread through 339 hundreds. The contrast vividly underlines the difference between *areal* production and *punctiform* production, symbolising one of the key differences between production in organic and industrialised societies.

Since almost two-thirds of the men engaged in manufacture were living in only 24 hundreds, it is instructive to consider how the hundreds in question were distributed. They are listed in Table 8.4. Sixteen of the hundreds are in the five counties that constitute the industrial group: Cheshire, Lancashire, Staffordshire, Warwickshire, and the West Riding. This conforms to expectation, but there are also eight hundreds in other counties – Cumberland, Leicestershire, Nottinghamshire, Wiltshire, and Worcestershire – and it is of interest to note the character of the employment which caused them to be among the hundreds most heavily committed to manufacture. In Carlisle in Cumberland cotton was the largest employer, with smaller totals in the manufacture of calico, ginghams, and woollens. In Leicestershire both in Leicester Borough and in Guthlaxton hundred (notably in Wigston Magna) stocking manufacture was the main employer. In Nottinghamshire stockings and lace were prominent in providing manufacturing employment in the town of Nottingham and in the hundred of Broxtow, notably in Mansfield and in Sutton-in-Ashfield. In Wiltshire the making of fine broadcloth and kerseymere was a major source of employment in both the hundred of Melksham, principally in the parish of Trowbridge, and in the hundred of Westbury, especially in the chapelry of Ditton. Carpet manufacture employed more than 2,000 men in the Worcestershire town of Kidderminster. The total of manufacturing employment in these eight hundreds was comparatively modest. In the 24 hundreds as a whole there were 193,859 men engaged in manufacture; in the eight hundreds 22,589, or 11.7 per cent of the total. Their presence among the industrial group of hundreds is, however, a reminder that long-established types of manufacture in textiles, clothing and fabrics, often using manufacturing methods which were little changed from previous centuries, were still affording substantial and strongly localised employment during the industrial revolution.

The decline of proto-industry

The fact that employment in manufacture was so heavily concentrated in a small number of hundreds and that 'manufacture' included all forms of textile manufacture suggests that if 'proto-industrial' activity had once been widespread and had provided employment for large numbers in making woollens and other textile goods, this was no longer the case in 1831. Employment in proto-industry was primarily in textiles and served widespread rather than local markets. At its peak, large numbers are thought to have been employed, often in rural areas. Little if any trace of this pattern is apparent in the1831 census.

Employment in textiles was always allocated to 'manufacture' in this census. In Table 8.3 the column headed 'per cent in manufacture' shows that manufacture was almost completely absent from the agricultural hundreds. Less than 1 per cent of the labour force, a total of 7,821 men, were engaged in manufacturing employment in these hundreds. A majority of the individual agricultural hundreds recorded zeros under this heading. In the retail and handicraft group, manufacturing employment, though only a minor element in the workforce as a whole, was slightly less restricted, with 3.9 per cent of workforce in this category.

In the retail trade and handicraft column (column (5)) the percentages for the agricultural and manufacturing hundreds reinforce one of the findings embodied in Table 8.1. In these two groups, to cater for the basic needs of their populations, about a quarter of the workforce was engaged in the kinds of activity represented in the ten large trades and the many smaller retail and handicraft occupations represented in the table. The comparable percentage in the retail trade and handicraft group was about double the percentage in the other two groups. These 'hundreds' were towns in which a relatively high percentage in retail trade and handicraft was to be expected.

The fact that the percentage of 'labourers not in agriculture' in the three main groups combined (agriculture, manufacture, and retail trade and handicraft) was relatively low at 57.9 per cent (Table 8.2, column (11)) means, of course, that the percentage in the rest of England was unusually high. The definition of the composition of this category, containing a very mixed assemblage of disparate occupational groups (see the note to Table 8.2), shows that coalminers were allocated to it. Coalmining employment was spatially concentrated and, since output per head showed little change over the nineteenth century, and coal output was rising strongly, the number of coalminers was increasing in parallel. For example, between 1831 and 1841 the number in England rose by 38 per cent, from 75,600 to 104,580.[15] Coal mining hundreds were very likely to fall into the 'Rest of England' category because in mining communities miners formed a large proportion of the active labour force. This may explain in part the strong showing of the 'Rest of England' in the 'labourers not in agriculture' column.

The 'finance and the professions' column (6) shows that 'merchants, bankers, capitalists, professional persons, artists, architects, teachers, clerks, surveyors, and other educated men' figured more prominently in the retail and handicraft group than elsewhere. They lived in towns, though no doubt their services were provided to the inhabitants of rural as well as urban areas. Such employment was rare in the agricultural hundreds and only slightly more prominent in the manufacturing hundreds. A broadly similar picture is visible in the employment of servants. They figured more prominently in the urban setting which characterised the retail trade and handicraft group, but the relative position of the other two groups was reversed. Servants were more widely employed in agricultural hundreds than in manufacturing hundreds where they formed less than 1 per cent of the workforce.

A final point to note in reviewing the data in Tables 8.2 and 8.3 is the very wide contrast between the average populations of hundreds in the three groups (Table 8.3). The average population of the 24 manufacturing hundreds was more than eight times larger than the average population of the 339 agricultural hundreds, a contrast so marked that the total population of the latter group was only 74 per cent greater than that of the former group. Since the average acreages of the two groups differed only modestly, the average population per 100 acres in the agricultural hundreds was 21 persons; the comparable figure for the industrial hundreds was 137 persons. Some of the industrial hundreds were small in area, but others were very large. The point is illustrated by the case

[15] Church, *The history of the British coal industry*, III, Table 3.1, p. 189.

of Macclesfield town and Macclesfield hundred. Both were included in the twenty-four manufacturing hundreds, with 41.3 and 34.4 per cent of their workforces, respectively, in manufacture, but whereas the first had an area of 2,410 acres the second occupied 148,030 acres. Large tracts of many of the industrial hundreds consisted of agricultural land. It would be possible, of course, to repeat this exercise using the parish rather than the hundred as the unit of measurement, and this would result in a much more accurate measure of the contrast between the three groups. This problem is far less serious with the retail and handicraft hundreds. Town and borough boundaries sometimes included considerable tracts of agricultural land, as was noted earlier in relation to Colchester,[16] but the far smaller average acreage of the retail and handicraft hundreds and the consequently far higher average population density (875 persons per 100 acres) results in a more realistic figure.

Concluding comment

In systems of classifying occupations which are based on the materials being manufactured – metals, wood products, textiles, leather goods, etc. – both enterprises operating on a large scale and selling to a widespread market and those serving a local market will be recorded under the same head. The same is true of many other occupational classifications, such as that using the primary, secondary, and tertiary distinction. The unusual system used in the 1831 census makes possible a valuable insight into one aspect of the changes involved in the industrial revolution.

In 1831 the twenty occupations employing the largest number of men in the retail trade and handicraft sector were the twelve that appear in Table 8.1 plus the following:

Wheelwright; miller; sawyer; carrier, carter; linen draper, haberdasher; glazier, plumber; huckster, hawker, pedlar, duffer; coach owner, driver, grooms, etc.

Between them, these twenty occupations alone employed 631,749 men, 20 per cent of the national labour force, and more than double the labour force in the whole manufacturing sector. The great bulk of the work carried out and business transacted by these men, and indeed by the men in the long list of occupations in the same sector employing fewer men than those in the top twenty, was performed locally. The retail trade and handicraft sector as a whole employed 957,569 men, and constituted 32.1 per cent of the total male labour force; manufacture employed only

16 See p. 164.

310,813 men or 10.4 per cent of the national total. The retail trade and handicraft sector was almost exactly the same size as the agricultural sector, which employed 32.6 per cent of the male labour force.

If it is fair to discount in general the possibility of substantial rises in individual productivity in small producers serving a local market; if bricklayers, blacksmiths, wheelwrights, and sawyers in the early decades of the nineteenth century were producing each year much the same quantity as their predecessors a century earlier, then the rise in individual productivity in industry as a whole would appear to have been due disproportionately to the relatively small labour force in the manufacturing sector who were working in larger enterprises serving national and international markets which offered greater scope for increasing individual productivity. In this sector, technical changes in production methods were common, often within workshops and factories that were making extensive use of the abundant energy that could be derived from fossil fuel. Lancashire cotton mills and Black Country foundries attracted much contemporary attention, and for good reason. But the proportion of the labour force engaged in such enterprises remained quite modest even at a date that would at one time have been regarded as marking the approaching completion of the industrial revolution. The same point intrigued McCloskey at an even later date. She wrote 'In 1861, at the end of the customary dating of the industrial revolution, only about 30 per cent of the labour force was employed in activities which had been radically transformed in technique since 1780 – Britain was not in 1861 a cotton mill'.

To the degree that the assumptions in the last paragraph are justified, they also underline the importance of the striking achievements of English agriculture over the period between the reigns of Elizabeth I and Victoria. All estimates of the rise in agricultural productivity per head are subject to significant margins of error, but that the rise was substantial is beyond doubt. Between 1600 and 1831 the population more than tripled from 4.2 million to 13.3 million. The proportion of the adult male workforce employed in agriculture more than halved from *c.* 70 per cent to 33 per cent. Ignoring complications such as the changing proportion of men of working age and changing sex ratios, this suggests that the agricultural workforce increased by about 50 per cent at most.[17] Once more simplifying, assume further that food consumption per head did not change over the period.[18] If so, the population increase suggests that

[17] See pp. 53–5 for a fuller discussion of productivity change in the agricultural workforce.

[18] It may well have risen. Inferences drawn from the trend of real wages in individual occupations may well fail to capture the trend in average family disposable incomes generally. The evidence collected by Muldrew suggests both that English agricultural labourers were substantially better fed than their equivalents on the continent and that

food consumption was 3.2 times larger at the end of the period than it had been at the beginning. However, in 1831 net imports of temperate foodstuffs provided perhaps a tenth of overall national consumption, so that home production accounted for only nine-tenths of the total.[19]

The implication of these estimates and assumptions is that output per head in agriculture doubled, a conclusion that is reinforced if the non-food production of agriculture is taken into account. The reduction in the proportion of arable land which was fallowed, and the expansion in both the range and volume of fodder crops, suggest both that farm animal numbers rose and that the animals matured more rapidly. Crafts' estimates of the size of the main British industries suggest that in 1801 the woollen and leather industries were the two largest measured by value added.[20] Both had expanded during the eighteenth century, and in both cases the raw material was mainly home produced. The output of wool rose substantially. Deane and Cole estimated that the output of the British woollen industry grew by *c.* 150 per cent in the eighteenth century, but imports of wool remained marginal.[21] Leather production probably rose by about two-thirds over the century, and again the hides were chiefly locally produced.[22] Fuller and more accurate information about the relevant parameters might well suggest a significantly larger increase in output per head in agriculture than suggested in the last paragraph.

What is indisputable is that the large reduction in the proportion of the labour force working on the land made possible a big increase in output from the secondary sector. Even if it was the case that the productivity of those engaged in what was termed in the 1831 census 'retail trade and handicraft' was increasing only slowly, the total output of the sector would be more than parallel with the rising number of those employed in it, to the overall benefit of the economy; and in large measure this would be due indirectly to the transformation in agriculture which released so many men from work on the land.

Because of the unusual character of the information in the 1831 census many aspects of the English economy are revealed which may prove a spur to future research. A notable example, considered briefly above,

between the early seventeenth and late eighteenth centuries their standard of living improved significantly: Muldrew, *Food, energy*, pp. 319–24.

19 See pp. 58–60 for a discussion of the complexities of estimating the net import percentage of temperate foodstuffs.

20 Crafts, *British economic growth*, Table 2.3, p. 22.

21 Deane and Cole, *British economic growth*, p. 61; Holderness, 'Prices, productivity, and output', p. 174.

22 Wrigley, *Energy and the English industrial revolution*, p. 87. Clarkson estimated that by the end of the eighteenth century approximately a fifth of the raw material used by the leather industry was imported: Clarkson, 'The manufacture of leather', p. 471.

was the virtual disappearance of proto-industrial activity from most of the country. Because all forms of textile manufacture were excluded from the retail trade and handicraft category, the bulk of proto-industrial employment would have been included under manufacture in 1831, and since there were so many hundreds in which there were either no men at all employed in manufacture, or the number was trivially small, it seems clear that employment in proto-industry had become insignificant. Taking advantage of the fact that this issue can be pursued down to the level of the individual parish or township, it should prove possible to investigate this issue more extensively in future.

More generally, the distinction between 'retail trade and handicraft' and 'manufacture', specified as the distinction between serving a purely local market and producing for sale to more distant markets, makes the 1831 census an informative source for establishing the scale and nature of the changes which had taken place in England over the two preceding centuries. An industrial revolution was still not fully accomplished, since the mechanical energy used in transport still came primarily from animal muscle rather than steam, but the scale of the contrast between England in 1831 and England at the beginning of the seventeenth century was vast.

9 The completion of the industrial revolution

During three centuries from the mid sixteenth to the mid nineteenth century the English economy changed from being a laggard compared to the most advanced economies on the continent to being the leader of the pack by a substantial margin. During the second half of the nineteenth century, however, the wheel turned again, and England ceased to be either a laggard or a leader. Consideration both of the circumstances that gave rise to the divergence between English experience and that of the bulk of the continent, and to the subsequent convergence which took place, is the subject matter of this chapter. Reviewing these changes also throws light on the timing of the completion of an industrial revolution in England. That its completion promoted further change whose character severely affected the regions of England closely identified with the initial accomplishment of an industrial revolution is briefly discussed in the final section of the chapter.

The concomitants of urban growth

A first topic to consider in relation to the period of divergence between England and her continental neighbours is the extent of the contrast in the scale and character of urban growth in the seventeenth and eighteenth centuries. It was both striking and significant. It offers an opportunity to explore the developments which gradually weakened the constraints on growth which were universal in organic economies, strengthening the prospect of securing prolonged growth and a sustained rise in the real incomes of the mass of the population: in short, of bringing about an industrial revolution. It also exemplifies the scale of the difference between changes on either side of the Channel, and suggests why comparable development was inhibited on the continent.

An increase in the proportion of the population living in towns is a reliable measure of the level of productivity in the agricultural sector (assuming, for convenience, that urban food supplies are locally produced rather than imported). Since those living both in towns and in the countryside must be fed, only if productivity is high enough to produce an increasing surplus above local rural requirements is urban growth possible. Bairoch concluded that in early modern Europe the maximum proportion of the population that could live in towns with 5,000 or more inhabitants was 13–15 per cent.[1] Where grain yields are low, *c.* 10–12 bushels per acre; a substantial proportion of arable land is fallowed each year; a proportion of each year's crop must be set aside as seed (which will involve a significantly higher proportion of the crop if the gross yield is modest); and draught animals must be fed, the scope for urban growth will be limited. Equally, if the urban percentage is low, traffic volumes are modest, roads are poor, and much of the rural population is living at a distance from the nearest town, the incentive to increase output will be slight in the absence of an accessible market. Local self-sufficiency will be the norm. Poor harvests may result in serious want and raised mortality. For the bulk of the population there will be little opportunity to acquire goods other than the four essentials of life: food, fuel, clothing, and shelter.

In continental Europe in the early modern period this situation prevailed over vast tracts of territory. It was not universal. The Netherlands was as much an outlier as England and from a much earlier date. Generally, however, a limited and largely unchanging level of urbanisation was the norm. In de Vries' study of urban growth in Europe, the urban percentage for the continent as a whole rises modestly from 10.8 to 13.0 per cent between 1600 and 1800, but if the European percentage is recalculated after excluding England and the Netherlands there is virtual stagnation in the urban percentage over the two centuries.[2] Though these two countries differed considerably, excluding them both makes sense in identifying the broader European pattern. Table 9.1 shows a rise from 10.7 to 11.6 per cent over the two centuries. The small apparent rise may well cloak a small 'real' fall in the continental urban percentage. For example, a European town with 4,000 inhabitants in 1600 whose population rose in parallel with the overall increase in the population of Europe over the next two centuries would have had more than 6,000 inhabitants in 1800 and would enter the calculation of urban totals if the lower limit for inclusion were 5,000 inhabitants. Its share of total population,

[1] See p. 56.

[2] Although the Netherlands and England both became much more heavily urbanised than the rest of Europe, they differed markedly from each other. The Dutch urban percentage for towns with 5,000 of more inhabitants had already reached 24 per cent in 1600 and rose further to 34 per cent in 1700, but then declined modestly to 29 per cent in 1800, whereas the comparable English percentages were 8, 16, and 27: Table 4.2, p. 49, and De Vries, *European urbanization*, Table 3.7, p. 39. Though these two countries differed considerably, excluding them both in Table 9.1 makes sense in identifying the broader European pattern.

Table 9.1 *Urban population totals and percentages (towns with 5,000 or more inhabitants)*

	1600	1700	1800
	Europe		
Population (million)	78.0	81.4	122.7
Urban population (million)	8.42	9.69	15.95
Per cent urban	**10.8**	**11.9**	**13.0**
Europe minus England and the Netherlands			
Population (million)	72.3	74.3	111.9
Urban population (million)	7.71	8.19	12.95
Per cent urban	**10.7**	**11.0**	**11.6**

Note: The urban totals for Europe were calculated by multiplying the European population totals for towns with 10,000 or more inhabitants at each date by the ratios suggested by de Vries to produce estimated totals for all towns with 5,000 or more inhabitants. De Vries, *European urbanization*, Table 3.2, p. 30 and 'Patterns of urbanization', Table 3.6, p. 88.
Sources: European and Dutch population totals: De Vries, *European urbanization*, Table 3.6, pp. 36–7; Dutch urban totals: *ibid.*, Appendix 1, pp. 770–8; English population and urban totals: Table 4.1.

however, would remain unchanged. Arguably, there is no best solution to this problem in measuring and interpreting urban percentages. With different purposes in mind different measures may be preferred, but there may be as much reason to regard the urban percentage in most of Europe as declining slightly between 1600 and 1800 as to view it as rising slightly.

The rapidly rising percentage of the population living in towns in England brought changes which enhanced the prospects of further growth, while at the same time further increasing the contrast between the experience of England and that of her neighbours. A major rise in the urban percentage necessarily meant a matching rise in the proportion of the workforce engaged in secondary and tertiary occupations, and a change in the structure of aggregate demand as an increasing share of incomes was spent on industrial products and services. The change in the structure of aggregate demand was strengthened by the fact that on average urban incomes were higher than rural incomes.[3] Living in towns also meant that its inhabitants secured a higher proportion of their wants through market exchange. The attitudinal changes that de Vries described when defining the nature of an industrious revolution, for example, came more naturally to the inhabitants of the town than

[3] Notably in London; see p. 91.

to those in the countryside. As Corfield noted: 'the growth of towns in eighteenth-century England encouraged a gradual shift away from the backward-sloping supply curve for labour that was often found in pre-industrial economies, where the hours worked varied inversely with real wages.'[4] She also suggested ways in which life in the countryside was increasingly changed through contact with urban life. Referring to the early decades of the eighteenth century, she wrote: 'Fashions spread from London to the provincial towns. And with the growing volume of routine shopping, the practice was gradually introduced (initially by the Quakers) of quoting fixed prices for all comers – instead of the slower and traditional bargaining and higgling over every sale.'[5]

Focusing initially on urban growth is convenient because it illustrates the way in which both progress within the context of an organic economy and a new element which foreshadowed more radical change were needed to make possible the transition from an organic economy to one in which an industrial revolution could occur. In England there was a major advance in the productivity of the land and of the agricultural labour force which allowed agricultural output to keep pace with urban food needs, and fuel needs were met increasingly from burning coal which also reduced the urban 'footprint'. In the past, prolonged urban growth had always produced negative feedback as the increasing urban demand gave rise to a decline in the productivity per head of the agricultural labour force, while at the same time the extent of forest cover was put under pressure both because of the increased demand for fuel wood and because the arable acreage was increased by taking previously forested land into cultivation.

The ceiling to urban growth to which Bairoch drew attention resulted from the inability of traditional European agriculture to respond to a rise in the proportion of the population living in towns by raising output sufficiently to cover a higher level of urbanisation. As a result, at some point the quantity of food available for urban consumption would tend to fall rather than rise. Yet in the absence of rising urban demand to provide an incentive for agricultural improvement, rural areas had little alternative to local self-sufficiency. Clay was pointing to the situation which resulted when he noted: 'English society in the early sixteenth century consisted largely of peasant farmers, whose propensity to consume goods manufactured outside their own homesteads was low, and who any way received little of their income in the form of money.'[6] If, however, an increased urban demand had the effect of bringing about an increase in

[4] Corfield, *The impact of English towns*, p. 84. [5] *Ibid.*, p. 19.
[6] Clay, *Economic expansion and social change*, II, p. 4.

the productivity of the workforce because agriculture moved away from a focus on local self-sufficiency to a market-orientated specialisation on the crops and livestock to which the locality was best suited, then negative feedback would be replaced by positive feedback, and a period of urban growth could occur without painful consequences. This was clearly evident in early modern England, especially in the period following the restoration of the monarchy after the civil war. Wilson perhaps had this in mind when remarking rather grandly that: 'The Restoration has a better claim than most other dates to be regarded as the economic exit from medievalism.'[7]

The success that England enjoyed in securing rapid urban growth, however, cannot be attributed solely to the sustained rise in agricultural productivity both per acre and per man. It was also greatly aided by the fact that town dwellers consumed no more of one vital 'crop' in 1800 than they had in 1600 in spite of an eight-fold rise in the urban population. Substituting coal for the product of coppiced woodland for domestic heating was almost as important as the rise in food grain yields in limiting the spread of the urban 'footprint' (Table 4.4). Whether urban growth would have ground to a halt without the joint benefit derived from rising agricultural productivity and the substitution of coal for firewood, though probable, must remain uncertain, but it is clear that absence of comparable change on the continent set limits to urban growth.

Energy supply

The second major reason setting England apart from the continent in the seventeenth and eighteenth centuries lay in a change in the sources from which heat energy was secured. The country moved from an almost exclusive dependence on a *flow* to gaining access to a *stock* of heat energy, from wood to coal, from the product of the annual round of plant photosynthesis to its accumulation over a geological age. The change was gradual and did not involve major innovations, or the widespread exercise of inventive genius. It might be said to have taken place naturally, a response to an age-old supply problem by the far greater use of a raw material which had long been used in relatively small quantities and whose production could be expanded at will. Coal had been a significant

[7] Wilson, *England's apprenticeship*, p. 236. In reference to the situation which had previously existed, he wrote: 'Almost everywhere, and especially in the remoter parts of the countryside, there survived the remains of an ancient and unspecialized economy in which many people lived a more or less self-sufficient life, growing a substantial proportion of the food they ate or drank, making their own clothes and footwear, cutting their own fuel, boiling their own soap.' *Ibid.*, p. 67.

source of heat energy in local areas for many centuries not only in England but in many other countries, notably in Sung China in the eleventh and twelfth centuries, where its use was industrial as well as domestic.[8]

The growing problem of using wood as a fuel in much of England in the sixteenth century is reflected in the statement made by James Roberts in a 1527 lawsuit in Lancashire; no-one, he said, had 'any need in time past to get coals for their fuel, by reason they had plenty of wood from the forests and turves in their liberty, which now be decayed and restrained from them'.[9] Coal's cheapness as a source of heat compared with burning wood became increasingly attractive in England in the sixteenth century as pressure on the available supply of fuel wood rose, especially if the quantity of heat required was large and concentrated at a notional point, as in a city. London faced a serious problem in meeting domestic fuel needs in the middle of the sixteenth century. Until *c.* 1550 wood and coal prices in the capital expressed in grams of silver per BTU were closely similar, but wood prices then increased sharply and during the rest of the century were between two and three times as high as the price of coal which fell moderately as the cost of shipping coal from Tyneside declined.[10] By 1600, coal had become the predominant domestic fuel source in London and also fed the brickworks and other industrial plants along the Thames. London is, of course, 300 miles distant from the north-east coalfields. Such a distance would normally have ruled out substituting coal for wood as supplies of wood became less accessible and more expensive but, in spite of its distance from the Thames, the low cost of transport by sailing vessels meant that 'sea-coal' from Tyneside became a cheaper alternative to fuel wood. In England generally coal gradually became the fuel of choice wherever the cost of transporting it from the nearest mine was sufficiently low to keep its price below that of fuel wood.

A convenient way of illustrating the progress of coal at the expense of wood as a source of heat energy is to consider the implication of the change in the consumption of coal per head of population in England over the early modern period. At the beginning of the period the figure was modest. In the 1560s the annual average consumption of coal per head was only 0.06 tons, approximately a hundredweight; in 1700 the average had risen to 0.47 tons; in 1750 to 0.73 tons; and in 1800 to

8 Jones, *Growth recurring*, pp. 75–6; Golas, '*Mining*', pp. 186–201; Debeir *et al.*, *In the servitude of power*, pp. 55–6. It seems clear that much of the large increase in coal production in China was linked to iron smelting. Iron production in China *c.* 1100 was as large as that for Europe as a whole *c.* 1700.

9 Swain, *Industry before the industrial revolution*, p. 163.

10 Allen, *The British industrial revolution*, Figure 4.3, p. 87.

1.29 tons.[11] An increasing proportion of the fuel consumed was used in industry rather than in the home. Hatcher suggested that: 'By the close of the seventeenth century industry and manufacturing may well have devoured more than a third of all the fuel burnt in Britain.'[12] In 1800, Flinn estimated that industry consumed about 59 per cent of total coal output.[13] On these estimates domestic fuel consumption per head in 1700 would have been approximately 0.31 tons per head per annum and in 1800 0.53 tons. The comparable figures for industrial consumption per head show a much sharper increase: from 0.16 tons in 1700 to 0.76 tons in 1800. Flinn considered that by the early nineteenth century most urban and many rural dwellers used coal for domestic heating and cooking, implying that a substantial majority of the population was burning coal rather than wood at home.[14] This squares well with the estimate of an average of 0.53 tons of coal per annum used for domestic heating and cooking in 1800. Average dry wood consumption for these purposes in past centuries has been estimated as 1.3 tons per head.[15] A ton of coal provides approximately as much heat as 2 tons of well-dried wood. Consuming just over than half a ton of coal should therefore provide as much heat as 1 ton of dry wood, a statistic that suggests that perhaps three-quarters or more of English houses were heated by coal rather than wood *c.* 1800.

English coal output continued to rise much faster than the population in the first half of the nineteenth century. In the early 1850s it had risen to 2.89 tons per head, more than twice the figure in 1800.[16] By this date, coal was almost universally the fuel used for domestic heating and cooking. If this is assumed to represent 0.65 tons per person per annum, it would suggest that the comparable figure for industrial usage tripled from 0.76 to 2.24 tons over the same period, an indication of the extent of the benefit arising from escaping from the energy constraints which inhibited growth in organic economies.[17]

[11] The coal production totals on which these figures were based may be found in Table 3.1, p. 32.

[12] Hatcher, *The history of the British coal industry*, I, pp. 419–20.

[13] Flinn, *The history of the British coal industry*, II, Table 7.13, pp. 252–3. The figure of 59 per cent was arrived at after deducting exports, waste coal, and coal consumed by collieries. There is, however, a slight uncertainty about the calculation since the total of individual items is 500,000 tons larger than the overall total shown at the foot of the column. I have assumed that the individual totals are correct and the overall total is an aberration.

[14] Flinn, *The history of the British coal industry*, II, p. 231.

[15] See p. 17. [16] See Table 3.1, p. 32.

[17] It is of interest that Jevons, writing in the 1860s, estimated domestic coal consumption per head to be about 0.75 tons: Jevons, *The coal question*, p. 138.

The estimate that coal consumption per head of population for industrial production rose almost five-fold during the eighteenth century and then tripled in the first half of the nineteenth century suggests how greatly industry benefited from being freed from dependence on wood fuel for heat energy. The bulk of the overall increase in coal consumption occurred because of rising industrial output. From the mid eighteenth century onwards this was due in large measure to the massive increase in coal consumption by the iron industry. In general, the substitution of coal for wood as a source of heat energy did not give rise to serious technical difficulties. Where the flame was separated from the object to be heated, as for example in heating a dye vat or in boiling a kettle, few problems were encountered in making the switch from wood to coal. Where no sheet of metal separated the flame from the object to be heated, as in smelting ores, chemical interactions could present difficulties, but in general these were overcome fairly quickly by a process of trial and error. There was a notable exception to this generalisation in the smelting of iron. It took several decades to overcome the problems which were experienced, but once this had been achieved iron production rose very rapidly and the industry became a major consumer of coal. In 1750 in Britain as a whole the iron industry consumed only 0.4 per cent of the national output of coal, rising to 16.8 per cent in 1805, 18.5 per cent in 1830, and 24.9 per cent in 1855. By the last date the consumption of coal by the iron industry alone comfortably exceeded the total of domestic consumption.[18]

The changes taking place in both food and fuel supply tended to foster other developments which benefited the economy. This was notably true in relation to transport. In organic economies the land was the source of almost all food and raw materials. As a result, production of these commodities was spread relatively evenly but thinly over huge tracts of land. This in turn meant that transport networks were dendritic – large mileages with a low volume of movement and therefore little incentive to invest in improving road surfaces. In the sixteenth century most country 'highways' were effectively 'bridle paths'.[19] Net yields per acre, however, rose substantially in the next two centuries and the volume of traffic in agricultural products generated from each square mile of farmland

[18] The consumption of coal in the production of iron rose from 21,000 tons in 1750 to 2,565,000 tons in 1805; 5,634,000 tons in 1830; and 19,000,000 tons in 1855. British coal output at the four dates was 5,230,000 tons, 15,045,000 tons, 30,500,000 tons, and 76,400,000 tons, respectively: Flinn, *The history of the British coal industry*, II, Table 1.2, p. 26, and Table 7.11, p. 242; Church, *The history of the British coal industry*, III, Table 1.3, p. 19. The second coal output total is for 1800 rather than 1805.

[19] Jackman, *The development of transportation in modern England*, p. 43.

rose proportionately. The quantity of agricultural produce moving on the road network was also multiplied by the rising urban population. Town dwellers in 1800 were seven times as numerous as they had been in 1600, implying a commensurate rise in the transfer of agricultural produce from the country to the town. Road surfaces were subject to much greater wear and tear, but the turnpike trust proved a reasonably effective institution for creating and maintaining better road surfaces. Large numbers of trusts were created during the eighteenth and early nineteenth centuries. As might be expected given the huge food requirements of the capital, turnpiking was initially more common in the vicinity of London than elsewhere. As the eighteenth century progressed, however, urban growth was especially rapid in the industrial counties in the north and the midlands and the turnpike network came to reflect this. Connection to the turnpike road system often also led to improvements in the urban environment and to facilities created for public benefit. Sweet, when discussing improvement acts for paving and lighting, noted that: 'In general, improvement almost always followed upon connecting the town to the turnpike road system.'[20]

The steady increase in the volume of coal output also created a powerful incentive for a change in transport facilities. Because the price of coal rose steeply when it was conveyed from the mine by horse and cart, the market accessible from the pithead was initially limited to a distance of about 10 miles surrounding the pit. However, because pitheads are fixed points often producing in large volumes and the demand for coal in towns and industrial centres, which may also be regarded as fixed points, was rising throughout the early modern period, there were an increasing number of routes between coalmines and their markets over which potential traffic volumes justified substantial investment in transport improvement. Hence the attraction of building canals linking production point and potential market.[21] Coal was cheap at the pithead and its final cost to the consumer therefore depended largely upon the cost per ton-mile of conveying it from A to B. Water transport was several times cheaper per ton-mile than carriage by horse and cart, and was cheapest of all at sea. Where sea transport linked coal mines to a suitable urban market, for example, access to cheap heat was readily possible even when the

[20] Sweet, *The English town*, p. 45.

[21] Although rural traffic volumes did not normally justify canal construction, agriculture nevertheless benefited substantially from access to a canal. In his discussion of this question, Duckham stated: 'In vast areas of England canal trade consisted very largely of an interchange of agricultural and industrial commodities.' He noted further that even commercially unsuccessful canals could bring great benefit to local agriculture: Duckham, 'Canals and river navigations', p. 134.

coal mine was a long way from its market, as households in London had found to their advantage already in the later sixteenth century. England benefited from being part of an island and having a very long coastline.

England and the continent

Rapid urban growth and the increasing use of coal as a source of heat energy in England produced a growing contrast between the English economy and the economies of most continental countries in the quarter-millennium between the reigns of Elizabeth I and Victoria. There had been a surge in agricultural productivity achieved without any substantial increase in the size of the agricultural labour force and a decreasing dependence on wood as the source of heat energy. Much higher net output per acre in arable agriculture, accompanied by a comparable rise in output per head in the agricultural labour force, combined with the substitution of coal for wood as a fuel, enabled England to avoid the fate which the classical economists regarded as inevitable following a period of economic growth.

With England making notable progress as a result of these developments in her economy, it might appear natural to expect other countries to follow suit, especially as the rapid expansion of England's economy, among other things, greatly increased her international standing and military power. This might have been expected to provoke attempts to emulate the English example. Yet in a lengthy period ending only in the mid nineteenth century, there were few if any comparable developments on the continent except in the Netherlands where peat had earlier produced changes similar to those taking place later in England with the increasing volume of coal use. Why was this the case? And why during the later nineteenth century, instead of there being a further widening of the English advantage, did it rapidly disappear?

Both the extent of the lead over other countries that England had obtained by the mid nineteenth century, and the speed with which it disappeared, can be illustrated by comparing England and three continental countries which rapidly closed the gap in the latter half of the century. In the reign of Elizabeth I England had been among the least developed and sophisticated of the European economies. By the start of Victoria's reign it had become, briefly, the most advanced of any economy world-wide. The Great Exhibition of 1851 symbolised this fact. At the time of the Exhibition the scale of output achieved in the industries that were particularly associated with the industrial revolution in Britain far exceeded that of other European countries. To illustrate this point, consider the output volumes in three of the most rapidly growing industries

Table 9.2 *The continent and the UK: change over half a century*

	Population (million) c.1850	Coal production (million tonnes) 1850–4	Pig iron production (000 tonnes) 1850–4	Cotton consumption (000 tonnes) 1850–4
Belgium, France, Germany	73.6	18.7	1,044	104
United Kingdom	20.8	58.0	2,716	320

Source: Mitchell, *European historical statistics*, Tables B1, pp. 29–37; E2, pp. 381–91; E8, pp. 412–19; E14, pp. 448–54.

of the industrial revolution era: coal, pig iron, and cotton. The statistics are striking. Table 9.2 shows that at the time of the Great Exhibition the United Kingdom's output in these three industries was in each case much larger than the comparable combined totals for the three countries whose economies were probably the most advanced on the continent: Belgium, France, and Germany. Production totals in all three industries were roughly three times as large in the United Kingdom as in the three continental countries combined. The disparity is far greater if expressed in output per head of population, since the UK population of 20.8 million was well under a third of the combined population of the three continental countries. The continental and British levels of output expressed per head of population were as follows, with the figure for the three continental countries listed first and the British figure second: coal, 0.25 tons, 2.79 tons; pig iron 14.2 kg, 131 kg; cotton consumption 1.4 kg, 15.4 kg. Expressed in this fashion the British output levels were roughly ten times those in the three continental countries used for comparison.

Although the Great Exhibition of 1851 took place when the relative advantage of the UK economy was marked, one aspect of its success already hinted at the brevity of the leadership of the British economy and presents a clue to the explanation both of the earlier development of a wide difference between the British economy and most continental economies and to its subsequent rapid disappearance.

The Liverpool and North Western Railway brought more than three-quarters of a million people from the north of England to the Exhibition on cheap excursion tickets and as many as 5 million people in all are thought to have made use of rail travel to attend.[22] In the two decades since the opening of the first railway that foreshadowed the future norm

[22] Bagwell, *The transport revolution*, pp. 127–8.

of railway operation, the Liverpool and Manchester Railway, there had been a striking expansion in the rail network in Britain. At the time of the Great Exhibition in 1851 there were 6,266 miles of railway in use. So powerful was the attraction of rail construction, however, that in this regard the continent was not far behind. In 1851, the length of railway open in Belgium, France, and Germany combined matched the UK figure almost exactly, standing at 6,372 miles. By 1875, the German total alone exceeded the UK figure, and ten years later the same was true of France.[23] After the mid century, industrial advance was a shared phenomenon in much of western Europe: the United Kingdom had ceased to be a pace-setter.

Even in the case of the three measures of production used in Table 9.2 by the early years of the twentieth century the British advantage had been greatly reduced. In the quinquennium 1905–9, for example, although the United Kingdom was still mining more coal than the three continental countries combined (the average annual totals were Belgium, France, and Germany 201 million tonnes; United Kingdom 260 million tonnes), in pig iron production the three continental countries had substantially outstripped the United Kingdom (15.4 million tonnes compared to 9.9 million tonnes). When 'new' industries arose Britain and the near continent were broadly on a par in the last years of Victoria's reign. Steel production on a large scale, for example, began only in the 1870s; compared with pig iron production it was a 'new' industry. Trends in production per head were similar on either side of the Channel. In 1905–9 the combined output of the three continental countries averaged 14.9 million tonnes compared to a UK figure of 6.1 million tonnes. Re-expressed per head of population there was little difference between the figures for the continental trio and the United Kingdom: 0.133 tonnes and 0.169 tonnes, respectively.[24] Steel production might be said to symbolise the disappearance of the advantage enjoyed half a century earlier by the 'first mover'. It is an interesting irony that the period in the later nineteenth century when the term 'industrial revolution' first became a commonplace was also the period when the wide gap which had opened up between the United Kingdom and other countries was rapidly closing.

The structure of the economies of all industrialising countries was much changed between the mid nineteenth century and the outbreak of the First World War by the advent of several new sectors of growing

[23] Mitchell, *European historical statistics*, Table G1, pp. 609–16.

[24] The note to Table 9.2 provides source details for population totals and coal and pig iron production. Steel production totals are taken from Mitchell, *European historical statistics*, Table E9, pp. 420–5.

importance. Coal remained the most important source of energy throughout the period, but its dominance was slowly reduced from the 1880s onwards by the increasing scale of oil and natural gas production. The development of the internal combustion engine led eventually to changes in transport facilities as fundamental as those that were brought about by the construction of rail networks, as cars, buses, and lorries transformed road transport. By the last decades of the nineteenth century the generation of electricity, its distribution through electricity grids, and its flexibility compared with power supplied from steam engines, was beginning to influence industrial location. Chemical industries grew rapidly in relative importance, and a list of this sort could be greatly extended. These were developments common to all the major economies of western Europe, and occurred at much the same time in all of them.

Although this very brief survey of the United Kingdom and the continent before and after the mid nineteenth century falls well short of what would be possible if the available information were more fully exploited and represented, it is clear that England remained the 'lead' country in the first half of the century, but that this ceased to be the case during its later decades. In attempting to account both for the long period when the gap grew larger and for its subsequent rapid disappearance, attention to energy supply reveals features that are suggestive. The key to explaining both the long period of increasing British advantage and its swift disappearance in the later decades of Victoria's reign may lie in the distinction between the differing histories of heat energy supply and mechanical energy supply.

Heat energy and mechanical energy

The steadily increasing production and consumption of coal in England from Tudor times onwards transformed the scale of heat energy which was available to meet both domestic and industrial needs, but it made no difference to the production of mechanical energy, which continued to be secured principally from human and animal muscle. When heat energy was first converted into mechanical energy to assist in the drainage of water from coalmines, the steam engines which were used were so inefficient in making the conversion that their use was confined almost exclusively to mine drainage. Their use involved burning large quantities of coal, and the price of coal rose steeply away from the minehead if conveyed overland, thus severely restricting the employment of steam engines. It was not until Watt's ingenuity had both greatly increased the efficiency of energy capture in the steam engine and made it possible to convert the movement of the piston into rotary motion that the burning of coal could begin to overcome the restrictions on the general availability of mechanical energy which had inhibited economic growth in all organic economies. In this process, the most significant single advance came with the railway engine. Unlike other industrial sectors, the transport sector had been exclusively dependent on mechanical rather than heat energy. In the other industrial sectors, which had already benefited markedly from burning coal to secure a much greater supply of heat energy, the increasing use of steam engines as a source of mechanical energy did not result in such a dramatic change as happened in the transport sector. Nevertheless, in the factory no less than on the railway the steam engine became the dominant source of mechanical energy in the middle decades of the nineteenth century. All forms of material production were able to embark on sustained, exponential growth.

It is not surprising that, in the centuries when coal was increasingly used in England to meet heat energy needs but when heat energy could not be converted economically into mechanical energy, what was happening in England was not paralleled on the continent. Coal was available locally in relatively few locations and the high cost of transporting it over land ruled out its use over great swathes of territory. The proportion of the land surface which was forested was generally higher and often much higher than in England. Fuel wood was therefore normally cheaper than coal as a source of heat energy on the continent. The good fortune which London enjoyed in being able to take advantage of the low cost of sea transport to obtain coal dug from pits which were also close to the sea but hundreds of miles distant from the capital was almost unique. In the bulk of continental Europe, as long as coal was the source only of heat energy, there was seldom any advantage in switching from wood to coal.

There were exceptions to this generalisation. Countries with little forest and where the bulk of the national territory was close to the coastline found advantages in importing coal. This was true of the Netherlands even in the seventeenth century,[25] and became true also of Denmark in the eighteenth century. The Danish example clarifies the circumstances in which a continental country might benefit from paralleling developments in England.

During the seventeenth and eighteenth centuries Denmark had experienced severe problems because the area of woodland had shrunk and heat energy was consequently in very short supply. The problems that this engendered led to desperate solutions. It became necessary in some extreme cases, for example, to use manure, cattle fodder, and straw as

[25] See p. 37.

fuel, which in turn tended to reduce soil fertility, producing what Kjaergaard termed a 'headlong course towards an ecological catastrophe'.[26] He noted that on the island of Fanø the inhabitants 'gave up heating completely and lit fires only to cook food'.[27] The Danish government attempted to arrest and reverse the trend towards environmental degradation but it was 'Thanks to coal and iron, the energy and raw materials crisis was overcome, and the sword of Damocles hanging over Denmark and the whole of Europe was removed'.[28] Though denuded of forest, Denmark was fortunate in that she was able to obtain coal cheaply from Newcastle much as London had long done. A ship leaving the Tyne laden with coal had a slightly longer journey to make when sailing to Denmark than if it sailed to the Thames estuary, but the difference was not substantial. Moreover, given the size and shape of Denmark's national territory, the distance from the coast to an inland market was always short. Already by the later eighteenth century coal was the normal domestic fuel in Copenhagen and was a major source of heat energy in its industry.[29] In the following century Denmark also provides a striking example of the way energy derived from coal could not only greatly change the nature of industrial production but might also produce radical change in agriculture.

Henriques and Sharp have recently described the close connection between cheap coal and the exceptional success of pastoral agriculture in Denmark. They note that it is sometimes assumed that, since the country did not have the benefit of local coal measures to provide cheap energy, in achieving economic growth 'it might appear that an increase of energy consumption is not needed, since specialization in non-energy intensive activities, perhaps agriculture, can solve the energy trap'.[30] They show that this assumption may sometimes be mistaken. 'Danish agriculture was actually a large consumer of coal, which was used to fuel the machinery of the cooperative creameries and to a lesser extent the related slaughterhouses for the pork industry. Indeed, this use of coal was not simply incidental to the development. The automatic cream separator, a centrifuge, relied almost exclusively on steam power from coal to function.'[31] In the later nineteenth century Danish agriculture, largely as a result of using energy derived from coal on a large scale, was able to increase its share of the market for butter in Britain from 15 to 40 per cent and of the market for bacon from 1 to 50 per cent. Henriques and Sharp noted that workers in the creameries were

[26] Kjaergaard, *The Danish revolution*, pp. 23, 33.
[27] *Ibid.*, p. 96. [28] *Ibid.*, p. 128. [29] *Ibid.*, pp. 120–1.
[30] Henriques and Sharp, *The Danish agricultural revolution*, p. 5. [31] *Ibid.*, pp. 5–6.

exceptionally heavy users of coal-derived energy. Their consumption of energy per worker was higher than in any other Danish industry, and aggregate energy consumption for these purposes was substantial. The creameries and slaughterhouses were consuming 16 per cent of the total of energy consumed in Danish industry as a whole. [32] Denmark became a relatively heavy user of energy; measured by consumption per head of population in the later nineteenth century it was at a similar level to that of France and the Netherlands and twice that of the southern European countries. In the late 1880s the proportion of national energy consumption derived from coal rose above 50 per cent.[33]

Relative cost meant that most continental countries continued to rely upon wood to generate heat energy during the centuries when in England coal largely replaced wood for this purpose. Wood had always been and long remained the prime source of heat energy on the continent both for domestic use and in industry. The radical improvements in the efficiency with which steam engines converted heat energy into mechanical energy which took place during the eighteenth and early nineteenth centuries, combined with the invention of a method for harnessing this energy to provide rotary motion, made it feasible with few exceptions to replace muscle energy by steam energy wherever mechanical energy was needed. Whereas the English example was not quickly matched on the continent when coal began to be used on a large scale in England to supply *heat energy*, there was much less time lag in adoption when the energy in coal was harnessed to provide *mechanical energy*. Coal was not cheaper than wood as a fuel in most of the continent in the early modern period, but with the advent of efficient steam engines its advantage over muscle as a source of mechanical energy for the transport both of goods and people was immediately evident, and the construction of rail networks made coal far more widely available at a lowered cost. As a result, coal rapidly replaced wood as the prime source of heat energy in continental countries, so that by the early years of the twentieth century the sources of both types of energy were increasingly met in the same way throughout Europe. By reducing the cost of coal at a distance from the coalfield, the construction of railway networks expedited change.

The transport sector therefore played a key role in initiating the convergence that took place. Since this sector depended exclusively on mechanical energy, it had long remained 'organic' in character both in England and on the continent. In 1800 just as in 1600, animal muscle was the dominant source of the energy consumed; hence the exceptional significance of the opening of the Liverpool and Manchester Railway in 1830.

[32] *Ibid.*, p. 11 and Table 1, p. 13. [33] *Ibid.*, Figure 3, p. 10.

It was very quickly apparent that traditional transport systems for conveying passengers and goods, whether by road or canal, were unable to compete with the railway in point-to-point transport. Movement by rail was far faster than by post coach or canal barge. Moreover, a train could transport far greater volumes of both passengers and goods than its predecessors on roads or canal. And, in addition, costs per ton-mile and per passenger-mile were normally lower by rail than by road or canal.

The railway engine and the construction of a rail network meant that transport no less than other sectors of the economy gained the benefit of an order of magnitude increase in the quantity of energy which could be employed. Whereas in the supply of heat energy whether or not coal rather than wood was the cheaper source varied in different parts of Europe, the advantage of the railway engine travelling over a rail network over the horse-powered alternatives was indisputable for long-distance transport. In relation to the provision of heat energy, areas with abundant forest cover had no reason to use coal in preference to wood as long as the transport system remained exclusively 'organic' in nature. When heat energy was converted into mechanical energy in the steam engine and used to drive the wheels of railway engines on iron tracks, a form of transport existed whose superiority over the existing alternatives was evident, leading to the rapid construction of rail networks throughout continental Europe.

Rail transport greatly reduced the cost of coal at a distance from the coalfield. The resulting rise in the demand for coal produced major increases in the volume of coal output. This change, however, proved a mixed blessing for the coalfields themselves since, when the price of coal no longer increased so markedly with the distance from the pit-head, the advantage of a coalfield location for industrial production was reduced. This effect was magnified as the efficiency of steam engines continued to rise so that a smaller tonnage of coal was needed to generate a given power output. The effect of this change is visible in the patterns revealed in Table 3.4, which showed the changing patterns of the fastest-growing English counties in the decades between 1801 and 1911. Over the period as a whole Durham was the fastest-growing county, and this was directly a function of the very rapid continued expansion of coalmining. It grew fast because output per head in coalmining was not rising and employment therefore rose in parallel with output. But the story was very different in counties that were major centres of industry as well as producing coal. In the earliest subperiod in Table 3.4, 1801–21, Lancashire was the fastest-growing county and it was still third fastest in 1851–81, but in the final subperiod 1881–1911 there was a notable change; Lancashire ranked only fifteenth among the forty-one English counties.

Lancashire's experience was typical of the leading English industrial counties in the period that culminated with the completion of an industrial revolution.

Similar changes took place on the continent due to the changing balance of locational advantage. A striking example of this occurred in Lorraine. Iron ore from Lorraine had been taken by rail to the Ruhr as raw material for the iron and steel industry during much of the second half of the nineteenth century but by the 1890s, as blast furnaces became more economical in their use of coke, it became cheaper to carry coke from the Ruhr to Lorraine than to transport the lean Lorraine iron ores to the Ruhr. As a result, the Ruhr lost its competitive advantage as a production site.[34] Even in the case of iron and steel manufacture a coalfield location no longer conferred a decisive advantage.

Whereas for a quarter-millennium before *c.* 1850 the pattern of change in England contrasted strongly with that on most of the continent, in the second half of the nineteenth century, in the wake of the completion of the industrial revolution, change on the island and on the continent displayed similar patterns. The era of English exceptionalism had ended.

Long-term change in England in the aftermath of the industrial revolution

When mechanical energy could be derived as readily from coal as heat energy, the industrial revolution was accomplished. Rather than producing greater stability, however, the completion of the industrial revolution in the mid nineteenth century provoked further radical change. Ironically perhaps, areas that in different ways had been prominent in bringing about the industrial revolution often experienced severe difficulties in the new situation.

Table 9.3 traces the population growth taking place in the industrial counties compared with the rest of the country and with England as a whole. The counties selected to form the industrial group were the five fastest-growing of the English counties over the period from 1700 to 1851 (Warwickshire, Staffordshire, Cheshire, Lancashire, West Riding). Their combined population rose by 553 per cent over the century-and-a-half, compared to a rise of 144 per cent in the rest of the country. In 1700, the industrial group contained 15 per cent of the national population; in 1851, the percentage had doubled to 30 per cent.

[34] Wrigley, *Industrial growth and population change*, p. 6.

Table 9.3 *Population growth over three centuries*

	Population (000)								
	1600	1700	1750	1801	1831	1851	1881	1901	1911
Industrial counties	603	768	1,049	2,028	3,555	5,093	8,149	10,310	11,353
Rest of England	3,559	4,442	4,873	6,628	9,678	11,911	16,227	20,183	22,278
England	**4,162**	**5,211**	**5,922**	**8,656**	**13,234**	**17,004**	**24,377**	**30,493**	**33,632**
		1600/1700	1700/1750	1750/1801	1801/1831	1831/1851	1851/1881	1881/1901	1901/1911
		Population growth ratios							
Industrial counties		127.4	136.5	193.4	175.3	143.2	160.0	126.5	110.1
Rest of England		124.8	109.7	136.0	146.0	123.1	136.2	124.4	110.4
England		**125.2**	**113.7**	**146.2**	**152.9**	**128.5**	**143.4**	**125.1**	**110.3**
		Annual population growth rates per cent							
Industrial counties		0.24	0.62	1.33	1.89	1.81	1.58	1.18	0.97
Rest of England		0.22	0.19	0.60	1.27	1.04	1.04	1.10	0.99

Note: The industrial counties are Cheshire, Lancashire, Staffordshire, Warwickshire, and Yorkshire, W.R.

Sources: Population totals for 1600, 1700, and 1750: Wrigley, *The early English censuses*, Table A2.6, pp. 224–5. Totals from 1801 to 1911 are taken from an exercise in which an attempt was made to provide comparable totals for individual units from the township and parish upwards. Since many boundaries changed during this period there are many amalgamated units and as a result the totals, even for large units such as the county, may differ slightly from the totals recorded in the later censuses.

Table 9.3 provides evidence of the length of the period during which the transformation of the economy that is conventionally termed an 'industrial revolution' took place and whose geographical heartland lay in the five industrial counties. Annual population growth rates in the seventeenth century had been almost identical in the industrial counties and the rest of England, but thereafter the rates diverged markedly. The contrast was striking in the century-and-a-half from 1700 to 1851, when population in the industrial counties was rising on average by 1.26 per cent annually, almost twice the rate in the rest of England, where the rate was 0.66 per cent. During the second half of the nineteenth century, however, the picture changed radically. In the successive periods

1831/51, 1851/81, 1881/1901, and 1901/11 the percentage rate of annual population growth in the industrial counties declined steadily as follows: 1.81, 1.58, 1.18, 0.97. In 1831–51 the industrial counties still enjoyed a marked superiority over other counties. Their annual rate of population growth was 1.81 per cent where the rate in the rest of the country was 1.04 per cent. In the decade 1901–11 the rate in the rest of England was almost unchanged over the intervening half-century at 0.99 per cent, but in the industrial counties the rate had fallen so steeply that, at 0.97 per cent, it was marginally below the rest of the country. The malaise which affected the traditional industrial centres in the north and midlands during the inter-war period was already making its mark in the last two or three decades before the outbreak of war. Coalfield location and dependence on industries that had long known rapid growth no longer denoted success. The creation of a national rail network, which symbolised the mastery of techniques for converting heat into mechanical energy, gradually undermined coalfield location as a decisive advantage. And if falling freight rates and speedier transit times were not enough, electricity generation and the increasing use of other fossil fuels further fostered the development of a very different pattern of locational advantage.

A case study of the changing fortunes of arable agriculture

It was not only the industrial counties whose fortunes changed with the completion of the industrial revolution. Agricultural counties also faced grave problems in the later nineteenth century. The striking gains in productivity during the early modern period had given rise to regional specialisation as each area concentrated on the products to which it was best suited by climate, soil, and distance to market. At the end of the sixteenth century, at a time when approaching three-quarters of the male labour force worked on the land, county population densities were notably similar if the calculation of density is related to land below 200 metres. The average county density was 14.1 persons per 100 acres and the standard deviation 2.9.[35] This uniformity appears to reflect a similarity of agricultural practice closely linked to local self-sufficiency.[36] By the early nineteenth century, as a result of regional specialization, the range of densities was far wider. Table 9.4 uses information drawn from the 1841 census that provides exact information about male agricultural employment. The density of this employment per 1,000 acres of land below 200 metres varies substantially between regions but within each region the variation is slight.

[35] See pp. 87–8. [36] See p. 88.

Table 9.4 *Density per 1,000 acres of male agricultural employment on land below 200 metres in 1841*

Region	**Males over 20 in agriculture**	**Area under 200 metres (acres)**	**Density per 1,000 acres**	**Number of counties in the region**	**Mean deviation of individual counties from average of constituent counties**
Northern	82,369	3,647,666	22.6	6	2.5
North western	139,024	3,703,000	37.5	5	2.0
Eastern (north)	128,459	4,376,523	29.4	6	1.1
Eastern (south)	196,638	5,101,792	38.5	8	1.4
Central western	140,245	4,088,655	34.3	7	1.3
South coastal	136,529	4,596,264	29.7	5	2.4
Welsh border	35,123	1,141,363	30.8	2	0.8
Somerset	34,985	862,062	40.6	1	
England	**903,529**	**27,699,375**	**32.6**	**40**	

Notes: The counties in each region were as follows (Middlesex is not included because so much of its area was urban land): *Northern*: Cumbria, Durham, Northumberland, Westmorland, East and North Riding of Yorkshire; *North western*: Cheshire, Derbyshire, Lancashire, Staffordshire, West Riding of Yorkshire; *Eastern (north)*: Huntingdonshire, Leicestershire, Lincolnshire, Norfolk, Nottinghamshire, Rutland; *Eastern (south)*: Bedfordshire, Buckinghamshire, Cambridgeshire, Essex, Hertfordshire, Kent, Suffolk, Surrey; *Central western*: Berkshire, Gloucestershire, Northamptonshire, Oxfordshire, Warwickshire, Wiltshire, Worcestershire; *South coastal*: Cornwall, Devon, Dorset, Hampshire, Sussex; *Welsh border*: Herefordshire, Shropshire.
Source: 1841 Census, Occupation Abstract, part I.

Table 9.4 displays patterns which would sustain a long discussion and analysis but is here included only to give context to the description of the changing fortunes of the agricultural Registration Districts (RDs) in a single county, Norfolk, one of six counties in the Eastern (north) group. Though agricultural fortunes in the later nineteenth century varied in different parts of the country, the contrasting nature of the situation before and after the mid nineteenth century, which was widely experienced, can be illustrated by considering them in outline in Norfolk.

In the later eighteenth and early nineteenth century, the period when national population growth rates reached their peak, the population trends in agricultural areas reflect their success in coping with the stresses that might have been expected to occur as a result. In Table 6.3 the 610 English hundreds were ordered by their growth rates. Growth rates in the bottom half of hundreds were modest, 0.43 per cent per annum, when compared with the rates in the top quarter, 1.66 per cent per annum. The slow-growing hundreds were predominantly agricultural in occupational structure, with 54 per cent of the labour force working on the land (Table 6.4). Over the ninety-year period covered in Table 6.3 the population of hundreds in the top quarter more than quadrupled; hundreds in the bottom half grew by less than a half. The relatively slow growth rate in the largely agricultural hundreds was beneficial. There was substantial migration from agricultural areas to industrial and commercial centres. As a result the country was able to accommodate very high rates of population growth overall without causing the deep distress in rural areas that would have occurred if high population growth rates had prevailed country-wide. Rates of growth in the agricultural counties in England, indeed, were similar to agricultural areas on the continent, even though the rate of growth in agricultural production per acre and per farm worker was far higher in England. But the benign period covered by Table 6.3, from 1761–1851, was followed by a half-century when the fortunes of many agricultural counties changed sharply and for the worse. The fortunes of the different agricultural regions varied somewhat but Norfolk's experience, even if the pattern of change was unusually clear-cut, illustrates the severity and abruptness of the move from relative prosperity to stress.

Population totals for RDs can be reconstructed for the whole of the nineteenth century for unchanging units. Hundredal totals are available at decadal intervals from 1761 to 1851. In Table 9.5 totals in 1801 for both hundreds and RDs are shown. They differ slightly, but the coverage is closely similar. The urban RDs are those for Yarmouth, King's Lynn, and Norwich. The others are treated as rural. Among the hundredal totals there are totals for the city of Norwich, and for the boroughs of King's Lynn and Yarmouth. The remaining hundreds are treated as rural. The rural totals for all periods relate to units in which agriculture was the dominant occupation. In 1831 in the rural RDs the census reveals that 65.5 per cent of adult males in the workforce were engaged in agriculture.

In the forty-year period from 1761 to 1801 and again in the first half of the nineteenth century the rural population was rising, by 11.5 per cent in the first period and by 46.8 per cent in the second. In both periods, the urban growth was the faster of the two, but the differences were relatively modest. What is noteworthy about the rise in rural numbers is that it was substantial in spite of the fact that agricultural employment was broadly stationary country-wide throughout the whole period.[37] Any increase in male agricultural employment was certainly substantially smaller than

[37] Wrigley, 'Men on the land'.

Table 9.5 *The rural and urban populations of Norfolk 1761–1901*

	Hundred		RD		
	1761	1801	1801	1851	1901
Rural	198,354	221,088	217,653	319,468	278,514
Urban	54,883	64,320	67,297	124,002	187,636
Total	253,237	285,408	284,950	443,470	466,150

	Percentage change		
	1761/1801	1801/1851	1851/1901
Rural	111.5	146.8	87.2
Urban	117.2	184.3	151.3
Total	112.7	155.6	105.1

Sources: Hundredal totals: Wrigley, *The early English censuses*, Table A2.7, pp. 226–53. The RD totals for 1801–51 are from *ibid.*, Table M1.2, pp. 256–77, which contains revisions of the totals published in the first six censuses. This exercise has now been brought forward to 1911 but the results are as yet unpublished.

the rise in the rural population total. This was, therefore, a period in which non-agricultural employment in rural areas of the county increased significantly. What was true of Norfolk was true of rural populations country-wide with some variation. The 1831 census reveals that in the rural hundreds of Norfolk two-thirds of adult males in rural areas were employed in agriculture, and that 70 per cent of the remainder were employed in the retail trade and handicraft category, providing goods and services for the local population. Much of the overall population increase in rural Norfolk before 1851 was therefore probably associated with a substantial increase in the number of men engaged in retail trade and handicraft. The change taking place in the second half of the century was abrupt and severe. Urban growth continued at much the same pace as previously but whereas the urban population of Norfolk rose by a half, the rural population declined by 13 per cent.

The contrast between the two halves of the century in rural Norfolk was both striking and very consistent. In every decade from 1801 to 1851 the rural population in Norfolk was increasing, though rate of growth slackened in the last two decades of the period; in every decade from 1851 to 1901 it was decreasing. Table 9.6 provides the details.

Table 9.6 *The population totals and decennial increase ratios of rural Registration Districts in Norfolk 1801–1901*

	Population totals		
1801	217,653	1861	302,259
1811	230,134	1871	294,174
1821	263,247	1881	289,215
1831	291,969	1891	286,436
1841	304,386	1901	278,514
1851	319,468		
	Increase ratios		
1801/11	105.7	1851/61	94.6
1811/21	114.4	1861/71	97.3
1821/31	110.9	1871/81	98.3
1831/41	104.3	1881/91	99.0
1841/51	105.0	1891/1901	97.2

Source: Wrigley, *Early English censuses*, Table M1.2, pp. 256–77.

There were nineteen rural RDs in Norfolk. The starkness of the contrast between the two halves of the century was as consistent when presented in a disaggregated form as when presented in summary form. If decennial increase ratios for each RD are calculated, it is remarkable that in the first half of the nineteenth century, when there were 95 decennial ratios for the rural RDs (19 RDs each with 5 decennial ratios), there was only one ratio of less than 100 in the RD, and even then the ratio was 99.7 (Aylsham in 1841–51). Growth was therefore virtually universal in every decade and in each hundred throughout the rural agricultural districts of the county. After 1851 the change was immediate and complete. In 1851–61 population fell in all 19 RDs and in the following decade in 18 of the 19. In the three final decades of the century the pattern was somewhat less clear-cut. Of the 57 ratios in question 14 revealed a population increase rather than the reverse. The contrast between the two halves of the century may well have been more complete in Norfolk than in most other counties, but the abrupt replacement of moderate growth by stagnation and decline was widespread.

My purpose in focusing on events in rural Norfolk was not to undertake an investigation into the changes elsewhere in the economy which induced such a dramatic reversal of fortune, but rather to illustrate the fact that the fulfilment of the requirements for escape from the restrictions common to all organic economies did not bring a new stability, but rather often stimulated further rapid change, and that this was true of many different aspects of national economic life. It was true of the wide swathes of rural England just as it was true also of the fortunes of the industrial counties. The nature of the industrial revolution meant that its completion, rather than heralding a reduction in further change, often entailed the opposite. When, and only when, both heat and mechanical energy could be secured without apparent limit in all locations and with much-reduced regional price variations, was it possible for exponential growth to become the norm, but completion of an industrial revolution proved to imply continued change rather than a new stability.

10 Review and reflection

The term 'industrial revolution' has had a wide currency for many decades. It can be misleading in that the changes taking place were not found solely in industry, nor were they always induced by a prior stimulus brought about through industrial advance. The term is, nonetheless, in all probability, through long usage, here to stay. Perhaps because of the inadequacy and ambivalence of the term 'industrial revolution', it has proved difficult to secure agreement on when it should be regarded as having been completed.

If a single, symbolic date is sought to mark the completion of the industrial revolution it might, in my view, be that of the Great Exhibition of 1851. Although the employment of the steam engine as the prime source of mechanical energy was only partially completed at this date, it was already clear that mechanical energy needs no less than heat energy needs could be met by burning coal. Two or three decades were to elapse before virtually all the industries which used mechanical energy on a considerable scale were securing their supply from the steam engine, but it was already clear at the time of the Great Exhibition that this change was under way. The rail network in Britain had already transformed inland transport and was in the process of radically revising the economic geography of the country. Further, the centuries during which there was a marked contrast between developments in England and on the continent had ended. Other countries were quick to realise where the future lay and to ensure that they were not left behind. It became clear that events in England had resulted in a 'package' of changes covering all major energy uses that it was both desirable and feasible to adopt elsewhere. Implementing the new 'package' involved changes that were largely technical rather than institutional and compatible with a wide range of different political and institutional structures. The 'package' was widely taken up in the second half of the nineteenth century, with striking results for the relative economic performance of Britain and her neighbours.

The first edition of Jevons' *The coal question* was published in 1865. In the opening sentence of the first chapter he stated:

Day by day it becomes more evident that the Coal we happily possess in excellent quality and abundance is the mainspring of modern civilization. As the source of fire, it is the source at once of mechanical motion and of chemical change. Accordingly it is the chief agent in almost every improvement or discovery in the arts which the present age brings forth.[1]

It is significant that, writing in the 1860s, Jevons could refer to coal as being the source of both mechanical motion and chemical change. His claim about chemical change, equivalent to what has been called heat energy in this book, could have been made with confidence more than a century earlier when coal had already become the prime source of heat energy both in the home and in many industries. But at that time it would not have been possible to make the same claim about mechanical motion. The mastery of fire, opening up the possibility of using heat energy for a wide range of different purposes, had begun almost half a million years earlier, and had made possible massive changes in many aspects of material life over the intervening period, even though in organic economies the absolute quantity of heat energy which could be secured was limited by the scale of the annual quantum of plant growth. Initially the use of coal rather than wood represented only a vast increase in the scale of heat energy available and a marked reduction in its cost but little change in the uses to which it was put.

With mechanical energy, it was very different. There had been no previous change comparable to that which the mastery of fire made possible in relation to heat energy. Societies had remained dependent on muscle power to provide mechanical energy, though assisted, of course, by the power generated from the wind by sails and windmills and from the rivers by water wheels. But wind and water power combined provided only a fraction of the mechanical energy that was derived from muscle power.[2] When a spade was used to turn the soil, an axe raised to cut down a tree, or a shuttle thrown in the manufacture of cloth, human muscle was employed. When the earth was ploughed, a wagon drawn, or a treadmill operated, animal muscle was the energy source, supplied largely by horses and oxen.

The most significant change in the provision of mechanical energy since the mastery of fire had transformed heat energy possibilities had been occasioned by the domestication of large animals, which substantially increased the quantity of available muscle power in many societies.

[1] Jevons, *The coal question*, p. 1.   [2] See Table 3.1, p. 32.

Horses, oxen, and donkeys could then be employed to carry people, pull carts and carriages, drag ploughs and canal barges, and for many other productive tasks. And muscle power retained its central importance in providing mechanical energy long after the use of coal had transformed the scale of heat energy usage. Musson laid emphasis on the continued importance of horses as a source of mechanical energy even in the late eighteenth and early nineteenth centuries. He considered that it had tended to be underplayed by comparison with steam power as industrialisation progressed. He provided a long list of examples of their use in a variety of industries.[3] Similarly, von Tunzelmann noted that 'many of the early textile inventions were developed for animal-powered mills, if not for man-power itself', and also estimated that even in the cotton industry 'it is likely that human beings supplied more motive power than steam-engines up to the 1820s'.[4]

Ironically, it had been a problem in providing sufficient coal to meet heat energy needs that had led to the development of a technique for converting heat energy into mechanical energy. Flinn noted that 'Probably the greatest proportion of water taken from coal-mines at the beginning of the eighteenth century was drawn to the surface by horse-power'.[5] Employing horses to provide the energy needed to evacuate water from coal mines severely limited the depth to which coal could be dug. In a general survey of the problem facing coalmining before the introduction of steam drainage, Flinn added:

> If drainage technology were to stand still at the point reached at the beginning of the eighteenth century, mining in Britain could scarcely have expanded and must probably have begun to show diminishing returns. At depths of between ninety and 150 feet the influx of water almost invariably created problems insoluble by the technology of the day, so that when seams of lesser depths were exhausted mining must cease. – There was a future for mining in Britain only if some more efficient drainage techniques became available.[6]

As the demand for coal continued to rise it became imperative to find a means to pump water from a greater depth to gain access to the huge quantity of coal in deeper beds and so to increase the quantity of coal that could be secured. Because coal was so cheaply available at the pithead even a very inefficient method of converting heat into work was acceptable. Newcomen engines provided an initial solution to the drainage problem but translated only a tiny fraction of the heat energy consumed into useful work. Watt's engine was substantially more efficient and by

[3] Musson, *The growth of British industry*, pp. 107–9.
[4] Von Tunzelmann, *Steam power*, pp. 117–18 and 295.
[5] Flinn, *The history of the British coal industry*, II, p. 113. [6] *Ibid.*, p. 114.

the early decades of the nineteenth century there had been further gains in the efficiency with which the energy in steam could be captured. A very important advance was that achieved when Watt solved the problem of converting the thrust of a piston into rotary motion. As a result, steam engines came to be employed almost universally in industry as the most convenient, powerful, and cheapest source of mechanical energy during the middle decades of the nineteenth century. The construction of rail networks provided the most striking single example of the fact that energy derived from burning coal could be employed as readily to supply mechanical energy for most purposes as to supply heat energy. The rail networks symbolised the ability to convert heat energy into mechanical energy in a manner to justify Jevons' claim that coal was 'the source at once of mechanical motion and of chemical change'.[7]

Although Jevons himself did not make use of the term 'industrial revolution', *The coal question* is a book whose content reflects the recognition that the industrial revolution was completed. 'Mechanical motion and chemical change' could be generated as required and a period of exponential economic growth was therefore possible.

Overview

This book has focused on a limited number of topics – energy consumption, agricultural productivity, urban growth, the changing occupational structure of England, consumer demand, the west European marriage system, and changes in transport facilities. In discussing them, other aspects of change in the economy have occasionally been mentioned but only as incidental to the topics just listed. Some topics which are central to the description and analysis of the industrial revolution in other discussions of its genesis have been entirely neglected, such as the improved availability of capital, and the downward trend in its cost; the scale and significance of the increased volume of overseas trade; and the striking advances in the scientific understanding of natural processes.

One reason for limiting the range of factors discussed was the wish to focus on the relationships between variables in terms of positive and negative feedback. The impossibility of conducting controlled experiments using historical data means that as a general rule it is not feasible to say of two variables which were changing that the change in A *caused* the change in B. This can be true even of relatively uncomplicated, individual events but the problem is greatly magnified where the change studied is intrinsically complex such as, for example, a rise in overall agricultural

[7] Jevons, *The coal question*, p. 1.

productivity. Hartwell, in his essay on methodology, plainly considered that historians could seldom resist the temptation to identify causation, and to do so primarily in terms of a single factor. He wrote: 'It is fair to say that historians, in their detailed analyses, have suggested *many* "causal factors", yet nearly all have sought "a main cause" and have elevated *one* variable, explicitly or implicitly, to the role of *chief cause*.'[8] The temptation to seek a cause is strong, but it is seldom possible to establish with certainty that it is demonstrable.[9]

This type of problem is sometimes finessed by making use of the distinction between necessary and sufficient causes. Because controlled experiments are not possible using historical data, the distinction, though of great value in defining the logical standing of a given proposed cause, can seldom be made with certainty. For example, if it is argued that it was a necessary condition for the scale of economic growth which took place in England in the later seventeenth and eighteenth centuries that the law governing the relations between creditors and debtors was clear and that its enforcement was predictable, then it would be illuminating to test the assertion. This is not possible because English history cannot be repeated with a different legal system to test the hypothesis, but it is also not possible for a second reason. It is inconceivable that an element in the social and political structure of a country as important as its legal system could be removed or replaced by another system without at the same time producing change in other elements in the system. The degree of interconnectedness between the different institutions that collectively compose a society is such that it is normally mistaken to suppose that the logical status of one feature or institution can be tested in a manner that would show that its presence was either necessary or sufficient to produce a given effect. Occasionally, it may be possible to justify the claim that a particular change was a necessary precursor of another event. For example, I consider that, given the nature of organic economies, it is reasonable to argue that it was necessary to discover an energy source other than that provided by the annual round of plant photosynthesis; but even though this is a necessary precondition, it does not imply that

[8] Hartwell, 'The causes of the industrial revolution', p. 56.

[9] In his recent review of the literature about the industrial revolution, A'Hearn summarised the current situation effectively: 'Explanations of Britain's industrial revolution draw from a long list of causal factors that range from culture to climate, from energy to empire. Because these causes are rarely mutually exclusive, because of reciprocal causation in a complex, interdependent society, and because there is but one British industrial revolution to study, it has proved difficult to build a consensus about which factors were important original causes and which were unimportant, merely permissive, or themselves the effect of industrialization.': A'Hearn, 'The British industrial revolution', p. 20.

employing the new energy source was sufficient to ensure an industrial revolution.

There are, in short, important limitations associated with making use of the concept of causation in historical explanation, whether expressed explicitly or by implication, but there is an alternative concept that can throw much light on change in the past. In relation to many of the topics discussed in this book the concept of positive and negative feedback is particularly helpful. This was the case in relation to the central theme of the book, which may be briefly summarised.

The key difference between the organic economies that developed in the wake of the neolithic agricultural revolution and the economies that were transformed by the industrial revolution is that in organic economies the nature of the growth process is such that prolonged growth is not possible. As the classical economists were vividly aware, land, no less than labour and capital, entered into all material production because it was the source both of the raw materials and of the energy used in almost all production processes. The supply of land is fixed and the process of growth therefore necessarily means attempting to raise productivity per acre, a process that at some point will reduce returns to both capital and labour and bring growth to a halt. Organic economies were inherently subject to negative feedback, whose character ruled out the possibility of exponential growth.

The raw materials produced by agriculture were all the product of plant photosynthesis, the process by which plants capture a fraction of the energy in incident sunlight. Almost all the energy available in organic economies was derived from plant photosynthesis. Some mechanical energy was obtained from the movement of wind and water but it represented only a tiny fraction of the total. The quantum of energy that a society could secure for productive purposes was quite small. It was necessary to devote a large proportion of the products of agricultural land to human nourishment. The productivity of men working on the land was so low that it was normal for three-quarters or more of the labour force to be engaged in agriculture. Indirectly it was for this reason that such a large proportion of income in organic economies was spent on food. It would have seemed absurd to anyone living in an organic economy to suggest that a day would come when less than a tenth of the labour force would work on the land and yet the population would suffer more from the effects of overeating than from malnourishment.

The industrial revolution produced radical change and raised the prospect of steadily rising living standards, even though populations were growing rapidly, because it replaced plant growth as the main source of energy by the mining of fossil fuels, initially coal. The nature of the growth process was transformed. Rather than the process of growth grinding to a halt by the negative feedback that was unavoidable in an organic economy, growth tended to clear the path to further growth. For example, rather than the unit cost of production tending to rise with expansion, as in the past, it tended to fall as higher volumes of output could be secured with falling marginal cost; and other cost elements, notably those associated with the movement of goods and people, also declined as expansion took place. Taking advantage of the existence of the immense *stock* of energy in coal removed the barrier which dependence on a *flow* of energy from the annual growth of plants had implied. It provided the possibility of vastly increasing the scale of material production and raising living standards commensurately but, given the perils of depending on a stock rather than a flow of energy, whether the new situation can be maintained or will prove fragile is uncertain.

Coda

The industrial revolution is usually depicted as a success story. Countless generations before it occurred had lived in organic economies whose nature was such that a period of relatively rapid growth was inevitably succeeded by stasis or decline. Living standards even in favourable circumstances were modest for the bulk of the population and a run of poor harvests commonly meant suffering and sometimes a heightened death rate. In an organic economy it was idle to expect that entire populations could enjoy not merely a sufficiency of the necessities of life but living standards rising from one generation to the next. The industrial revolution brought liberation from these age-old restrictions.

There was always a chance, however, that making use of energy provided by fossil fuel radically to expand the productivity of the economy and of individual workers was equivalent to living in a fool's paradise. If, the energy *stock* represented by a fossil fuel becomes depleted, and no way is found to replace it by an energy *flow* of the same magnitude, the potential penalty is horrific. Using fossil fuel has, among other things, led to very large increases in population. Their continued existence depends upon finding an alternative to fossil fuels that can supply comparable amounts of energy, and ideally to do this without greatly increasing its unit cost. If the depletion in the *stock* of fossil fuel is not matched by success in securing energy on the same scale from alternative energy *flows*, the future is bleak indeed. Even providing food for the increased populations would then probably prove beyond achievement. The fact that, in securing the high yields that are currently normal, more energy is often consumed than is made available in the crops which are harvested points to the nature of the problem.

And this is not the only problem with using fossil fuel on a large scale. The environmental pollution that their use produces is potentially an equally serious danger, and one that is more immediate. We face the challenge encapsulated by the concept of intergenerational justice. Environmental pollution raises this issue in a particularly acute fashion. The life of those in the middle and later decades of life, the generations who occupy positions of power and must make decisions, is unlikely to be greatly affected by the environmental changes associated with the large-scale use of fossil fuels. The lives of their grandchildren and great-grandchildren, in contrast, appear certain to be very severely affected unless there is a world-wide recognition of the urgent need to act decisively over the decades immediately in front of us. It is to be hoped (but perhaps not confidently expected) that the implications of doing justice to later generations is recognised by the generations in power today.

There appear to be viable methods for avoiding both dangers provided that co-ordinated action is agreed and implemented. In the absence of such action, however, the industrial revolution may come to be regarded not as a beneficial event which liberated mankind from the shackles which limited growth possibilities in all organic economies but as the precursor of an overwhelming tragedy – assuming that there are still survivors to tell the tale.

Bibliography

A'Hearn, B., 'The British industrial revolution in a European mirror, in R. Floud, J. Humphries, and P. Johnson (eds.), *The Cambridge economic history of modern Britain, I, 1700–1870* (Cambridge, 2014), pp. 1–52.

Aikin, J., *A description of the country from thirty to forty miles round Manchester* (London, 1793).

Albert, W., 'The turnpike trusts', in D.H. Aldcroft and M.J. Freeman (eds.), *Transport in the industrial revolution* (Manchester, 1983), pp. 31–63.

Allen, R., *The British industrial revolution in global perspective* (Cambridge, 2009).

Bagwell, P.S., *The transport revolution from 1770* (London, 1974).

Baines, D., *Migration in a mature economy: emigration and internal migration in England and Wales, 1861–1900* (Cambridge, 1985).

Bairoch, P., 'The impact of crop yields, agricultural productivity, and transport costs on urban growth between 1800 and 1910', in A. van der Woude, A. Hayami, and J. de Vries (eds.), *Urbanization in history: a process of dynamic interactions* (Oxford, 1990), pp. 134–51.

Beier, A.L. and Finlay, R. (eds.), *London 1500–1700: the making of the metropolis* (London, 1986).

Bogart, D., 'The transport revolution in industrialising Britain', in R. Floud, J. Humphries, and P. Johnson (eds.), *The Cambridge economic history of modern Britain, I, 1700–1870* (Cambridge, 2014), pp. 368–91.

Botham, F.W. and Hunt, E.H., 'Wages in Britain during the industrial revolution', *Economic History Review*, 2nd series, 40 (1987), pp. 380–99.

Broadberry, S., Campbell, B.M.S, Klein, A., Overton, M., and van Leeuwen, B., *British economic growth, 1270–1870* (Cambridge, 2015).

Burnette, J., 'Agriculture, 1700–1870', in R. Floud, J. Humphries, and P. Johnson (eds.), *The Cambridge economic history of modern Britain, I, 1700–1870* (Cambridge, 2014), pp. 89–117.

Campbell, B.M.S., 'Land, labour, livestock, and productivity trends in English seigniorial agriculture, 1208–1450, in B.M.S. Campbell and M. Overton (eds.), *Land, labour and livestock: historical studies in European agricultural productivity* (Manchester, 1991), pp. 144–82.

Chalklin, C., *The rise of the English town 1650–1850* (Cambridge, 2001).

Chambers, J.D., 'Population change in a provincial town: Nottingham 1700–1800', in L.S. Pressnell (ed.), *Studies in the industrial revolution* (London, 1960), pp. 97–124.

Population, economy, and society in pre-industrial England (Oxford, 1972).

Chartres, J.A., 'Food consumption and internal trade', in A.L Beier and R. Finlay (eds.), *London 1500–1700* (London, 1986), pp. 168–96.

Chartres, J.A. and Turnbull, G.L. 'Road transport', in D.H. Aldcroft and M.J. Freeman (eds.), *Transport in the industrial revolution* (Manchester, 1983), pp. 64–99.

Church, R., *The history of the British coal industry, III, 1830–1913: Victorian pre-eminence* (Oxford, 1986).

Clapham, J.H., *An economic history of modern Britain*, 2nd edn. reprinted, 3 vols. (Cambridge, 1950–2).

Clark, P. and Slack, P., *English towns in transition 1500–1700* (Oxford, 1976).

Clarkson, L.A., 'The manufacture of leather', in J. Thirsk (ed.), *The agrarian history of England and Wales, VI, 1750–1850* (Cambridge, 1989), pp. 466–83.

Clay, C.G.A., *Economic expansion and social change: England 1500–1700*, 2 vols. (Cambridge, 1984).

Coale, A.J. and Demeny, P., *Regional model life tables and stable populations* (New Jersey, 1966).

Coleman, D.C., *The economy of England 1450–1750* (Oxford, 1977).

Corfield, P.J., *The impact of English towns 1700–1800* (Oxford, 1982).

Cottrell, F., *Energy and society: the relation between energy, social change, and economic development* (New York, 1955).

Court, W.H.B., *The rise of the Midland industries 1600–1838* (Oxford, 1938).

Crafts, N.F.R., *British economic growth during the industrial revolution* (Oxford, 1985).

'The industrial revolution', in R. Floud and D. McCloskey, *The economic history of Britain since 1700*, 2nd edn., vol. I (Cambridge, 1994), pp. 44–59.

Cressy, D., *Literacy and the social order: reading and writing in Tudor and Stuart England* (Cambridge, 1980).

Darwin, C., *The descent of man and selection in relation to sex* (2nd edn., 1877), in P.H Barrett and R.B. Freeman (eds.), *The works of Charles Darwin*, vols. 21–22 (London, 1989).

Davis, R., *The industrial revolution and British overseas trade* (Leicester, 1979).

Deane, P., 'The industrial revolution in Great Britain', in C.M. Cipolla (ed.), *The Fontana economic history of Europe: the emergence of industrial societies*, part 1 (London, 1973), pp. 161–227.

'The British industrial revolution', in M. Teich and R. Porter (eds.), *The industrial revolution in national context: Europe and the USA* (Cambridge, 1996), pp. 13–35.

Deane, P. and Cole, W.A., *British economic growth 1688–1959* (Cambridge, 1962).

Debeir, J.-C., Deléage, J.-P., and Hémery, D., *In the servitude of power: energy and civilisation through the ages* (London and New Jersey, 1991).

De Vries, J., 'Patterns of urbanization in pre-industrial Europe 1500–1800', in H. Schmal (ed.), *Patterns of European urbanization since 1500* (London, 1981), pp. 77–109.

European urbanization 1500–1800 (Cambridge, Mass., 1984).

The industrious revolution: consumer behaviour and the household economy, 1650 to the present (Cambridge, 2008).

De Vries, J. and van der Woude, A., *The first modern economy: success, failure, and perseverance of the Dutch economy, 1500–1815* (Cambridge, 1997).

De Zeeuw, J.W., 'Peat and the Dutch golden age: the historical meaning of energy-attainability', in *A.A.G. Bijdragen*, 21 (Wageningen, 1978), pp. 3–31.

Dejongh, G. and Thoen, E., 'Arable productivity in Flanders and the former territory of Belgium in a long-term perspective (from the middle ages to the end of the Ancien Régime)', in B.J.P. van Bavel and E. Thoen (eds.), *Land productivity and agro-systems in the North Sea area (middle ages–20th century)*, CORN publications, series 2 (Turnhout, 1999), pp. 30–64.

Duckham, B.F., 'Canals and river navigations', in D. Aldcroft and M. Freeman (eds.), *Transport in the industrial revolution* (Manchester, 1983), pp. 100–41.

Feinstein, C.H., 'Pessimism perpetuated: real wages and the standard of living in Britain during and after the Industrial Revolution', *Journal of Economic History*, 58 (1998), pp. 625–58.

Flinn, M.W., *The history of the British coal industry, II, 1700–1830: the industrial revolution* (Oxford, 1984).

Freeman, M.J., 'Introduction', in D.H. Aldcroft and M.J. Freeman (eds.), *Transport in the industrial revolution* (Manchester, 1983), pp. 1–30.

Galloway, J.A., Keene, D., and Murphy, M., 'Fuelling the city: production and distribution of firewood and fuel in London's region', *Economic History Review*, 49 (1996), pp. 447–72.

Gatley, D.A., *An introduction to the 1831 census* (Victorian Census Project, Staffordshire University, 2003).

Geertz, C., *Agricultural involution: the process of ecological change in Indonesia* (Berkeley, 1963).

Gerhold, D., 'Productivity change in road transport before and after turnpiking, 1690–1840', *Economic History Review*, 49 (1996), pp. 491–515.

'The development of stage coaching and the impact of turnpike roads, 1653–1840', *Economic History Review*, 67 (2014), pp. 818–45.

Glennie, P. and Whyte, I., 'Towns in an agrarian economy 1540–1700', in P. Clark (ed.), *The Cambridge urban history of Britain, II, 1540–1840* (Cambridge, 2000), pp. 167–93.

Golas, P.J., 'Mining', in J. Needham (ed.), *Science and civilisation in China*, V, part XIII (Cambridge, 1999), pp. 186–201.

Goubert, P., *Beauvais et le Beauvaisis*, 2 vols. (Paris, 1960).

Goudsblom, J., *Fire and civilization* (London, 1992).

Gough, R., *The history of Myddle*, ed. D. Hey (London, 1983).

Greene, A.N., *Horses at work: harnessing power in industrial America* (Harvard, 2008).

Griffin, E., *Liberty's dawn: a people's history of the industrial revolution* (New Haven and London, 2013).

Grigg, D.B., *Population growth and agrarian change: an historical perspective* (Cambridge, 1980).

Hajnal, J., 'European marriage patterns in perspective', in D.V.Glass and D.E.C. Eversley (eds.), *Population in history* (London, 1965), pp. 101–43.

Hartwell, R.M., 'The causes of the industrial revolution: an essay on methodology', in R.M. Hartwell (ed.), *The causes of the industrial revolution in England* (London, 1967), pp. 53–79.

Hatcher, J., *The history of the British coal industry, I, Before 1700: towards the age of coal* (Oxford, 1993).

Hawke, G.R. and Higgins, J.P.P., 'Transport and social overhead capital', in R. Floud and D. McCloskey (eds.), *The economic history of Britain since 1700, I, 1700–1860* (Cambridge) 1981, pp. 227–52.

Henriques, S.T. and Sharp, P., *The Danish agricultural revolution in an energy perspective: a case of development with few domestic energy sources*, University of Southern Denmark, Discussion Papers on Business and Economics, 9 (2014).

Holderness, B.A., 'Prices, productivity, and output', in J. Thirsk (ed.), *The agrarian history of England and Wales, VI, 1750–1850* (Cambridge, 1989), pp. 84–189.

Hunt, E.H., 'Industrialization and regional inequality: wages in Britain, 1760–1914', *Journal of Economic History*, 46 (1986), pp. 935–66.

Jackman, W.T., *The development of transportation in modern England*, 3rd edn. (London, 1966).

Jevons, W.S., *The coal question: an inquiry concerning the progress of the nation, and the probable exhaustion of our coal-mines*, Reprints of Economic Classics (New York, 1965).

John, A.H., 'Statistical appendix', in J. Thirsk (ed.), *The agrarian history of England and Wales, VI, 1750–1850* (Cambridge, 1989), pp. 972–1155.

Jones, E.L., *Agriculture and the industrial revolution* (Oxford, 1974).

'Agriculture, 1700–80', in R. Floud and D.N. McCloskey (eds.), *The economic history of Britain since 1700, I, 1700–1860* (Cambridge, 1981), pp. 66–86.

Growth recurring: economic change in world history (Oxford, 1988).

Kander, A., Malanima, P., and Warde, P., *Power to the people: energy in Europe over the last five centuries* (New Jersey, 2013).

Kjaergaard, T., *The Danish revolution, 1500–1800; an ecohistorical interpretation* (Cambridge, 1994).

Kussmaul, A., *A general view of the rural economy of England 1538–1840* (Cambridge, 1990).

'The pattern of work as the eighteenth century began', in R. Floud and D. McCloskey (eds.), *The economic history of Britain since 1700*, 2nd edn., vol. 1 (Cambridge, 1994), pp. 1–11.

Landers, J., *Death and the metropolis: studies in the demographic history of London 1670–1830* (Cambridge, 1993).

Langton, J., *Geographical change and industrial revolution: coalmining in south west Lancashire, 1590–1799* (Cambridge, 1979).

Laxton, P. and Williams, N., 'Urbanization and infant mortality in England: a long term perspective and review', in M.C. Nelson and J. Rogers (eds.), *Urbanisation and the epidemiologic transition* (Uppsala, 1989), pp. 109–35.

Lee, R., 'Short-term variation: vital rates, prices, and weather', in E.A. Wrigley and R.S. Schofield, *The population history of England 1541–1871: a reconstruction* (London, 1981), pp. 356–401.

Levasseur, E., *La population française*, 3 vols. (Paris, 1889–92).

Livi-Bacci, M., *The population of Europe: a history* (Oxford, 2000).

McLeod, C., 'The European origins of British technological predominance', in L. Prados de la Escosura (ed.), *Exceptionalism and industrialisation: Britain and its European rivals, 1688–1815* (Cambridge, 2004).

Malanima, P., *L'economia italiana: dalla crescita medieval all crescita contemporanea* (Bologna, 2002).

Energy consumption in Italy in the 19th and 20th centuries: a statistical outline (Rome, 2006).

Malthus, T.R., *An essay on the principle of population as it affects the future improvement of society* [London, 1798], in *The works of Thomas Robert Malthus*, ed. E.A. Wrigley and D. Souden, 8 vols. (London, 1986), vol. 1.

'The amendment of the poor laws, 1807', *Essays on population*, in *The Works of Thomas Robert Malthus*, ed. E.A. Wrigley and D. Souden, 8 vols. (London, 1986), vol. 4.

Principles of political economy considered with a view to their practical application, 2nd edn. [London, 1836], in *The works of Thomas Robert Malthus*, ed. E.A. Wrigley and D. Souden, 8 vols. (London, 1986), vol. 5.

An investigation of the cause of the present high price of provisions [London, 1800], in *The works of Thomas Robert Malthus*, ed. E.A. Wrigley and D. Souden, 8 vols. (London, 1986), vol 7.

Mandeville, B., *The fable of the bees*, ed. and with an introduction by P. Harth (London, 1989).

Mathias, P., 'The social structure in the eighteenth century: a calculation by Joseph Massie', *Economic History Review*, 2nd series, 10 (1957), pp. 30–45.

'Agriculture and the brewing and distilling industries in the eighteenth century', in E.L. Jones (ed.), *Agriculture and economic growth in England 1650–1815* (London, 1967), pp. 80–93.

McCloskey, D.N., 'The industrial revolution 1780–1860: a survey', in R. Floud and D.N. McCloskey (eds.), *The economic history of Britain since 1700, I, 1700–1860* (Cambridge, 1981), pp. 103–27.

McKendrick, N., 'Commercialization and the economy', in N. McKendrick, J. Brewer, and J.H. Plumb, *The birth of a consumer society: the commercialization of eighteenth-century England* (London, 1982), pp. 9–194.

Meredith, D. and Oxley, D., 'Food and fodder: feeding England, 1700–1900', *Past and Present*, 222 (2014), pp. 163–214.

Mill, J.S., *Principles of political economy with some of their applications to social philosophy*, ed. J.M. Robson, 2 vols. (Toronto, 1965).

Mitchell, B.R., *European historical statistics 1750–1975*, 2nd rev. edn. (London, 1980).

British historical statistics (Cambridge, 1988).

More, T., *Utopia and a dialogue of comfort*, Everyman's Library, 461, rev. edn. (London, 1951).

Muldrew, C., *Food, energy and the creation of industriousness: work and material culture in agrarian England, 1550–1780* (Cambridge, 2011).

Musson, A.E., *The growth of British industry* (London, 1981).

Nef, J.U., *The rise of the British coal industry*, 2 vols., first published 1932 (reprinted, New York, 1972).

Ogilvie, S., 'Choices and constraints in the pre-industrial countryside', in C. Briggs, P.M. Kitson, and S.J. Thompson, *Population, welfare and economic change in Britain 1290–1834* (Woodbridge, 2014), pp. 269–305.

Overton, M., *Agricultural revolution in England: the transformation of the agrarian economy 1500–1850* (Cambridge, 1996).

Overton, M. and Campbell, B.M.S., 'Statistics of production and productivity in English agriculture 1086–1871', in B.J.P. Bavel and E. Thoen (eds.), *Land productivity and agro-systems in the North Sea area (middle ages – 20th century)*, CORN publication, series 2 (Turnhout, 1999), pp. 189–208.

Overton, M., Whittle, J., Dean, D., and Hann, A., *Production and consumption in English households 1600–1750* (London, 2004).

Petersen, C., *Bread and the British economy, c. 1770–1870* (Aldershot, 1995).

Pimentel, D., 'Energy flow in the food system', in D. Pimentel and C.W. Hall (eds.), *Food and energy resources* (London, 1984), pp. 1–24.

Pollard, S., *Peaceful conquest: the industrialization of Europe 1760–1970* (Oxford, 1981).

Postan, M.M., 'Village livestock in the thirteenth century', *Economic History Review*, 2nd series, 15 (1962), pp. 219–49.

Poussou, J.-P., 'Les villes anglaises, du milieu du XVIIe siècle à la fin du XVIIIe siècle', in A. Lottin, J.-P. Poussou, H. Soly, B. Vogler, and A. van der Woude, *Études sur les villes en Europe occidentale* (Paris, 1983), pp. 7–212.

Rappaport, S., *Worlds with worlds: structures of life in sixteenth-century London* (Cambridge, 1989).

Ricardo, D., On the principles of political economy and taxation, in *The works and correspondence of David Ricardo*, I, ed. P. Sraffa with the collaboration of M.H. Dobb (Cambridge, 1951).

Schofield, R.S., 'Dimensions of illiteracy, 1750–1850', *Explorations in Economic History*, 10 (1972–3), pp. 437–54.

'The relationship between demographic structure and environment in pre-industrial Europe', in W. Conze (ed.), *Sozialgeschichte der Familie in der Neuzeit Europas* (Stuttgart, 1976), pp. 147–60.

Sen, A., *Poverty and famines: an essay on entitlement and deprivation* (Oxford, 1981).

Shammas, C., *The pre-industrial consumer in England and America* (Oxford, 1990).

Shaw-Taylor, L. and Wrigley, E.A.,'Occupational structure and population change', in R. Floud, J. Humphries, and P. Johnson (eds.), *The Cambridge economic history of modern Britain, I, 1700–1870* (Cambridge, 2014), pp. 53–88.

Sieferle, R.P., *The subterranean forest: energy systems and the industrial revolution* (Knapwell, 2001).

Smith, A., *An inquiry into the nature and causes of the wealth of nations*, ed. E. Cannan, 5th edn, 2 vols. (London, 1961).

Söderberg, J., Jonsson, U., and Persson, C., *A stagnating metropolis: the economy and demography of Stockholm 1750–1850* (Cambridge, 1991).

Souden, D., 'Migrants and the population structure of later seventeenth-century provincial cities and market towns', in P. Clark (ed.), *The transformation of English provincial towns 1600–1800* (London, 1984), pp. 133–68.

Stone, R., *Some British empiricists in the social sciences 1650–1900* (Cambridge, 1997).

Swain, J.T., *Industry before the industrial revolution: north-east Lancashire c. 1540–1640* (Manchester, 1986).

Sweet, R., *The English town 1680–1840: government, society and culture* (Harlow, 1999).

Szostak, R., *The role of transportation in the industrial revolution: a comparison of England and France* (Montreal and Kingston, 1991).

Thirsk, J. (ed.), *The agrarian history of England and Wales, VI, 1750–1850* (Cambridge, 1989).

Thomas, B., *The industrial revolution and the Atlantic economy: selected essays* (London and New York, 1993).

Thompson, F.M.L., 'Nineteenth-century horse sense', *Economic History Review*, 2nd series, 29 (1976), pp. 60–81.

Turnbull, G., 'Canals, coal and regional growth during the industrial revolution', *Economic History Review*, 2nd series, 40 (1987), pp. 537–60.

Unger, R.W., 'Energy sources for the Dutch golden age: peat, wind, and coal', *Research in Economic History*, 9 (1948), pp. 221–53.

Van der Woude, A., Hayami, A., and de Vries, J., 'Introduction', in A. van der Woude, A. Hayami, and J. de Vries (eds.), *Urbanization in history: a process of dynamic interactions* (Oxford, 1990), pp. 1–19.

(eds.), *Urbanization in history: a process of dynamic interactions* (Oxford, 1990).

Von Thünen, J.H., *The isolated state*, ed. with introduction by P. Hall (Oxford, 1966).

Von Tunzelmann, G.N., *Steam power and British industrialization* (Oxford, 1978).

Voth, H.-J., 'Time and work in eighteenth-century London', *Journal of Economic History*, 58 (1998), pp. 29–58.

Warde, P., *Energy consumption in England and Wales 1560–2000* (Consiglio Nazionale delle Ricerche, 2007).

'The first industrial revolution', in A. Kander, P. Malanima, and P. Warde, *Power to the people: energy in Europe over the last five centuries* (New Jersey, 2013), pp. 129–247.

White, L.P. and Plaskett, L.G., *Biomass as fuel* (London, 1981).

Whittle, J., *The development of agrarian capitalism: land and labour in Norfolk 1440–1580* (Oxford, 2000).

Willan, T.S., *The inland trade: studies in English internal trade in the sixteenth and seventeenth centuries* (Manchester, 1976).

Wilson, C., *England's apprenticeship 1603–1763* (London, 1965).

Wrigley, E.A., *Industrial growth and population change: a regional study of the coal-field areas of north-west Europe in the later nineteenth century* (Cambridge, 1961).

'Marriage, fertility and population growth in eighteenth-century England', in R.B. Outhwaite (ed.), *Marriage and society: studies in the social history of marriage* (London, 1981), pp. 137–85.

'Men on the land and men in the countryside: employment in agriculture in early nineteenth-century England', in in L. Bonfield, R.M. Smith, and K. Wrightson (eds.), *The world we have gained: histories of population and social structure* (Oxford, 1986), pp. 295–336.

'A simple model of London's importance in changing English society and economy, 1650–1750', in E.A. Wrigley, *People, cities and wealth: the transformation of traditional society* (Oxford, 1987), pp. 133–56.

'No death without birth: the implications of English mortality in the early modern period', in R. Porter and A. Wear (eds.), *Problems and methods in the history of medicine* (Beckenham, 1987), pp. 133–50.

'Urban growth and agricultural change: England and the continent in the early modern period', in E.A. Wrigley, *People, cities and wealth: the transformation of traditional society* (Oxford, 1987), pp. 157–93.

'British population during the "long" eighteenth century, 1680–1840', in R. Floud and P. Johnson (eds.), *The Cambridge economic history of modern Britain, I, Industrialisation, 1700–1860* (Cambridge, 2004), pp. 57–95.

'Corn and crisis: Malthus on the high price of provisions', in E.A. Wrigley, *Poverty, progress, and population* (Cambridge, 2004), pp. 204–11.

'Men on the land and men in the countryside: employment in agriculture in early nineteenth-century England', in E.A. Wrigley, *Poverty, progress, and population* (Cambridge, 2004), pp. 87–128.

'The occupational structure of England in the mid-nineteenth century', in E.A. Wrigley, *Poverty, progress, and population* (Cambridge, 2004), pp. 129–203.

'The transition to an advanced organic economy', *Economic History Review*, 59 (2006), pp. 435–80.

'Rickman revisited: the population growth rates of English counties in the early modern period', *Economic History Review*, 62 (2009), pp. 711–35.

Energy and the English industrial revolution (Cambridge, 2010).

'Coping with rapid population growth: how England fared in the century preceding the Great Exhibition of 1851', in D. Feldman and J. Lawrence (eds.), *Structures and transformations in modern British history: essays for Gareth Stedman Jones* (Cambridge, 2011), pp. 24–53.

The early English censuses, British Academy Records of Social and Economic History, new series, 46 (Oxford, 2011).

'European marriage patterns and their implications: John Hajnal's essay and historical demography during the last half century', in C. Briggs, P.M. Kitson, and S.J. Thompson (eds.), *Population, welfare and economic change in Britain 1290–1834* (Woodbridge, 2014), pp. 15–41.

Wrigley, E.A., Davies, R.S., Oeppen, J.E., and Schofield, R.S., *English population history from family reconstitution 1580–1837* (Cambridge, 1997).

Wrigley, E.A. and Schofield, R.S., *The population history of England 1541–1871: a reconstruction* (London, 1981).

Wrigley, E.A. and Souden, D. (eds.), *The works of Thomas Robert Malthus*, 8 vols. (London, 1986).

Young, A., *Travels in France and Italy during the years 1787, 1788 and 1789*, Everyman's Library (London, n.d.).

OFFICIAL PUBLICATIONS

Annual Report of Registrar General for England and Wales, 1838– (London, 1839–).

1831 *Census*

Comparative Account of the Population of Great Britain, *PP* 1831, XVIII.

Enumeration Abstract, I and II, *PP* 1833, XXXVI–XXXVII.

1841 *Census*

Occupation Abstract, part I, England and Wales, and islands in the British Seas, *PP* 1844, XXVII.

Age Abstract, part I, England and Wales, *PP* 1843, XXII.

1851 *Census*

Population tables, II, vol. 1, England and Wales, *PP* 1852–3, LXXXVIII, part 1.

Index